"C. J. Hopkins is our modern Jeremiah. No other prophet has described the strategies or predicted the perils of the emerging totalitarianism with such persistence and eloquence."

—Robert F. Kennedy Jr.

"C. J.'s case is an example of egregious censorship, and the free world should be repulsed by it."

—JD Vance

"C. J. Hopkins is the modern Western version of a Samizdat writer, i.e., a forbidden wit who loudly says things that are obvious but Not Spoken Of in officialdom. Probably this is not a profitable life choice, but it is a hilarious enterprise, and his furious columns have increasingly become required reading as 'normal' media discourse strays further and further from reality."

—Matt Taibbi

"Earlier this year, I interviewed @CJHopkins_Z23 before a German court annulled a lower court's finding in his favor. He now faces three years in jail for writing satire. C. J.'s case is a central front on the battle over censorship and free speech."

—Jay Bhattacharya

"C. J. Hopkins belongs to a dying breed: an old-school leftist who has stayed true to his anti-capitalist (or anti-globocapitalist, as he would say) and anti-authoritarian roots, resisting both the lure of liberal-progressive neoliberalism and the temptations of faux-revolutionary rightism. This kind of 'intellectual sovereignty' is exactly what we need to navigate these tumultuous times—and that is perhaps why he is being so harshly persecuted by the justice system."

—Thomas Fazi, writer and journalist, coauthor of *The Covid Consensus: The Global Assault on Democracy and the Poor—A Critique from the Left*

"Reading these pages is like sitting with Hopkins and Kafka as they humorously compare their stories. Thank you, C. J., for making the madness of recent years a bit easier."

—Gavin de Becker, bestselling author of *The Gift of Fear*

"C. J. Hopkins is a stone-cold hero. Remember that picture taken in Germany in the 1930s of the one guy not doing the Nazi salute while everyone surrounding him is? That's C. J. Hopkins."

—**Toby Young, director of the Free Speech Union, editor in chief of *Daily Sceptic*, and associate editor of *The Spectator***

"This book is a must-read. C. J,'s journey through the German legal system is a breathtaking commentary on bureaucratic excess. The most benign allusion to historical iconography becomes a delusional pursuit of the author by the legal system. The totalitarian impulse seems to be alive and well."

—**Drew Pinsky, MD**

"We live in a dark age. Oppression sucks the oxygen from our days with ill-intended interruptions and interventions. And then, marvelously, in marches C. J. Hopkins with his verbal lightsaber signing the air with honor. And our belly laughs bring back the oxygen and we can breathe again."

—**Catherine Austin Fitts, the *Solari Report***

"Not every writer is persecuted by their government. Fewer have the courage to stand up to their persecutors and risk jail time and financial ruin. C. J. Hopkins paid the price to vindicate his right to speak and write freely. The words in these pages represent his brave acts of protest and defiance."

—**Nico Perrino, executive vice president of the Foundation for Individual Rights and Expression**

"Hopkins's writing on the New Normal Reich is a beacon of light, humour, and grace in these dark times. If I had to don a beret and head to the bunkers for a revolution, I'd want C. J. by my side. Buy this book for your 'not awake' friends and family if you want them to understand what we will lose when the censorship gates slam fully shut on free thought."

—**Trish Wood, award-winning investigative journalist and host of *Trish Wood Is Critical* podcast**

FEAR & LOATHING
IN THE NEW NORMAL REICH

FEAR & LOATHING
IN THE NEW NORMAL REICH

C. J. HOPKINS
Consent Factory Essays, Vol. IV (2022–2024)

FOREWORD BY MATT TAIBBI

Skyhorse Publishing

Copyright © 2025 by C. J. Hopkins
Foreword copyright © 2025 by Matt Taibbi

All Rights Reserved. No part of this book may be reproduced in any manner without the express written consent of the publisher, except in the case of brief excerpts in critical reviews or articles. All inquiries should be addressed to Skyhorse Publishing, 307 West 36th Street, 11th Floor, New York, NY 10018.

Skyhorse Publishing books may be purchased in bulk at special discounts for sales promotion, corporate gifts, fund-raising, or educational purposes. Special editions can also be created to specifications. For details, contact the Special Sales Department, Skyhorse Publishing, 307 West 36th Street, 11th Floor, New York, NY 10018 or info@skyhorsepublishing.com.

Skyhorse® and Skyhorse Publishing® are registered trademarks of Skyhorse Publishing, Inc.®, a Delaware corporation.

Visit our website at www.skyhorsepublishing.com.
Please follow our publisher Tony Lyons on Instagram @tonylyonsisuncertain.

10 9 8 7 6 5 4 3 2 1

Library of Congress Cataloging-in-Publication Data is available on file.

Hardcover ISBN: 978-1-5107-8392-8
eBook ISBN: 978-1-5107-8393-5

Cover design by Anthony Freda

Printed in the United States of America

Contents

Foreword by Matt Taibbi	ix
Fear and Loathing in the New Normal Reich	1

2022

The Last Days of the Covidian Cult	27
Attack of the Transphobic Putin-Nazi Truckers!	32
The Naked Face of New Normal Fascism	36
Revenge of the Putin-Nazis	41
Springtime for GloboCap	48
The Normalization of the New Normal Reich	54
The Unvaccinated Question Revisited	58
The Rise of the New Normal Reich Banned	64
The Morning After	72
The Gaslighting of the Masses	77
The Road to Totalitarianism Revisited	83
The Year of the Gaslighter	89

2023

The Mother of All Limited Hangouts	99
The War on Insensitivity	104
The New Normal Left	111
A Twitter Files Requiem	117
The Great Divide	121
The War on Reality Revisited	125
New Normal Germany Blues	131

The Criminalization of Dissent Revisited	137
The "Free-Speech Twitter" PSYOP	143
The Order of Punishment	148
The Criminalization of Dissent Ad Absurdum	153
Israel's 9/11	158
The Year of the Mindfuck	162

2024

Not Guilty	173
The Resistible Rise of the New Normal Reich	178
The Palestine Congress	184
Fighting Monsters	188
The Anti-Zionist Inquisition	193
The Civil War Simulation	197
The People's Court of New Normal Germany	202
The New Normal Right	215
Political Justice	222
Guilty	230
Fear and Loathing in New Normal Germany	235
The Revenge of Trumpenstein	241
A Tale of Two PSYOPS	244
The Year of the Zealot	251

Acknowledgments   259

Foreword

by Matt Taibbi

We expect artists to be brave. Using imagination at all usually requires some rebelliousness of spirit. But we live in an age when Western writers and thinkers chose a different path, embracing cowardice, groupthink, and shunning as principles. If they could have worn badges announcing their devotion to the creed, they would have. In fact, they did.

C. J. Hopkins was not one of the groupthinkers. An American playwright who chose the expat life in Germany, C. J. began publishing a unique form of fulminating, obscene, defiant, and often hilarious essay online just as the Great Shrinking era began. His curse was he couldn't believe small lies, and beginning in 2016 or so, life was suddenly packed with big ones: America was James Bond stalking a cat-stroking supervillain named Putin-Hitler, anti-Semites had devoured Labour, Cubans were melting diplomat brains with invisible sound weapons, and Nord Stream was blown up not by Western armies but an escapee from one of Winslow Homer's rowboats.

Hopkins earned Internet celebrity for calling out all these things, and his cutting nicknames for the new forces that ruled us ("The New Normal," "GloboCap") were being bandied about as countercultural code by the end of Donald Trump's first term. But it wasn't until the arrival of COVID-19, and what C. J. quickly dubbed the "Covidian Cult," that he really found his groove. His essays during this period read like one contiguous dystopian novel, written from some underground depot of a society falsely told the surface had been contaminated—think *The Machine Stops*, *Never Let Me Go*, or even *Silo*.

I mentioned that artists and thinkers of this period would have worn badges of cowardice if they could and did in fact do this. This happened in 2020, 2021, 2022, 2023, 2024 . . . I'm still seeing people walking around with at least one mask on. It's not easy to define the current political movement—C. J. calls it a form of Global Capitalist Totalitarianism—but one of its main features has been its constant search for public symbols of conformity. In the United States, it started with de-eroticized fashion choices: black rimmed glasses, unisex haircuts, tie-sweatervest combos for men, dress sneakers, an Ibram Kendi book sticking out of a Tumi bag . . .

None of this did quite enough, but when the pandemic came, opportunities for conformism blossomed. Strict home-stay regimes and social-distancing rules were implemented, giving citizens the power now to bark at the noncompliant. The mask soon became all-important, as the person without one, or who slipped one down too long while chewing food in a restaurant (we'll look back in awe at how absurd some of this was), was soon liable to be publicly excoriated or even made the target of a Call to Authorities. As calls for mandates grew (bills for which were introduced in many parts of the world, including C. J.'s Germany), there began to be dreams of the mask coming with a new accessory: the vaccine passport. The desire to get this shiny new badge was, for many during this period, stronger than the urge for companionship, family, even sex.

C. J. quickly identified all this as cult behavior and referenced Margaret Singer's Six Conditions for Mind Control in essays about the disorder. This made him new enemies; he'd already been denounced using the other terms for suppressive persons he'd described previously. "It is now virtually impossible to refute it in any mainstream forum without being dismissed as a 'conspiracy theorist,' or an 'anti-Semite,' or a 'Russian asset,'" he wrote in 2019. But laughing at the Mask and the Six-Foot Rule now put him in the category of those who were "killing people" with their shit attitudes about the virus, and it was not long before he became one of the first Americans to be arrested for wrong-speak.

C. J. was arrested in Germany for the alleged crime of seeking to further "the aims of a former National Socialist Organization" through a tweet of the cover of his book, *The New Normal Reich*. The ostensible crime was that the mask featured prominently on the cover had the faintest of faint outlines of a white swastika on it, a very deliberate and (I think) clever satirical image meant to make a point about the enforced conformism and totalitarian instincts of global health authorities.

In fact, the circumstances of the "crime" showed the determination to preserve the principle of conformism. When German health minister Karl Lauterbach said, "The masks always send out a signal," C. J. tweeted his book cover back at him, starting the train of justice rolling. For the crime of saying, *You are acting like Nazis when you make us wear these fucking things* he was arrested and convicted! With the exception of a future Health and Human Services Secretary in America almost no one of prominence in our country stood up for C. J.'s right to speak. It was shameful.

In the early 2000s, America faced a crisis. The government told a great big lie to start a war, and everyone but artists and intellectuals believed it. This made the latter groups feel impotent and disconnected from society.

Beginning in 2016 and continuing through the events described in C. J.'s book, a new series of crises arrived. The government told not one but many Big Lies, none bigger than the ones about Covid and vaccine efficacy and social distancing (a standard created totally arbitrarily, it turned out). This time, the government created Lies designed to appeal to the smart set, so no one believed in them more than artists and intellectuals. Everyone cheered each one. This was rigidly enforced, through financial consequences, shunning, censorship, and in C. J.'s case, arrest.

The essays in this book tell this whole story, and because it includes a true tale of pursuit and arrest over something simultaneously comical and horrifying, and takes place in Germany besides, it will remind some of Kafka. I hear other voices in C. J., from Burroughs to Bukowski to Hunter Thompson, but none of those writers ever had to live this kind of dystopian experience. This is a true story, a document for history, and a great read.

One last note. As this book goes to print, a great confrontation is taking place, between a deprogramming America and aggrandized Europe, now protected by a powerful censorship law called the DSA that is (forgive the analogy, but it works) the intellectual version of the Atlantic Wall.

For the first time, there are American politicians speaking out against these tactics, but people like German foreign minister Boris Pistorius have said such criticism is "unacceptable." I wonder how long we'll put up with that. But if we do ever make a priority of lifting that Atlantic Wall, the citizens who spoke up first, like C. J., should be remembered for sounding the alarm.

Fear and Loathing in the New Normal Reich

December 23, 2024

The Order of Punishment arrived in the mail.

It arrived in a scary-looking "Nazi-brown" envelope stamped by hand with the official stamp of the *Amtsgericht Tiergarten* (i.e., the Berlin District Court) and covered with little boxes containing other little boxes and instructions in German indicating which box should be checked when, and stickers with bar codes and an inscrutable 16-digit number that the Deutsche Post man had presumably scanned to establish delivery of the Order of Punishment to my registered address.

I tore the envelope open carefully, so as not to mutilate it, as my attorney had instructed. There it was, the Order of Punishment. The Berlin District Court had pronounced me guilty of thought crimes against the New Normal Reich (without a trial or any other type of proceeding) and sentenced me to sixty days in prison or to pay a fine of 3,600 Euros.

And so began my journey through the legal system of New Normal Germany.

Actually, my journey through the German legal system had begun five months earlier, in May of 2023, when I was notified by the Berlin state prosecutor, this time in a regular envelope without the stamp and all the boxes and the stickers, that I was being criminally investigated on suspicion of "disseminating propaganda, the contents of which are intended to further the aims of a former National Socialist organization," which is punishable by up to three years in prison.

The "propaganda" at issue, I would find out later, was two tweets I had tweeted in August of 2022, both featuring the cover artwork of my book, *The Rise of the New Normal Reich: Consent Factory Essays, Vol. III (2020–2021)*, and lampooning the official "Covid" narrative that government leaders, health authorities, and the media had been systematically terrorizing the public with for over two years.

According to that narrative, in the Spring of 2020, as the US election season was getting underway, with Donald Trump poised for a second term as president and "populist" movements still on the rise in Europe, humanity was suddenly attacked without warning by an apocalyptic coronavirus with a projected death rate of 3.4 percent.[1] One hundred sixty million people were going to die! Governments had no choice but to declare a "global state of health emergency," suspend constitutional rights, order a series of "lockdowns," force everyone to walk around wearing medical-looking masks in public, bombard us with lies and official propaganda, demonize and censor dissent, segregate anyone who wouldn't follow orders,[2] and otherwise transform society into a pathologized de facto police state.

Apparently, we had no immunity to this virus, which had spread from Chinese bats or pangolins and was nothing like the other coronaviruses that humanity has been infected with for millennia, and which are among the main causes of the common cold. People were dropping dead in the streets![3] Our only hope of survival as a species was to cancel democracy and coerce everyone into submitting to a series of experimental "vaccinations,"

---

1 Lovelace, Jr., Berkeley and Noah Higgins-Dunn, "WHO says coronavirus death rate is 3.4 percent globally, higher than previously thought," CNBC, March 3, 2020.
2 Hubbard, Kaia, "Germany Locks Down the Unvaccinated, Weighs Vaccine Mandate," *US News & World Report*, December 2, 2021.
3 "A man lies dead in the street: the image that captures the Wuhan coronavirus crisis," *The Guardian*, January 31, 2020.

which were being developed by global pharmaceutical corporations like Pfizer, BioNTech, and Moderna and were absolutely "side effect free."[4]

All of which was lies and propaganda, of course, the most formidable official propaganda campaign in the history of official propaganda campaigns. As early as the Spring of 2020, it was clear that, whatever "Covid" was, or wasn't, it certainly was not the apocalyptic plague that the authorities and the media were making it out to be. Anyone who was paying attention could see that there was no justification whatsoever for the totalitarian "emergency measures" that were being implemented all across the planet in almost perfect synchronization.

No, something much simpler and more insidious was happening. Our official "reality" was being revised, like that scene in *1984* in which the Party switches official enemies in the middle of the Hate Week celebrations. But, in our case, they weren't just switching official enemies. They were radically revising our entire official "reality." And they wanted us to know it. They made sure we knew it. Government officials, the corporate media, health authorities, celebrities, pundits, the entire global-capitalist propaganda apparatus was relentlessly pumping out the message. The message was unmistakably clear. Our lives, as we knew them, were over.[5] The whole "Western democracy" show was over. It was time to click heels and follow orders, because from now on there was going to be a "New Normal."[6,7,8,9,10]

---

4   "And it's also about why a minority of society doesn't want a vaccination that has no side effects, even though it's free and can save their lives and those of many others," Karl Lauterbach, Twitter, August 14, 2021.
5   Harris, Mary, "We're Not Going 'Back to Normal'—So What Will the New Normal Look Like?," *Slate*, April 16, 2020.
6   Sanchez, Ray, "America's 'new normal' will be anything but ordinary," CNN, April 17, 2020.
7   Florida, Richard, "The New Normal After the Coronavirus Pandemic," *Bloomberg*, June 25, 2020.
8   Kirkey, Sharon, "After the COVID-19 crisis ends, what does our 'new normal' look like?," *National Post*, May 2, 2020.
9   Fisher, Max, "What Will Our New Normal Feel Like? Hints Are Beginning to Emerge," *New York Times*, April 21, 2020.
10 "Our new normal in pictures," CNN, May 20, 2020.

I had reported on the rollout of the so-called "New Normal" during 2020 and 2021, and had published a selection of those essays in the book that had brought me to the attention of the German authorities. The cover art, created by Anthony Freda, was an homage to one of the well-known covers of William Shirer's 1960 classic, *The Rise and Fall of the Third Reich: A History of Nazi Germany*.

However, back in May of 2023, when I was officially notified that I was being investigated for . . . well, basically, "disseminating pro-Nazi propaganda," I had no idea what the accusation referred to. I sat there at one of my local cafés in a state of semi-shock for a while, trying to decipher the German legalese in the prosecutor's notice of *Ermittlungsverfahren*. The notice claimed that I had tweeted two tweets containing an image of a *Mund-Nasen-Bedeckung* (i.e., a "mouth-nose covering") with a swastika "on" it. That had to be my book cover artwork, but that didn't make sense, because the swastika on the cover is behind the mask, partially obscured by it, not "on" it, as the prosecutor was claiming. The prosecutor gave me two weeks to submit a written response to the accusation. Or what? Was I going to be arrested? Were the New Normal Thought Police going to raid my apartment, confiscate my propaganda-disseminating equipment, and haul me off to some former Stasi enhanced-interrogation facility? Or maybe the whole thing was just a practical joke. I checked the notice and the envelope again for signs that one of my German friends was having me on. No, it was real. The actual state prosecutor (i.e., district attorney) had launched a criminal investigation of me . . . for tweeting. German detectives were probably poring through my Twitter timeline right that minute, searching for any further evidence of my "hate crimes," or my "delegitimization of the democratic state," or any other seditious satirical activity. I briefly considered fleeing to Sweden, or Florida, and living out my days as a political exile under an assumed identity, but I was pretty sure my wife wouldn't go for it. Also, the longer I sat there staring at the prosecutor's notice, the more pissed off I got. My book had already been banned in Germany. And now the authorities were actually going to charge me with a criminal offense and prosecute me for comparing the rollout of the "New Normal"—the suspension of constitutional rights, the segregation and demonization of "the Unvaccinated," the forced public ideological-conformity rituals, the coerced "vaccinations," the censorship, et cetera, all based on a fabricated "state of emergency"—to the rise of Nazi Germany in the 1930s?

I went home and got myself a German lawyer.

I have lived in Berlin for twenty years now. I fled New York in 2004, in the throes of a classic midlife crisis, divorced, broke, burned out by the city, disgusted with the "War on Terror" and the flag-waving atmosphere in the USA at the time. The occupation of Iraq was in full swing. The US military, its coalition partners, and assorted corporate mercenary forces had invaded the country in March 2003. I had watched the shock-and-awe campaign on a miniature TV in a cheap hotel room in London, where one of my plays was being performed at the time. My future second wife and I attended the demo on the day it began. A procession of tens of thousands of us marched along the Thames to Westminster, and then stood around in Parliament Square with our DON'T ATTACK

IRAQ and STOP THE WAR placards, calling George W. Bush and Tony Blair "Hitler" and chanting anti-war slogans at each other. The mood was funereal. Nothing was going to stop what was coming and everyone knew it. A few hours later, the night-vision footage of the bombing started running on the BBC.

A couple months earlier, back in New York City, we (i.e., my future wife and I) had helped to organize the theater community for the demonstrations that took place in cities all around the world on February 15. The preparations went on for weeks in advance. Anarchist general assemblies were held. Diversities of tactics were extensively discussed. Temporary autonomous zones were established. Teenagers with asymmetrical haircuts arrived from all across the country, some of whom slept on my floor in Brooklyn. Bread and Puppet Theater came down from Vermont with a school bus full of giant puppets.

On the day, approximately half a million of us marched through the icy streets of Midtown, theater people, union people, students, teachers, families with kids in strollers, Trotskyists, anarchists, DNC operatives, Hare Krishnas, those Black Hebrew Israelites, and people who had never attended a protest in their lives. Bread and Puppet did their thing. The black-bloc militants restrained themselves. The authorities and media called us "terrorist sympathizers, "Saddam apologists," "traitors," et cetera. Mounted police rode their horses into the crowd. It didn't matter. The world was united. There were demonstrations in London, Berlin, Rome, Paris, Athens, Madrid, Amsterdam, Dublin, Montreal, everywhere. Ten million people in six hundred cities in sixty countries around the world, exercising their democratic rights, demanding that their voices be heard. It was the largest protest event in history.

It didn't accomplish one fucking thing.

What we didn't understand back in 2003, and still don't really understand today, is what we are up against. It isn't a country. It isn't a cabal. It isn't a conspiracy. Yes, of course, there are conspiracies and cabals, and there are countries, and they all compete with each other, just as global corporations compete with each other, but they do so within a supranational, hegemonic metasystem, upon which they are entirely dependent, and within which they are interdependent, inextricably linked at the systemic level, the trajectory and scope of their evolution delimited by the evolution of the system.

That system is global capitalism.

It is one big global-capitalist world now. It has been for about thirty-five years, since the fall of the former Soviet Union. Communism, the final ideological adversary of global capitalism, is dead. One supranational ideological system dominates the entire planet. It is our ideological operating system, to which all systems running on it must conform. It is the map that dictates the territory. The ontological lingua franca. It is our official "reality." It is the only game in town.

It is evolving into a new form of totalitarianism, because it doesn't have anything else to do. It has no outside enemies, because there is no outside, so it is doing what any self-respecting occupying power would do. It is neutralizing internal resistance to its global dominance and its ideology. Any and all forms of internal resistance. It is conducting a global "clear-and-hold" op.

The destabilization and restructuring of the Middle East is an essential part of that "clear-and-hold" op. The disintegration of national sovereignty is an essential part of that "clear-and-hold" op. The dissolution of borders. The homogenization of culture. The neutering of religion. The erasure of history. The commodification of "identity." The "visibility-filtering" of speech. The surveillance of the social. The criminalization of dissent. The pathologization of emotions and beliefs. And so on.

It's all part of that "clear-and-hold" op.

The disillusionment we experienced in 2003—the millions of us all around the world who took to the streets and otherwise attempted to stop a textbook war of aggression—was the result of a fundamental misperception. A misperception that persists today. We were focused on the USA, and other Western countries, and on the governments of those countries, as if those governments and their leaders were driving events, which of course they were at a certain level, but on another level, a higher level, a systemic level, they were being driven by the evolutionary needs of the system. Bush, Cheney, Rumsfeld, et al., were not Napoleonic autocrats; they were functionaries, glorified factotums. They were just doing their jobs, "just following orders." We, the protesters out in the streets, thought we were "speaking truth to power," but we were really just a bunch of irate callers complaining to the customer service representatives of the wholly owned subsidiaries of a company we didn't even know existed.

In other words, we couldn't see the forest for the trees.

The New World Order

George W. Bush, Dick Cheney, Donald Rumsfeld, and the rest of their gang of beady-eyed sociopaths will be remembered as the ones who launched the "Global War on Terror," but it was George H. W. Bush and Michael Gorbachev who had ushered in the "New World Order." Bush described it in an address to Congress on September 11, 1990:

> We stand today at a unique and extraordinary moment. The crisis in the Persian Gulf, as grave as it is, also offers a rare opportunity to move toward an historic period of cooperation. Out of these troubled times, our fifth objective—a new world order—can emerge: a new era—freer from the threat of terror, stronger in the pursuit of justice, and more secure in the quest for peace. An era in which the nations of the world, East and West, North and South, can prosper and live in harmony.

The "unique and extraordinary moment" we were standing at in 1990 was not the dawn of a new era of "prosperity" and "harmony." It was the birth of the first truly globally hegemonic ideological power system in human history.

Of course, neither Bush nor Gorbachev, nor Francis Fukuyama,[11] nor neoconservatives like William Kristol and Robert Kagan, who would later found the Project for the New American Century, nor anyone else entirely understood the new leviathan that was coming into being. Michael Hardt and Antonio Negri perhaps came the closest to capturing it in *Empire*.[12] Their portrait of the "empire" as a metasystem occupying the entire

---

11 Francis Fukuyama, *The End of History and the Last Man*, Free Press, 1992.
12 Michael Hardt and Antonio Negri, *Empire*, Harvard University Press, 2000.

geopolitical territory—and thus there being no outside of the system—and of the terrorist or insurgent as the empire's new official enemy was certainly accurate.

As for me, I have been writing about the New World Order, one way or another, for the last thirty-five years. I first explored it in my early plays and experimental stage-texts in the 1990s and 2000s, and I have continued to focus on it in my essays and fiction. It has been the overarching theme of my work, and the backdrop of most of my personal life, and the lives of everyone in my generation, despite the fact that most of us are either unaware of it or unable to talk about it, not because we're ignorant or stupid, but because none of us really understand the magnitude of the historic transformation we have all been living through.

I was born in 1961, at the tail end of the post-war baby boom, in what in those days was still the segregated South. The Cold War was a fact of everyday life. We recited the Pledge of Allegiance in school. I was two years old when John F. Kennedy was assassinated. I was six when Dr. King and Bobby Kennedy were assassinated. I grew up watching the war in Vietnam and assorted acts of international and domestic terrorism on television. My recollection of the 1970s is rather hazy. Sex, drugs, rock and roll, et cetera. I had just started college when Ronald Reagan was elected. Not that I cared about politics at the time. I was assiduously misspending what was left of my youth. I barely made it through university. After graduating, I took off for San Francisco, where I generated an abundance of bad pseudo-beat poetry, until my future ex-wife pulled me back into the theater—I had been an actor for a while as a kid—and filled my head full of radical politics. We hit the road for New York City in October 1989, just after the Loma Prieta earthquake. A few weeks later, as we were settling in at our illegal sublet loft in Greenwich Village, the Berlin Wall came tumbling down.

One month later, the Cold War was over.

The world I had grown up and come of age in, the "reality" I had come of age in, ended. It didn't happen all at once. It happened gradually over the decades that followed. First, there were the celebrations. "America" had defeated the Rooskies! The Germans were getting back together!

Then the "New World Order" talk began. Then we had to bomb Iraq and Yugoslavia. Bill Clinton executed a mentally challenged Black guy, won the election, moved into the White House, and began receiving presidential blow jobs. The post-Cold-War party started winding down. It felt like we were in some kind of limbo. Then people started getting fat. Not regular fat. Serious fat. Walrus fat. Elephant seal fat. There had always been fat people, regular fat people. But this was different. Something was happening. Suddenly, everywhere you went, you were surrounded by hordes of these enormous fat people, many of them stuffing Big Macs into their faces or sucking up super-sized buckets of soda as they waddled directly at you on the sidewalk or took up two or three seats on the subway. And then, one day, as if an edict had been issued, you weren't allowed to call them "fat" anymore. They weren't "fat." They suffered from "obesity." Obesity was an official disease, a condition. There were guidelines, charts with body-fat percentages, according to which the majority of Americans were technically "obese" or "borderline obese." And then, at some point— I don't recall exactly when—obesity became an official "identity." People no longer suffered from obesity. They were "differently bodied persons." They were "People of Obesity." At the same time, again, as if an edict had been issued, everyone had to join a gym or fitness studio or take up yoga or Pilates and rack up 150 minutes of aerobic activity a week, or start obsessively running or power-walking while wearing a plastic pulse-oximeter wristband, and consuming an assortment of dietary supplements, antioxidants, and a carefully calibrated cocktail of serotonin-selective reuptake inhibitors, and benzodiazepines, like Fluoxetine and Alprazolam, and other psychiatric medications to treat the ever-increasing array of psychiatric disorders that everyone was suffering ... anxiety disorder, personality disorder, post-traumatic stress disorder, bipolar disorder, eating disorder, disruptive mood disregulation disorder, cognitive disorder, conduct disorder, oppositional defiant disorder, the list went on and on and on. Also, the condoms. You had to wear them. Everyone had to, or we were going to die! It didn't matter whether you were gay or straight. Penises needed to be covered with latex, or polyurethane, or polyisoprene, or some other synthetic prophylactic material. Oh, and the smoking. No more smoking! The secondhand smoke was giving everyone cancer, especially kids not in rear-facing car seats, and helmetless bikers, and unregistered gun owners, so laws needed to be passed to mandate the affixing of warning labels with disgusting photographs of rotted-out teeth and amputees and dead fetuses and unopenable childproof caps on potentially dangerous or offensive products and those plastic anti-shoplifting devices and the installing of scanners and metal detectors and police and active-shooter drills in schools and the relentless bombardment of everyone's brain with corporate-speak and behavioral conditioning like an endless stream of memos from Human Resources regarding the replacement of inappropriate words with marketing gibberish, and if you didn't like that you could take it up with Jesus in your corporate megachurch, or join a white-supremacist cult in Idaho, or shave your genitals, bleach your anus, and post monetized homemade porn on the Internet, which, while everyone was busy quitting smoking and medicating and meditating and reinvesting and wrapping their dicks in plastic, had slithered its immaterial tendrils up into our perceptual orifices and replaced us with images of ourselves on Facebook ... until we woke up one day in some infinite virtual antechamber of corporate purgatory, the identical, interchangeable avatars of an insatiable consumer deity consuming itself in perpetuity, hypnotized by reflections of reflections of reflections of ourselves ...

And then, before anyone could get their bearings and try to work out what was actually happening, terrorists were flying planes into buildings, and the "Global War on Terror" was on. Yes, that's right, it was a "state of emergency." America was under attack! It was time to suspend constitutional rights,[13] unleash the armored Urban-Assault Vehicles and heavily armed soldiers to patrol the streets, illegally surveil everyone, and start conditioning us to unquestioningly follow orders, like putting our "fluids" in little plastic bottles and letting the TSA creeps grope our kids at the airport (because otherwise the terrorists would win!), and the rest of the "Global War-on-Terror-Perpetual-State-of-Emergency" show.

None of which had anything to do with "America," or defending America from terrorism. By that time, "America" had already disappeared. "America" disappeared with the Soviet Union. The world in which they

---

13 Are you beginning to see a recurring pattern here?

both existed had disappeared. The "America" and "Russia" that fought the Cold War were products of our collective imagination, mythical projections of the last two major ideologies competing for global dominance in a world where, finally, global dominance had become possible.

Global capitalism won the competition. Having won, it didn't need "America" anymore. Unleashed on the entire territory of the planet, freed from the need to maintain a simulation of "democracy" to justify itself, it was doing what it was designed to do, the only thing it knows how to do, destabilizing, restructuring, and privatizing everything, transforming societies into marketplaces, and rendering everything and everyone an interchangeable commodity.[14]

By the turn of the century, it was clear where we were headed. It was going to happen everywhere, eventually, the globalization of the post-social marketplace, the disassembly of the simulation of democracy, the destabilization, restructuring, and privatization of everything, the commodification of every single aspect of our lives. The USA was already halfway there. No, it wasn't quite a pure marketplace yet—and it still isn't; vestiges of the social remain—but it was getting there at breakneck speed.

On my return from Europe in 2003, I decided that I had had enough. I had had enough of the increasingly pathologized, military-occupied corporate theme park the USA and New York City were becoming. The downtown theater scene I came up in was being decimated by real-estate developers. I was broke, deep in credit-card debt, and being evicted from my basement apartment in Brooklyn. My plays were being celebrated and

---

14 This is usually where I inform my pro-capitalism readers that I am not attacking or condemning capitalism per se. I have no problem with capitalism per se. The thing is, if it isn't controlled by actual societies, i.e., people, with actual values, it destroys society and eradicates any and all values that interfere with the flows of capital. What many conservatives and libertarians understand as "Wokeness," "Cultural Marxism," or "Libtardism," is actually just global capitalism, unrestrained by any higher authority, doing precisely what it is designed to do, i.e., decoding values, *any and all values that interfere with the commodification of everything*. I explain this at length in the following essays. In the meantime, if my use of the term "capitalism" offends you, just mentally replace it with "corporatism," or "crony capitalism," or whatever term you prefer.

published in the UK. Europeans were against the "War on Terror." The coffee in France and Germany was better. A friend of a friend had a sublet in Berlin.

Over the course of the next year, I learned a little German, sold most of what remained of my personal possessions, fought my landlady in New York Housing Court, won, and collected a bit of cash in overcharged rent. I flew back to London in the Summer of 2004, crashed with an old Greek theater friend who had somehow become a BBC producer, and eventually made my way to Berlin.

Back then, Berlin was still "poor but sexy." In the former East German neighborhood where I landed, Russian bullet holes pocked the facades of the buildings. There were dogs in the bars and coal ovens in the apartments. Most of the city was still under reconstruction. Everyone was broke, or inexplicably wealthy. Underground art galleries, music venues, and sex clubs of every variety abounded. My first few years here were a little crazy. I had emigrated to a foreign country in which I didn't know anyone and could barely speak the language. I was flying by the seat of my pants. I remember tripping on mushrooms with a beautiful German cinematographer in the *Volkspark Friedrichshain*, where a debate between Walter Ulbricht and Joseph Goebbels had devolved into a running brawl, which was not unusual in the Weimar era. I remember snorting snuff with a certain German television news presenter in an after-hours club off the *Fasanenstraße*. I was commissioned to write and stage a play in the Philological Library of the *Freie Universität*, the *Berlin Brain*, designed by Norman Foster, in conjunction with a national marketing campaign to promote Germany as the "Land of Ideas" during the lead-up to the 2006 FIFA World Cup. A Deutsche Bank executive attended the show, and started screaming insults at the naked performers, who were tearing apart and eating the books. Later, I was commissioned by a technical university, way out in the boondocks on the edge of the city, to write and stage a multimedia performance, which ended up being the most aggressively offensive theater piece I have ever written. I had assumed it was going to be performed for the student body. Instead, it was performed for an invited audience of academics, business leaders, and the local Catholic congregation, the majority of whom stormed out in droves after multiple enormous close-up projections of one of the actors' lipsticked mouths started shouting about burning down the Library of Alexandria, and the Library of Congress, and assorted other libraries, and Ronald McDonald fucking the Pope. That was my last German library commission, but there were other commissions, in Berlin and the UK, and I made good friends, and traveled around Europe, and took a cheap apartment near a scenic canal, and my wife (i.e., my second wife) eventually abandoned New York City and joined me, and I taught people English and mentored young scriptwriters, and ... well, basically, life was good.

That Berlin is no more. It disappeared in the blink of an eye in the Spring of 2020.

The New Normal Reich

I documented the rollout of the New Normal Reich during 2020 and 2021 in the book that has now made me a "hate criminal" in Germany. The title does not refer exclusively to Germany. The New Normal Reich is a global Reich. It is what the New World Order has evolved into. We all experienced its coming into being, whether in the USA, the UK, Ireland, Canada, Australia, Italy, or wherever. I just happened to experience it here in Germany, which, as an American, I found extremely disturbing. I won't go on and on about it here and spoil the essays collected in that volume, and the ones you are about to read in this one, and I honestly don't want to single out the Germans, because people in other countries were just as fascistic, fanatical, and hate-drunk, and would have gladly helped load "the Unvaccinated" and the "Covid deniers" and the "mask refuseniks" onto the trains to the camps,[15] but there is something uniquely horrifying about

---

15   The following is a 2020 Facebook post by Paul Street, a fairly well-known leftist journalist who often writes for *CounterPunch*. "So, I am not kidding here: when is someone going to draft legislation for internment camps and separate quarantine regions for Amerikaners who simply refuse vaccination and masks? I'm sorry to have to say this but we get [sic] a big fourth wave because of this partisan and social Darwinian and individualist madness and I'll draft the legislation myself. I am so not an anarchist and so much an authoritarian on this issue. I mean perhaps we need to stake out some

how the German masses go full-bore totalitarian at the drop of a hat. If you listened closely back in the Spring of 2020, you could hear the collective sigh of relief whooshing out all across the Fatherland as the veneer of democracy was abruptly torn away again. Suddenly, Germany was back in its element. Government leaders started barking out paranoid propaganda like Hitler on crack, whipping the German masses up into a frenzy of sadomasochistic hysteria. The corporate and state media began pumping out lies and fear like the proverbial Goebbelsian piano. A new "Enabling Act" was rushed through the *Bundestag*,[16] empowering the government to rule by decree. Protests against the "Covid measures" and the abrogation of the German Constitution were banned. Anyone challenging the official Covid narrative was demonized as a "far-right extremist," an "anti-Semite," or a "conspiracy theorist." Police goon squads raided businesses and homes where "social-distancing violations" had been reported. Mobs chased down maskless passengers on trains. A projection on a TV tower in Düsseldorf proclaimed "*Impfung=Freiheit*" (i.e., "vaccination=freedom"), which, OK, was not quite "*Arbeit macht frei*," but it was close enough to get the message across. By late 2021, the New Normal goon squads were brutally attacking the so-called "*Spaziergänger*" (i.e., people going on communal evening walks) and measuring the mandated "social distance" between people at the outdoor Christmas markets, literally, with big wooden measuring sticks. By April of 2022, the fanatical lunatics running the government would be attempting to pass an *Allgemeine Impfpflicht* (i.e., a "Covid vaccination mandate"), forcibly experimentally "vaccinating" every man, woman, and child in the country. TV celebrities were calling "the Unvaccinated" "a useless appendix on the body of society," exactly as the Nazis had described the Jews. Signage was posted outside

---

tens of thousand [sic] of acres of Western public lands and keep these people there. If they want to achieve herd immunity through mass death, fine, that's their choice, but maybe do it under lock and key in Covidiot Banustans under the coordinated control of the Department of the Interior, Homeland Security, the CDC, Department of Defense, and Border Control. Go ahead, call me a fascist, whatever, I can take it."

16 The revised "Infektionsschutzgesetz" ("Infection Protection Act") was passed by the German Bundestag on November 18, 2020.

restaurants, shops, theaters, museums, and on trains and buses, barring maskless people and "the Unvaccinated" from entering. There was an alphanumeric coding system that designated whether you were "vaccinated" or "recovered" and stipulated the documents you had to present to officials, and waiters, and shopkeepers, and all the other "good Germans" (or, rather, "good New Normals") who had been empowered to demand that you "show your papers."

And so on.

Yes, once again, "the land of poets and thinkers" had devolved into the land of mindless order-following fascists. Although there was, and there remains today, a sizable minority of courageous Germans willing to challenge the New Normal madness (for which many are still paying a price), the overwhelming majority of Germans started clicking heels and following orders, and unleashing their hatred on anyone who didn't. The entirety of mainstream German society—politicians, state and corporate media, scientific authorities, the judiciary, academia, cultural figures, celebrities, et cetera—started marching, or goose-stepping, in perfect sync.

The most disturbing aspect of it all for me, both personally and philosophically, was how thrilled people were to be taking part in the rollout of a new totalitarian movement. Again, this was not unique to the Germans, and, naturally, they didn't perceive themselves as members of a totalitarian movement. Totalitarians never do. They perceive themselves as participants in some beneficent, historic crusade, the justification for which is axiomatic and unquestionable. The Nazis didn't see themselves as the "bad guys" either. Neither did the Stalinists, nor the Maoists, nor the members of any other infamous totalitarian movement. They saw themselves as heroes, saviors of humanity, agents of destiny, or history, or whatever. Or they were just swept up in the exhilaration of the moment.

The thing is—and most of us don't want to acknowledge this—totalitarianism is exhilarating. It's like a powerful drug, a "power" drug . . . a mystical experience most modern religions cannot provide to their spiritually impoverished adherents. Surrendering oneself to an overwhelming force, an incontestable, godlike power, an inscrutable, impervious, immutable master that is literally remaking "reality," rewriting history, transmuting facts, is like mainlining pharmaceutical morphine.

It floods the dopamine receptors in the brain with irresistible orgasmic ecstasy. All your little mundane worries disappear. There is no you. And there is only you. You are everything, and nothing. You are pure sensation. You are fused with the Ultimate Power of the Universe, beyond good and evil, beyond humanity, and all its petty morals and judgments. You have jacked into the Cosmic Orgy. You are literally being fucked by God. Which particular god doesn't really matter, for it is the totalitarian movement itself, the sheer power of it, and not its ideology, that is seductive, that is almost irresistible.

As for the ideology of the New Normal Reich, it is subtler than that of the Nazis and the Communists, but totalitarianism is totalitarianism. Its essence, the attempt to establish complete control over society and everyone in it, down to the most intimate aspects of our lives, our very thoughts and perceptions, remains the same.

The fundamental distinction between the ideology of the New Normal Reich and twentieth-century totalitarian systems is that the New Normal Reich doesn't have an ideology. Its official ideology is "reality." I have written quite a lot about that, for example, in one of the essays in the book that has prompted the Germans to prosecute me for "hate crime" (as opposed to "sedition," a political charge, which is clearly what I am actually being punished for). Understanding this distinction is crucial to understanding the nature of the new totalitarianism. Here's an excerpt from that 2021 essay, *Pathologized Totalitarianism 101*:

> The most significant difference between 20th-century totalitarianism and this nascent, global totalitarianism is how New Normal totalitarianism pathologizes its political nature, effectively rendering itself invisible, and thus *immune to political opposition*. Whereas 20th-century totalitarianism wore its politics on its sleeve, New Normal totalitarianism presents itself as a non-ideological (i.e., supra-political) reaction to a global public health emergency. And, thus, its classic totalitarian features—e.g., the revocation of basic rights and freedoms, centralization of power, rule by decree, oppressive policing of the population, demonization and persecution of a scapegoat underclass, censorship, propaganda, etc.—are

not hidden, because they are impossible to hide, but are recontextualized in a pathologized official narrative. The *Untermenschen* become "the Unvaccinated." Swastika lapel pins become medical-looking masks. Aryan ID papers become "vaccination passes." Irrefutably senseless social restrictions and mandatory public-obedience rituals become "lockdowns," "social distancing," and so on. The world is united in a Goebbelsian total war, not against an external enemy (i.e., a racial or political enemy), but against an internal, pathological enemy.

This "pathologization" feature of the new totalitarianism does not only pertain to what people now refer to as "the Covid years," i.e., the rollout of the New Normal during 2020 to 2022. The pathologization of the political, and of the social itself, has been in progress for over three decades. And of course it has. It was predictable, inevitable. In a world united under a single ideology, there can be no legitimate ideological opposition, no actual political opposition. There can only be "deviants," "thought criminals," "deniers," "conspiracy theorists," "terrorists," "extremists." Such people are not political opponents. They are aberrations. They are cancerous tumors, malignant cells in the body of the empire, which need to be shrunk down to a harmless size, or, if all else fails, surgically removed.

The proclaimed ideology of such "deviants" doesn't matter. It is their deviance, and not their political or religious beliefs, that make them a threat. Neo-nationalists, "populists," Islamic fundamentalists, Christian fundamentalists, actual anarchists,[17] "gender skeptics," anti-Zionists," "anti-vaxxers," "Covid deniers," anyone who challenges the post-ideological ideology of the global-capitalist empire, whether they realize what they are challenging or not. Anyone who refuses to surrender their values—regardless of the nature of their values—to the values-devouring machinery of the market and be reconstituted as an interchangeable consumer.

Such people are not content to wear the desiccated husks of their former values like so many meaningless fashion accessories, as the vast majority of Western consumers do, so they attack the body of the empire from

---

17   i.e., not the global-capitalist "antifa" brownshirts.

within, or are perceived by the empire as an attack from within. Their very existence amounts to such an attack, an insurgency, or at least the threat of insurgency, as it contradicts the "reality" of the empire, and, of course, there can only be one "reality."

I am one of those people. Perhaps you are too. Unfortunately, our numbers are rapidly diminishing. Some of us are being criminally prosecuted, or canceled, or otherwise unpersoned. Others are being "visibility-filtered" into oblivion, herded into virtual ghettos, demographically segregated cul-de-sacs, where, as they say in the movies, "no one can hear you scream." Others have been captured and psychologically conditioned into a fanatical, cult-like, reactionary mass that is being molded into the official enemy that the New Normal Reich needs to confront and defeat—or perpetually confront and never quite defeat—in order to consolidate its dominance.

This is also a key feature of the New Normal Reich, the capture, conditioning, and commodification of opposition forces that cannot be eliminated. (Remember, this is global-capitalist totalitarianism, not the ham-fisted twentieth-century version.) Any internal resistance to the empire that cannot be annihilated, or otherwise silenced, can be commodified, branded, and then marketed back to its members as a simulacrum of itself. Ultimately, it can be instrumentalized, like "the Brotherhood" in Orwell's *1984*. It can be molded into a "resistance movement," which simultaneously exists and does not exist, because it only exists as a simulacrum (i.e., a copy of a thing that no longer exists, which conceals the fact that it no longer exists), and is deployed to lure political opposition into an endless war against other simulacra, a war that is itself a simulacrum (i.e., a copy of a war which is not being fought, and was never fought, and will never be fought, because it was already over before it began).

"Free-speech X" is a prime example. The ease with which Elon Musk and a consortium of serious global-capitalist behemoths, Saudi royalty, and assorted other oligarchs purchased the platform formerly known as Twitter,[18] rebranded it as "The Bastion of Free Speech" (despite the fact that X continues to collaborate with the empire to censor dissent),

---

18 Pringle, Eleanor, "Elon Musk was just forced to reveal who really owns X. Here's the list," *Fortune*, August 22, 2024.

corralled the majority of the "populist" opposition to the emergence of the New Normal Reich, and transformed it into a global personality cult, is a testament to the versatility of capitalism, and to the advantage of having no official ideology. When you don't have to conform to any specific ideology, you can wear whatever mask you need to wear. You can play whichever role is called for. It's all just marketing, advertising, branding. It's about selling images. The images don't *mean* anything. They're just Pavlovian stimuli designed to trigger a reaction in the target consumer.

The transformation of Twitter/X into the Musk Cult and its merger with (or takeover of) the MAGA movement has been fascinating, if extremely depressing, to watch. At the moment, it appears to be on the verge of morphing into exactly the official enemy that the empire has been desperately simulating for years. Musk and his minions are whipping the cult up into a frenzy of unbridled racial hatred in the wake of an attack by a Saudi immigrant on a Christmas market in Magdeburg, Germany. Musk has endorsed the AfD (i.e., the *Alternativ für Deutschland* party), and his followers are shrieking for mass deportations. X is systematically "boosting" neo-Nazis and other race-obsessed geeks who are posting anti-Muslim propaganda reminiscent of the anti-Semitic propaganda published in *Der Stürmer* in the 1930s. Algorithmically boosted influencers are posting about the "Zionist Occupation Government." The "Jewish Question" is being openly discussed.[19]

---

19   N.B. A few days after I wrote that paragraph, Musk fomented an internecine conflict within the cult, ostensibly over the issue of skilled immigration. In a series of "confrontational" tweets, he provoked the hardcore MAGA faction into "attacking" him for not being anti-immigrant enough, thus (a) whitewashing his image by enabling him to portray himself as "anti-racist," and (b) eliciting a flood of ugly bigoted posts from MAGA influencers, the visibility of which X algorithmically amplified. Once the dust had settled, his lieutenants set about scolding cult members for "divisiveness" and demanding "unity" and loyalty to Elon. Then Musk started tweeting about Pakistani rape gangs in the UK, which unleashed a torrent of outrage, bigotry, and reaffirmed devotion from the wayward cult members who had forgotten why they had attacked him in the first place. All of which is textbook cult-management strategy. It doesn't really matter how much of this is calculated behavior on Elon Musk's part. Cults (and larger authoritarian systems) are organisms. They function predictably, regardless of who leads them.

All of which is music to the ears of the empire, what with Trump about to assume office again and its political functionaries on the ropes here in Europe. Since 2016, The Powers That Be have been portraying themselves as the "defenders of democracy," as the only alternative to "the return of fascism." Despite their best efforts, it hasn't quite worked. The "populists" were never fascist enough. Trump never went balls-out-Hitler as prophesied. "Russiagate" and "Hitlergate" screwed the pooch. The corporate media have lost their credibility. Trump and MAGA are back with a vengeance. In Germany, the ruling coalition has collapsed. The government in France has collapsed. And so on. What the empire desperately needs at the moment is a bona fide fascistic official enemy, or at least a plausible simulacrum thereof, to terrorize the masses with, which is exactly what the Musk Cult is providing.

Seriously, if you called up Central Casting and asked for a neo-fascist antagonist, they couldn't do any better than what the "populist" resistance is being molded into by Elon and his cadre of influencers. Everything seems to be building toward a Hollywood-formula Act-Three showdown. The protagonist (i.e., the global-capitalist empire) has suffered the obligatory end-of-Act-Two major setback. The antagonists are in the catbird seat. The Musk Cult, MAGA, the AfD, and other neo-nationalist parties and movements are uniting into an Axis of Literal Hitlerosity! Emboldened bigots are hopping around in public beating their chests and hooting like a troop of crack-addled chimpanzees in heat. The stage is being perfectly set for our protagonist to make a final push, save "Western democracy" from the Populist Menace, and implement another slew of permanent "temporary emergency measures."

If all of that sounds like some sort of phantasmagoria, well, that's because it is. There is no actual political opposition. There never is in a totalitarian system, even a nascent totalitarian system like ours.

What there is, in our global-capitalist system, is a game in which the "red team" and the "blue team" take turns playing "the establishment" and "the resistance," whipping their fans up into a series of fervors over "culture war" issues guaranteed to keep them perpetually polarized, apoplectic with mindless hatred, paralyzed by fear and loathing, and clawing at each others' throats, while the destabilization, restructuring, and commodification of virtually everything in existence continues, while the atomization of society continues, while the decommissioning of national sovereignty continues, while the pathologization of the political continues, while the criminalization of dissent continues, while the dismantling of democracy continues, while the New Normal Reich continues to emerge from the chrysalis of the New World Order . . .

And, of course, this is just the beginning. I don't know how it is going to end or exactly how we're going to get where we're going, but we are all going to end up there together, all of us, if we continue down this road we are on.

I do not know how to not end up there. A number of my readers have asked me to offer "solutions" to the "problems" I have been writing about. I do not have any "solutions" to offer, and I do not trust anyone who claims to. What I've been writing about—i.e., in my more serious pieces, when I'm not just trying to make people laugh—is not a "problem" that has a "solution." It is the evolution of global ideological power system, the first of its kind in human history. That system is roughly thirty-five years old, which is nothing in historical terms. I have been trying to understand and explain its evolution, not wave the flag of any of the forces attempting to further or retard its advance . . . or furtively attempting to further its advance by pretending to attempt to retard its advance.

I hope that you will keep that in mind as you read the essays collected in this volume. Many of them have to do with my journey through the legal system of New Normal Germany, but that story is not really a story about Germany, or even a story about me, personally. It is a story about the evolution of that system. It is a story about where this road we are on leads.[20]

This part of that journey begins in 2022, as the pandemic hysteria was finally subsiding and the official Covid narrative was being exposed for

---

20 I'll spare you a repetition of the Martin Niemöller quote. I'm pretty sure you know it by heart. The point is, we're all headed to the same destination. It's just that some of us are getting there first.

the propaganda that it always was. That feels like a million years ago now. The Orwellian "memory hole" is working overtime, erasing and rewriting the past. Which is part of why I've been publishing these collections.[21] If nothing else, I hope they might serve as an unofficial history of events, a document, a reminder of what really happened, because, sometimes, in order to see where we are going, we have to look back and recall where we've been.

Ready? OK, here we go.

---

21 I'm grateful to Skyhorse for publishing this one. I'm a bit worn out from my adventures with the German authorities over the past few years.

2022

The past is whatever the records and the memories agree upon.
　　　　　　　　　　　　　　　　—George Orwell, *1984*

The Last Days of the Covidian Cult

January 18, 2022

This isn't going to be pretty, folks. The downfall of a death cult rarely is. There is going to be wailing and gnashing of teeth, incoherent fanatical jabbering, mass deleting of embarrassing tweets. There's going to be a veritable tsunami of desperate rationalizing, strenuous denying, shameless blame-shifting, and other forms of ass-covering, as suddenly former Covidian Cult members make a last-minute break for the jungle before the fully vaxxed-and-boosted "Safe and Effective Kool-Aid" servers get to them.

Yes, that's right, as I'm sure you've noticed, the official Covid narrative is finally falling apart, or is being hastily disassembled, or historically revised, right before our eyes. The "experts" and "authorities" are finally acknowledging that the "Covid deaths" and "hospitalization" statistics are artificially inflated and totally unreliable,[22] which they have been from the very beginning, and they are admitting that their miracle "vaccines" don't work,[23] (unless you change the definition of the word "vaccine"),[24] and

---

[22] Cole, Brendan, "Jake Tapper Rails Against 'Misleading' CDC COVID Hospitalization Numbers," *Newsweek*, January 11, 2022.
[23] Nolen, Stephanie, "Most of the World's Vaccines Likely Won't Prevent Infection from Omicron," *New York Times*, December 19, 2021.
[24] Camero, Katie, "Why did CDC change its definition for 'vaccine'?," *Miami Herald*, September 27, 2021.

that they have killed a few people,[25] or maybe more than a few people, and that lockdowns were probably "a serious mistake."[26]

I am not going to bother with further citations. You can surf the Internet as well as I can. The point is, the "Apocalyptic Pandemic" PSYOP has reached its expiration date. After almost two years of mass hysteria over a virus that causes mild-to-moderate common-cold or flu-like symptoms (or absolutely no symptoms whatsoever) in about 95 percent of the infected and the overall infection fatality rate of which is approximately 0.1 percent to 0.5 percent, people's nerves are shot. We are all exhausted. Even the Covidian cultists are exhausted. And they are starting to abandon the cult en masse.

It was always mostly just a matter of time. As Klaus Schwab said, "the pandemic represent[ed] a rare but narrow window of opportunity to reflect, re-imagine, and reset our world."

It isn't over, but that window is closing, and our world has not been "re-imagined" and "reset," not irrevocably, not just yet. Clearly, GloboCap underestimated the potential resistance to the Great Reset, and the time it would take to crush that resistance. And now the clock is running down, and the resistance isn't crushed . . . on the contrary, it is growing. And there is nothing GloboCap can do to stop it, other than go openly totalitarian, which it can't, as that would be suicidal. As I noted in a recent column:

> New Normal totalitarianism (and any global-capitalist form of totalitarianism) cannot display itself as totalitarianism, or even authoritarianism. It cannot acknowledge its political nature. In order to exist, it must not exist. Above all, it must erase its violence (the violence that all politics ultimately comes down to) and appear to us as an essentially beneficent response to a legitimate global health crisis.

---

25 "Lisa Shaw: Presenter's death due to complications of Covid vaccine," BBC, August 26, 2021.
26 Merrick, Rob, "David Frost brands Covid lockdowns a 'serious mistake' and says No 10 failed to 'challenge' scientists," *The Independent*, January 13, 2022.

The simulated "global health crisis" is, for all intents and purposes, over. Which means that GloboCap has screwed the pooch. The thing is, if you intend to keep the masses whipped up into a mindless frenzy of anus-puckering paranoia over an "apocalyptic global pandemic," at some point, you have to produce an actual apocalyptic global pandemic. Faked statistics and propaganda will carry you for a while, but eventually people are going to need to experience something at least resembling an actual devastating worldwide plague, in *reality*, not just on their phones and TVs.

Also, GloboCap seriously overplayed their hand with the miracle "vaccines." Covidian cultists really believed that the "vaccines" would protect them from infection. Epidemiology experts like Rachel Maddow assured them that they would.

"Now we know that the vaccines work well enough that the virus stops with every vaccinated person," Maddow said on her show the evening of March 29, 2021. "A vaccinated person gets exposed to the virus, the virus does not infect them, the virus cannot then use that person to go anywhere else," she added with a shrug. "It cannot use a vaccinated person as a host to go get more people."

And now they are all sick with . . . well, a cold, basically, or are "asymptomatically infected," or whatever. And they are looking at a future in which they will have to submit to "vaccinations" and "boosters" every three or four months to keep their "compliance certificates" current, in order to be allowed to hold a job, attend a school, or eat at a restaurant, which, OK, hardcore cultists are fine with, but there are millions of people who have been complying, not because they are delusional fanatics who would wrap their children's heads in cellophane if Anthony Fauci ordered them to, but purely out of "solidarity," or convenience, or herd instinct, or . . . you know, cowardice.

Many of these people (i.e., the non-fanatics) are starting to suspect that maybe what we "tin-foil-hat-wearing, Covid-denying, anti-vax, conspiracy-theorist extremists" have been telling them for the past twenty-two months might not be as crazy as they originally thought. They are backpedaling, rationalizing, revising history, and just making up all kinds of self-serving bullshit, like how we are now in "a post-vaccine world," or how "the Science has changed," or how "Omicron is different," in order to avoid being forced to admit that they're the victims of a GloboCap PSYOP and the worldwide mass hysteria it has generated.

Which ... fine, let them tell themselves whatever they need to for the sake of their vanity, or their reputations as investigative journalists, celebrity leftists, or Twitter revolutionaries. If you think these "recovering" Covidian Cult members are ever going to publicly acknowledge all the damage they have done to society, and to people and their families, since March 2020, much less apologize for all the abuse they heaped onto those of us who have been reporting the facts ... well, they're not. They are going to spin, equivocate, rationalize, and lie through their teeth, whatever it takes to convince themselves and their audience that, when the shit hit the fan, they didn't click heels and go full "Good German."

Give these people hell if you need to. I feel just as angry and betrayed as you do. But let's not lose sight of the ultimate stakes here. Yes, the official narrative is finally crumbling, and the Covidian Cult is starting to implode, but that does not mean that this fight is over. GloboCap and their puppets in government are not going to cancel the whole "New Normal" program, pretend the last two years never happened, and gracefully retreat to their lavish bunkers in New Zealand and their mega-yachts.

Totalitarian movements and death cults do not typically go down gracefully. They usually go down in a gratuitous orgy of wanton, nihilistic violence as the cult or movement desperately attempts to maintain its hold over its wavering members and defend itself from encroaching reality. And that is where we are at the moment ... or where we are going to be very shortly.

Cities, states, and countries around the world are pushing ahead with implementing the New Normal biosecurity society, despite the fact that there is no longer any plausible justification for it. Austria is going ahead with forced "vaccination."[27] Germany is preparing to do the same.[28] France is rolling out a national segregation system to pun-

---

27 Weise, Zia, "Austria's vaccine mandate to apply from February 1, Unvaccinated people face police checks and fines of up to €3,600 from mid-March," *Politico*, January 16, 2022.
28 "Germany's SPD expects vote on general vaccine mandate in March," Reuters, January 12, 2022.

ish "the Unvaccinated."[29] Greece is fining "unvaccinated" pensioners.[30] Australia is operating "quarantine camps."[31] Scotland. Italy. Spain. The Netherlands. New York City. San Francisco. Toronto. The list goes on, and on, and on.

I don't know what is going to happen. I'm not an oracle. I'm just a satirist. But we are getting dangerously close to the point where GloboCap will need to go full-blown fascist if they want to finish what they started. If that happens, things are going to get very ugly. I know, things are already ugly, but I'm talking a whole different kind of ugly. Think Jonestown, or Hitler's final days in the bunker, or the last few months of the Manson family.

That is what happens to totalitarian movements and death cults once the spell is broken and their official narratives fall apart. When they go down, they try to take the whole world with them. I don't know about you, but I'm hoping we can avoid that. From what I have heard and read, it isn't much fun.

---

29 "French parliament approves vaccine pass law to tackle Covid," Reuters, January 16, 2022.
30 "Greece punishes unvaccinated elderly with monthly fines - People above 60 in the southern European country face fines of up to 100 euros a month if they refuse COVID jabs," *Aljazeera*, January 17, 2022.
31 "Howard Springs: Australia police arrest quarantine escapees," BBC, December 1, 2021.

Attack of the Transphobic Putin-Nazi Truckers!

February 4, 2022

They rolled up on Ottawa's Parliament Hill like one of the plagues in the Book of Revelation, honking their infernal air horns, the grills of their tractors grinning demonically, the sides of their dry vans painted with blasphemies like "FREEDOM TO CHOOSE," "MANDATE FREEDOM," "NO VACCINE MANDATES," and "UNITED AGAINST TYRANNY."

Yes, that's right, New Normal Canada has been invaded and now is under siege by hordes of transphobic Putin-Nazi truckers, racist homophobes, anti-Semitic Islamaphobes, and other members of the working classes!

According to the corporate media, these racist, Russia-backed, working-class berserkers are running amok through the streets of Ottawa, waving giant "swastika flags," defecating on war memorials, sacking multi-million-dollar "soup kitchens," and eating the food right out of homeless people's mouths. Rumor has it, a kill-squad of truckers has been prowling the postnatal wards of hospitals, looking for helpless Kuwaiti babies to yank out of their incubators.

I know, this is Canada, so that sounds a little dubious, but this has all been thoroughly fact-checked by the fact checkers at the New Normal Ministry of Truth . . . you know, the ones that fact-checked Russiagate, and the Attempted Putin-Nazi Insurrection of January 6 at the US Capitol, and the safety and effectiveness of the Covid "vaccines," and the masks, and the inflated Covid statistics, and the rest of the official Covid narrative.

Or just take it from Prime Minister Justin Trudeau, who took to Twitter to condemn the protests as "a display of antisemitism, Islamophobia, anti-Black racism, homophobia, and transphobia!"[32] Now, this is the actual prime minister of Canada, not just some woke fanatic on Twitter. He was tweeting from his fortified Covid Bunker in an undisclosed location somewhere in the Yukon, or possibly the United States, where he fled as the transphobic Putin-Nazi truckers rolled up outside his office in Ottawa. Trudeau had vowed to stand and fight, but he had no choice but to flee the capital after he mysteriously tested positive for Covid, which also might have been the work of the Russians, possibly the same professional team of weed-smoking, hooker-banging Novichok assassins that got to the Skripals back in 2018!

Russian involvement has not yet been confirmed by the ex-CIA and NSA officials posing as "analysts" on CNN, but according to the CBC, "there's concern that Russian actors could be continuing to fuel things as the protest grows, and perhaps even instigating it from the outset."[33]

And, in light of the exposure of Putin's plot to produce a "very graphic" false-flag video "involving the deployment of corpses"[34] as a pretext to invade the Ukraine and set off nuclear Armageddon, or at least a raft of economic sanctions and DEFCON 1-level bellicose verbiage, it's possible that the entire "Covid pandemic" was an elaborate Putin-Nazi ruse designed to bring down the Trudeau government, and sabotage the implementation of the New Normal global-segregation system, and the compulsory mRNA "vaccination" of every man, woman, and child on earth, and "democracy," and transgender rights . . . or whatever.

---

32 "Today in the House members of Parliament unanimously condemned the antisemitism, Islamophobia, anti-Black racism, homophobia, and transphobia that we've seen on display in Ottawa over the past number of days. Together, let's keep working to make Canada more inclusive," Justin Trudeau, Twitter, February 2, 2022.
33 Colton, Emma, "Canadian news host slammed for suggesting Russia behind massive 'freedom' trucker protest," Fox News, January 30, 2022.
34 Borger, Julian, Shaun Walker and Dan Sabbagh, "Russia plans 'very graphic' fake video as pretext for Ukraine invasion, US claims," *The Guardian*, February 3, 2022.

But, seriously, this is where we are at the moment. We are in that dangerous, absurdist end-stage of the collapse of a totalitarian system or movement where chaos reigns and anything can happen. The official Covid narrative is rapidly evaporating. More and more people are taking to the streets to demand an end to whole fascist charade . . . no, not "transphobic white supremacists" or "anti-vax extremists," or "Russian-backed Nazis," but working-class people of all colors and creeds, families, with children, all over the world.

The Covidian Cult has lost control. Even hardcore mask-wearing, social-distancing, triple-vaxxed-double-boosted members are defecting. Formerly fanatical New Normal fascists are mass-deleting their 2020 tweets and switching uniforms as fast as they can. No, it isn't over yet, but the jig is up, and GloboCap knows it. And their functionaries in government know it.

And therein lies the current danger.

There is a narrow window, a month or two, maybe, for governments to declare "victory over the virus" and roll back their segregation systems, mask-wearing mandates, "vaccine" mandates, and the rest of the so-called "Covid restrictions." Many governments are already doing so, England, Norway, Denmark, Sweden, Switzerland, Finland, Ireland, et cetera. They have seen which way the wind is blowing, and are rushing to dismantle the New Normal in their countries before . . . well, before a convoy of extremely angry truckers arrives at their doors.

If they let that happen, they will find themselves in the unenviable position that Trudeau is now in. The Canadian truckers appear to be serious about staying there until their demands are met, which means Trudeau only has two options: (1) give in to the truckers' demands, or (2) attempt to remove them by force. There's already talk about bringing in the military.[35] Imagine what an unholy mess that would be. Odds are, the military would disobey his orders, and, if not, the world would be treated to the spectacle of full-blown New Normal Fascism in action.

---

35 Newton, Paula, "Ottawa officials say they're looking at 'every single option' to help end the trucker protest as demonstrations enter 6th day," CNN, February 2, 2022.

Either way, Trudeau is history, as long as the truckers stand their ground. I pray they do not give an inch, and I hope the leaders of other New Normal countries, like Australia, Germany, Austria, Italy, and France, are paying close attention.

Some of my readers will probably recall a previous column in which I wrote: "This isn't an abstract argument over 'the science.' It is a fight . . . a political, ideological fight. On one side is democracy, on the other is totalitarianism. Pick a fucking side, and live with it."

This is it. This is that fight. It is not a protest. It is a game of chicken. A high-stakes game of political chicken. In the end, politics comes down to power. The power to force your will on your adversary. GloboCap has been forcing the New Normal on people around the world for the past two years. What we are witnessing in Canada is the power of the people, the power the people have always had, and which we will always have, when we decide to use it, the power to shut down the whole GloboCap show, city after city if necessary.

So get out there and support the Canadian transphobic Putin-Nazi truckers, or your local transphobic Putin-Nazi truckers. And don't worry if you don't have a swastika flag. The agents provocateurs and the official propagandists in the corporate media will take care of that!

The Naked Face of New Normal Fascism

February 20, 2022

I told you this part wasn't going to be pretty. The collapse of fascist ideological movements and fanatical death cults never is. The New Normal is proving to be no exception.

After three weeks of non-violent civil disobedience outside the Canadian parliament in Ottawa by truckers and other Canadian citizens struggling to uphold their right to not be subjected to forced "vaccination," Justin Trudeau unleashed the goon squads. Thousands of militarized riot police (and other unidentified heavily armed operatives) swarmed the area, surrounded the protesters, started breaking into trucks and arresting people, and beating them with batons and the butts of their rifles.

In one particularly ugly episode, the New Normal stormtroopers rode their horses directly into a crowd of non-violent protesters, trampling an elderly lady with a walker.[36] She had just finished saying something to the police along the lines of "you break my heart . . . this is about peace, and love, and happiness." Then they knocked her down and rode their horses over her.

Despite an abundance of video evidence clearly depicting exactly what happened,[37] the Ottawa Police tried to spin it on Twitter . . .

---

36 Warmington, Joe, "Police horses trample demonstrators at Freedom Convoy protest in Ottawa," *Toronto Sun*, February 18, 2022.
37 McKnight, Patricia, "Video Appears to Show Police Horses Trampling Canadian Trucker Protesters," *Newsweek*, February 21, 2022.

We hear your concern for people on the ground after horses dispersed a crowd. Anyone who fell got up and walked away. We're unaware of any injuries. A bicycle was thrown at the horse further down the line and caused the horse to trip. The horse was uninjured.[38]

A photo of the incident that went viral on Twitter captured the moment when the Ottawa police and their horses brutally "dispersed" the crowd, trampling the old lady, whose walker might have been the alleged "horse-assaulting bicycle." The face of the gentlemen on the ground beside her might have also caused the horse "to trip," or was in the process of causing the horse "to trip," at the moment this now infamous photo was taken.

And that wasn't all. Oh no, far from it. The "show of force" was just getting started. After all, this was not a "mostly peaceful" outbreak of rioting, looting, and arson. This was non-violent civil disobedience, with children's bouncy castles, makeshift saunas, honking, dancing, illegal barbecuing, and other forms of "terrorist" activity, which had to be crushed with an iron fist.

On Saturday, the goon squads broke out the stun grenades, the pepper spray, and the big wooden sticks. By Sunday morning, they were shooting people with "non-lethal, mid-range impact weapons." "Tow truck operators" wearing bright green horror-movie ski masks to conceal their identities were brought in to haul away the big rigs.

Before he turned the goon squads loose on Friday, Trudeau invoked the "Emergencies Act," suspending the Canadian Constitution, which he had already suspended back in 2020 due to the "Apocalyptic Pandemic," which is why the protesters were protesting in the first place. Parliament was scheduled to debate his authority to declare another "state of emergency," but, of course, the debate was abruptly suspended due to the massive "police operation" that his invocation of the Act had enabled.

Acting under the Emergencies Act, he immediately canceled the right of assembly, outlawed the protests, and started threatening to kill

---

38 Ottawa Police, Twitter, February 18, 2022.

people's dogs and take away their kids. Then he and his fascist New Normal lieutenants started freezing the bank accounts of anyone and everyone even vaguely connected to the trucker protest. According to a *Bloomberg* report:

> The emergency orders require virtually every participant in the Canadian financial system—banks, investment firms, credit unions, loan companies, securities dealers, fundraising platforms and payment and clearing services—to determine whether they possess or control property of a person who's attending an illegal protest or providing supplies to demonstrators.[39]

And, as if all that wasn't fascist enough, Ottawa's police chief has made it clear that, once the crackdown is finally over, they will hunt down anyone involved in the protests, arrest them and charge them with "criminal offenses," subject them to "financial sanctions," and otherwise destroy their lives and families.

The crackdown in Ottawa is hardly an aberration. As my readers might recall, New Normal Germany outlawed protesting against the New Normal (i.e., the new official ideology) back in September of 2020, and the German police have been absolutely brutal. Anyone deemed a "Covid denier" is subject to surveillance by Germany's intelligence services. The US Department of Homeland Security designates us "domestic violent extremists." Same story in Australia, France, Belgium, the Netherlands, and assorted other countries.

I have been describing the New Normal as a new form of totalitarianism (or fascism, if you prefer) for the past two years, and I have been documenting it from the very beginning (see, e.g., my Twitter threads from March 2020[40] and April 2020,[41] which the *OffGuardian* editors have

---

[39] Orland, Kevin and Brian Platt, "Banks Get Protesters' Names as Canada Financial Squeeze Unfolds," *Bloomberg*, February 17, 2022.
[40] "50 Headlines: Welcome to the 'new normal,'" *OffGuardian*, April 14, 2020.
[41] "50 Headlines Darker: More of the 'New Normal,'" *OffGuardian*, April 25, 2020.

preserved for posterity). It has been there all along, right out in the open, but rendered invisible by the official Covid narrative.

The official narrative is rapidly dissolving, rendering the fascism of the New Normal visible. This is happening now because those of us who have seen it from the beginning, and have been resisting it all along, have held out long enough to run out the clock. GloboCap can't keep the narrative going, so all they have left is brute fascist force.

We need to make GloboCap deploy that force, and to shine a big, bright spotlight on it, as the truckers and protesters in Ottawa have just done. In case anyone is confused about the tactic, it's called classic non-violent civil disobedience. I described it in a recent column:

> In other words, we need to make GloboCap (and its minions) go openly totalitarian . . . because it can't. If it could, it would have done so already. Global capitalism cannot function that way. Going openly totalitarian will cause it to implode . . . no, not global capitalism itself, but this totalitarian version of it. In fact, this is starting to happen already. It needs the simulation of "reality," and "democracy," and "normality," to keep the masses docile. So we need to attack that simulation. We need to hammer on it until it cracks, and the monster hiding within in appears. That is the weakness of the system . . . New Normal totalitarianism will not work if the masses perceive it as totalitarianism, as a political/ideological program, rather than as a response to a deadly pandemic.

The official narrative is dead or dying. The Covidian Cult is coming apart. No one but the most fanatical New Normals believes there is any real justification for imposing mandatory "vaccination," "quarantine camps," segregation of "the Unvaccinated," or any of the other "Covid restrictions." "The virus" is no longer an excuse for mindlessly following ridiculous orders and persecuting those of us who refuse.

Apocalyptic Pandemic Theater is over. It is a purely political fight from now on.

Ottawa is not the end. It is just the beginning. Protests and other forms of civil disobedience are growing all around the world . . . yes, even here in New Normal Germany. That does not mean it is time to relax. On the contrary, it is time to step up the pressure. It is time to make the monster show itself, in all its naked fascist ugliness, and to force everyone to pick a side.

Revenge of the Putin-Nazis
March 7, 2024

And they're back! It's like one of those 1960s Hammer Film Productions horror-movie series with Peter Cushing and Christopher Lee... Return of the Putin-Nazis! Revenge of the Putin-Nazis! Return of the Revenge of the Bride of the Putin-Nazis! And this time they're not horsing around with stealing elections from Hillary Clinton with anti-masturbation Facebook ads. They are going straight for "democracy's" jugular!

Yes, that's right, folks, Vladimir Putin, leader of the Putin-Nazis and official "Evil Dictator of the Day," has launched a kamikaze attack on the United Forces of Goodness and Freedom to provoke us into losing our temper and waging a global thermonuclear war that will wipe out the entire human species and most other forms of life on earth!

I'm referring, of course, to Putin's inexplicable and totally unprovoked invasion of Ukraine, a totally peaceful, Nazi-free country which was just sitting there minding its non-Nazi business, singing Kumbaya, and so on, and not in any way collaborating with or being cynically used by GloboCap to menace and eventually destabilize Russia so that the GloboCap boys can get back in there and resume the Caligulan orgy of "privatization" they enjoyed throughout the 1990s.

No, clearly, Putin has just lost his mind, and has no strategic objective whatsoever (other than the total extermination of humanity), and is just running around the Kremlin shouting "DROP THE BOMBS! EXTERMINATE THE BRUTES!" all crazy-eyed and with his face painted green like Colonel Kurtz in *Apocalypse Now*, because what other explanation is there?

Or, OK, sure, there *are* other explanations, but they're all just "Russian disinformation" and "Putin-Nazi propaganda" disseminated by "Putin-apologizing, Trump-loving, discord-sowing racists," "transphobic, anti-vax conspiracy theorists," "Covid-denying domestic extremists," and other traitorous blasphemers and heretics, who are being paid by Putin to infect us with doubt, historical knowledge, and critical thinking, because they hate us for our freedom . . . or whatever.

Let's take a quick look at some of that "Russian disinformation" and "propaganda," purely to inoculate ourselves against it. We need to be familiar with it so we can switch off our minds and shout thought-terminating clichés and official platitudes at it whenever we encounter it on the Internet. It might be a little uncomfortable to do this, but just think of it as a Russian-propaganda "vaccine," like an ideological mRNA fact-check booster (guaranteed to be "safe and effective")!

OK, the first thing we need to look at, and dismiss, and deny, and pretend we never learned about, is this nonsense about "Ukrainian Nazis." Just because Ukraine is full of neo-Nazis,[42] and recent members of its government were neo-Nazis, and its military has neo-Nazi units (e.g., the notorious Azov Battalion),[43] and it has a national holiday celebrating a Nazi,[44] and government officials hang his portrait in their offices, and the military and neo-Nazi militias have been terrorizing and murdering ethnic Russians since the USA and the United Forces of Goodness supported and stage-managed a "revolution" (i.e., a coup) back in 2014 with the assistance of a lot of neo-Nazis,[45] that doesn't mean Ukraine has a "Nazi problem."

After all, its current president is Jewish!

---

42 Golinkin, Lev, "Neo-Nazis and the Far Right Are On the March in Ukraine," *The Nation*, February 22, 2019.
43 Rubinstein, Alexander and Max Blumenthal, "How Ukraine's Jewish president Zelenskyy made peace with neo-Nazi paramilitaries on front lines of war with Russia," *The Grayzone*, March 4, 2022.
44 JTA and Cnaan Liphshiz, "Ukraine Designates National Holiday to Commemorate Nazi Collaborator," *Haaretz*, December 27, 2018.
45 Marcetic, Branko, "A US-Backed, Far Right–Led Revolution in Ukraine Helped Bring Us to the Brink of War," *Jacobin*, February 2022.

If a traitor mentions the Ukrainian Nazis, switch your mind off as quickly as you can and hit them with that thought-terminating cliché ... "THE PRESIDENT OF THE UKRAINE IS JEWISH!" Or "EVERY COUNTRY HAS NAZIS!" That's another good one!

The other thing we need to look at, and dismiss, and never think about again, is the role the United Forces of Goodness played in orchestrating this mess, starting with how members of the US government stage-managed that coup in 2014,[46] and how they funded and worked with known neo-Nazis,[47]—not secret, dog-whistling, half-assed Nazis, but big fat, Jew-hating, Sieg-heiling Nazis—to foment and eventually execute it. All that, of course, is just "Russian propaganda," despite the fact that it has been thoroughly documented, not just by the usual "conspiracy theory outlets," but by official mouthpieces of the Forces of Goodness, like the BBC,[48] *The Nation*,[49] and even *The Guardian*.[50]

If some Putin-Nazi traitor mentions these facts, or sends you links to the numerous articles documenting the 2014 coup, again, switch your mind off immediately and shout "ANCIENT HISTORY! ANCIENT HISTORY!" and then shoot yourself up with a massive "booster" of fact-checked Truth from the Forces-of-Goodness media. I recommend *The Guardian* and the *New York Times*, but if you want to go directly to the source, just follow Illia Ponomarenko of the *Kyiv Independent* on Twitter, where he is tweeting old photos of himself and his neo-Nazi Azov-Battalion "brothers in arms" lounging around on crates of ammo following a training exercise or something.[51]

---

46 Parry, Robert, "The Ukraine Mess That Nuland Made," *Truthout*, July 15, 2015.
47 Whelan, Brian, "Far-right group at heart of Ukraine protests meet US senator," Channel 4 News, December 16, 2013.
48 "Ukraine crisis: Transcript of leaked Nuland-Pyatt call," BBC, February 7, 2014.
49 Luhn, Alec, "The Ukrainian Nationalism at the Heart of 'Euromaidan,'" *The Nation*, January 21, 2014.
50 Milne, Seumas, "It's not Russia that's pushed Ukraine to the brink of war," *The Guardian*, April 30, 2014.
51 "Brothers in arms. It was a fine day in August 2017 when Azov guys consecrated me an artillery guy," Illia Ponomarenko, Twitter, April 22, 2019.

OK, that's enough "inoculation" for now. We don't want to expose ourselves to too much of that stuff, or we're liable to end up supporting the wrong Nazis.

Fortunately, the United Forces of Goodness (and Freedom) are censoring most of it anyway, and instead are feeding us sentimental stories, like the one about "the Ghost of Kyiv,"[52] the completely fictional Ukrainian fighter pilot who shot down the entire Putin-Nazi Air Force while delivering pithy one-liners like Bruce Willis in the *Die Hard* films!

As the *New York Times* explained,[53] fake stories like that, or the one about the Snake Island martyrs who told the Russians to "go fuck themselves"[54] and so were genocided by a Putin-Nazi kill squad[55] but then turned up alive a few days later,[56] are not disinformation, and even if they are, it doesn't matter, because they're good for morale!

And that's the important thing, after all. If we're ever going to defeat these Putin-Nazis, and the imaginary apocalyptic plague, and Trump, and terrorism, and domestic extremism, and climate change, and racism, and whatever, we need to keep the Western masses whipped up into a perpetual state of utterly mindless, hate-drunk hysteria like an eternal episode of the Two Minutes Hate from Orwell's *1984*.

It doesn't really matter who the masses are being told to hate this week . . . the Russians, "the Unvaccinated," the Terrorists, the Populists, the Assad-Apologists, the Conspiracy Theorists, the Anti-Vaxxers, the Disinformationists . . . or whoever. In the end, there is only one enemy,

---

52 Simko-Bednarski, Evan, "Who is the 'Ghost of Kyiv'? Story of Ukrainian ace pilot goes viral," *New York Post*, February 25, 2022.
53 "Viral stories like the Ghost of Kyiv—a Ukrainian pilot who supposedly single-handedly shot down several Russian fighter jets—are of questionable veracity. But they're a key part of Ukraine's war plan, experts say, as it tries to keep morale high," *New York Times*, Twitter, March 3, 2022.
54 Visontay, Elias, "Ukraine soldiers told Russian officer 'go fuck yourself' before they died on island," *The Guardian*, February 25, 2022.
55 "Snake Island: Ukraine says soldiers killed after refusing to surrender," BBC, February 25, 2022.
56 Curet, Monique, "Ukrainian Snake Island soldiers are believed to be alive, but details of their captivity are unclear," *Poynter*, March 4, 2022.

the enemy of the United Forces of Goodness, the enemy of the unaccountable, supranational global-capitalist empire (or "GloboCap" as I like to call it).

This multiplicitous, Goldstein-like enemy of GloboCap is an internal enemy. GloboCap has no external enemies. It dominates the entire planet. It is one big global-capitalist world. It has been for the last thirty years or so. Most of us can't quite get our heads around that bit of reality yet, so we still see the world as a competition between sovereign nation states, like the USA and Russia. It is not. Yes, there *are* still nation states, and they compete with each other (like corporations compete for advantage within the system they comprise), but the fundamental conflict of our age is a global counter-insurgency op.

What we've been experiencing for the last thirty years, over and over, in many different forms, is a globally hegemonic power system carrying out a "clear-and-hold" operation. GloboCap has been gradually destabilizing, restructuring, and privatizing the post-Cold-War world, first, in Eastern Europe and the Greater Middle East, and, more recently, here at home in the Western nations. For those not familiar with the term "clear and hold," it is a standard counter-insurgency strategy in which military (or private military) personnel clear an area of guerrillas, or other insurgents, and then keep the area "clear" of such insurgents while winning the support of the populace for the government (or the occupation) and its policies.

Take a minute and think about that. Think about the last two years. Think about the last thirty years. Seriously, just as an exercise, imagine GloboCap as an occupying army and the entire world as the territory it is occupying. Imagine GloboCap establishing control, targeting and neutralizing a variety of insurgencies, *any* insurgency, regardless of its nature, any and all resistance to its occupation, or lack of support for its "government and policies." It does not matter who the insurgents are, die-hard communists, Islamic fundamentalists, nationalists, populists . . . it makes no difference. The occupation couldn't care less what they believe in or why they're resisting. The objective of the op is to control the territory and get the populace on board with the new "reality."

Welcome to the new reality... a "reality" in which "history has stopped [and] nothing exists except an endless present in which the Party is always right." Yes, I know you are sick of me quoting Orwell, but, given the circumstances, I cannot help it. Just reflect on how seamlessly GloboCap segued from the Apocalyptic Pandemic narrative back to the Putin-Nazi narrative, which had seamlessly replaced the Global War on Terror narrative in the Summer of 2016, and how instantly the New Normals switched from hating "the Unvaccinated" to hating the Russians, and then scold me again for quoting Orwell.

Look, I hate to disappoint Edward Norton and millions of other fanatical liberals, but the USA is not going to war with Russia, not intentionally in any event. Russia has ballistic missiles with thermonuclear warheads on them. This isn't a rerun of World War II. And it isn't World War III or the Cold War redux. That is not what is happening in Ukraine.

What is happening in Ukraine is, Russia is not playing ball. For some reason, it does not want to be destabilized, restructured, and privatized by GloboCap. It is acting like a sovereign nation-state... which it is, and isn't, which paradoxical fact GloboCap is trying to impress on Russia, just as countries throughout the global-capitalist empire impressed it on us for the past two years, as Trudeau impressed it on those protesters in Ottawa when he canceled their rights and went full-fascist.

What is happening is, Russia is rebelling against GloboCap, and, unlike the other rebellious parties that GloboCap has been dealing with recently, Russia has thermonuclear weapons.

I'm not trying to tell you who to root for. Root for GloboCap if you want. I'm just urging you, before you fly over to Kyiv[57] and join the fight against the Putin-Nazis, or make a jackass of yourself on the Internet shrieking for nuclear Armageddon, or fire-bomb your local Russian restaurant, or beat the crap out of some Russian-looking person, to maybe take a moment or two and try to understand what is actually going on, and who the major players actually are, and where GloboCap's efforts to "clear and hold" the entire planet are inexorably taking us.

---

57   Formerly known as "Kiev," until Ukraine de-Russified it in 1995.

I know, that's a lot to ask these days, but I can't help thinking about all those nukes, and the fallibility of human beings, and yes, all the Ukrainians who are going to needlessly suffer and die while we watch the action on TV, and root for our favorite characters to win, and so on . . . as if it were a fucking movie.

Springtime for GloboCap
March 27, 2022

Warm up the Wagnerian orchestra and call in the goose-stepping chorus girls, because . . . yes, that's right, it's Springtime for GloboCap! "The Winter of Severe Illness and Death"[58] is over! The big Black Sun is shining again! God's in his heaven, all's right with the world!

OK, sure, the vast majority of humanity are suffering from post-traumatic stress, having been terrorized, gaslighted, threatened, bullied, and otherwise systematically mindfucked by their governments, the media, and "health authorities" on a daily basis for the past two years, and we're all exhausted and at each other's throats, and many of our businesses and incomes have been ruined, and inflation is spiraling out of control, and a lot of us are still being gratuitously demonized, segregated from society, banned from traveling, and forced to submit to invasive procedures and wear medically pointless symbols of ideological conformity on our faces, so we're not quite in the spirit of the season . . . but, for GloboCap, things couldn't be going any better!

Not only is the final phase of their rollout of the new pathologized totalitarianism (i.e., the New Normal) going more or less to plan, but those pesky, non-ball-playing Russians have been baited into a military quagmire in Ukraine that could be dragged out for years! Think of all the destabilization, restructuring, and privatization opportunities, and not just in Russia and Eastern Europe, and not just during the next few years,

---

58 Malloy, Allie and Maegan Vazquez, "Biden warns of winter of 'severe illness and death' for unvaccinated due to Omicron," CNN, December 16, 2021.

but throughout the world and well into the future! With the majority of the Western masses brain-buggered into a state of almost catatonic credulity and obedience, who's going to stop them? The sky's the limit!

We're talking *radical* social and economic restructuring, a brave new GloboCap-curated world! A world of constant chaos and crisis, eternally recurring "Apocalyptic Pandemics," intramural proxy wars, climate-change lockdowns, "disinformation" attacks, mandatory genetic-therapy, digital currencies . . . the whole nine yards. A world not governed as much as "guided" by non-governmental global-governance entities, global corporations, benevolent billionaires, banks, investment management firms, and, of course, the military and intelligence communities.

But I'm getting a little ahead of myself. It will be a while before GloboCap can blossom into its full expression. In the meantime, the global "clear-and-hold" op continues . . . and appears to have abruptly shifted into an extremely psychotic and fascist phase.

This shift was executed in Orwellian fashion, like that scene in *1984* where the Party switches official enemies right in the middle of a Hate Week speech. But, in our case, the switch was a little more complicated, because GloboCap didn't just switch official enemies—like they did in the Summer of 2016, and then again in the Spring of 2020—they revised the *identity* of the official enemy, not just its name, but its fundamental character, or, more accurately, and more psychotically, they split the identity of the official enemy, stripping off and embracing its fascism while simultaneously maintaining and magnifying its fascism, simulating a moral spectrum of fascism, and thus subjecting the New Normal masses to a mind-bending level of Orwellian double-think.

In the blink of an eye, without missing a beat, both the white-supremacist Putin-Nazis that plagued Democracy throughout the Trumpian Reich and the Covid-denying Anti-Vax Nazis that plagued the New Normals throughout the Global Pandemic were seamlessly replaced by the GloboCap Nazis . . . but, the thing is, the GloboCap Nazis are the good guys, and the Putin-Nazis and Anti-Vax Nazis are . . . well, I guess they're still technically Nazis, except for the fact that they aren't actual Nazis and are mostly just regular working-class people, whereas the GloboCap Nazis *are* actual Nazis (i.e., Sieg-heiling,

Jew-hating, Hitler-worshiping Nazis), who the US military and intelligence community, NATO, and assorted private "military advisors" have been funding, arming, and otherwise supporting since the 2014 Ukrainian "revolution" (i.e., coup) that they orchestrated to destabilize Russia as part of that global clear-and-hold operation, which operation, of course, doesn't actually exist, and is just another conspiracy theory disseminated by Putin-Nazi traitors like me to erode support for the GloboCap Nazis, who are really just wholesome young Aryan boys who are trying to defend Democracy from Evil, and cleanse their country of the Jews and the Roma, and exterminate the Russian race, starting with the children, apparently.

> **Consent Factory**
> @consent_factory
>
> We couldn't believe this was real at first, but it seems this is an actual broadcast from an actual TV channel in #Ukraine ...
>
> I can allow myself to quote the words of Adolf Eichmann, who said that in order to destroy a nation, it is necessary to destroy, first of all, children.

OK, I know this is getting confusing, what with all the various Nazis, and so on, but that's only because you're still trying to make sense of the utterly psychotic official propaganda that GloboCap is relentlessly bombarding us with. For example, the recent BBC segment in which Ros Atkins explained how the neo-Nazi Azov Detachment is actually "mainstream." Or a recent NBC piece by Allan Ripp, explaining how, yes, there is definitely a serious neo-Nazi problem in Ukraine, but if the Ukrainian Nazis (i.e., the GloboCap Nazis) persecute and murder Ukrainian Jews, it's actually Putin's fault for invading the country and creating "chaos and insurgency," or whatever.[59] Or the *Unherd* article by Aris Roussinos,[60] explaining that arming and supporting neo-Nazis "may be one of the hard choices forced by war," and advising Zelenskyy to disarm them once the war is over and "freedom" is restored, which, obviously, he intends to do. After all, the man is Jewish! He will probably ban the neo-Nazis outright, like he banned all the non-neo-Nazi parties.[61]

Or, if you prefer your propaganda less nuanced, you can go with CNN and get it straight from the source, for example, from Major Denis Prokopenko of the neo-Nazi Azov Regiment,[62] or the neo-Nazi squad that Jeremy Bowen of the BBC was hanging out with.[63] Apparently, CNN and the BBC were unable to locate any non-neo-Nazis to bring us the "fact-checked Truth" from the battlefield.

---

59 Ripp, Allan, "Ukraine's Nazi problem is real, even if Putin's 'denazification' claim isn't," NBC, March 5, 2022.
60 Roussinos, Aris, "The truth about Ukraine's far-Right militias Russia has empowered dangerous factions," *Unherd*, June 1, 2022.
61 "Zelenskyy suspends parties with Russian links - Ukraine's President Volodymyr Zelenskyy has ordered to suspend activities of 11 political parties with links to Russia," *The Independent*/AP, March 20, 2022.
62 Norton, Ben, "CNN promotes neo-Nazi commander from Ukraine's white-supremacist Azov regiment—Top US media outlet CNN promoted a commander from Ukraine's neo-Nazi Azov regiment, failing to mention his militia's white-supremacist ideology," *Geopolitical Economy Report*, March 21, 2022.
63 "Exclusive: BBC claims Ukrainian nazis are exaggerated—but shows video of Bowen with nazi unit," *Skwawkbox*, March 26, 2022.

Or... wait. Sorry, I got all confused again. These are the *good* Nazis... the GloboCap Nazis! The *actual* Nazis, not the fictional Nazis. Or... wait, no... never mind. I mean, it's not like it really matters anyway, right? The point is, it's Spring, and the goat-footed balloon-Man whistles... no, strike the balloon-Man. This is no time for balloon-Man references. It's New Normal Spring! The birds are buzzing! The bees are chirping! The ICBMs are tumescent with rocket fuel and throbbing in their silos! The New Normal masses are out prancing around with their "vaccination passes" and medical-looking masks, in their official neo-Nazi Azov hoodies, waving their Ukrainian flags, and otherwise desperately trying to pretend that they haven't just been colossally mindfucked by GloboCap for the last two years!

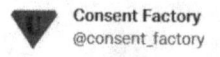

> **Consent Factory**
> @consent_factory
>
> Here's the perfect gift for your fanatical, brainwashed loved ones this Spring. Yes, it's official neo-Nazi Azov Battalion sweaters and hoodies! Suitable for pogroms, doing NATO's dirty work, or simply wearing around the house. Available in all sizes from Amazon.com!
>
> +2 colors/patterns
> **GR8Shop**
> Fight Azov Battalion Ukraine Forces Unisex Sweater
> ★☆☆☆☆ ⌄1
> $44⁹⁹
> $8.00 shipping
>
> +2 colors/patterns
> **GR8Shop**
> Fight Azov Battalion Ukraine Forces Unisex Hoodie
> $49⁹⁹
> $8.00 shipping
>
> 12:03 AM · Mar 3, 2022 · Twitter Web App

But, there I go, getting negative again. I really need to try to focus on the positive, no matter how psychotic things are in reality. Here in New Normal Germany, it's almost Freedom Day again! Technically, Freedom Day was March 18, but they rewrote the Infection Protection Act (again) to postpone Freedom Day until April 2, after which date "the Unvaccinated" will be allowed to go back out into society and everyone will only be forced to wear symbols of conformity to official ideology on their faces on public transport, and trains, and planes, and in hospitals, and various other places, unless federal states declare themselves "hotspots"—which several states have already done—in which case Freedom Day will be postponed indefinitely.

But whatever. It's Springtime for GloboCap! Freedom is slavery! Ignorance is strength! The GloboCap Nazis are winning the war! Sure, Pfizer has just released nine pages of "adverse events of special interest" connected to their Covid "vaccine," but they "may not have any causal relationship" to each other![64] And all those videos of the GloboCap Nazis duct-taping men, women, and children to lampposts, painting their faces with chemicals, stripping them half naked, and whipping and beating them?[65] Those people are all "saboteurs" or "looters,"[66] or "Putin-Nazi collaborators," and it's all just Russian disinformation! And whatever. Trust the "Science" . . . or something!

All right, I think that's quite enough from me. I'll sign off and let you get back to the show. Look, here come the triple-vaxxed, double-boosted, goose-stepping GloboCap chorus girls!

---

64 "Fact Check: Pages of suspected side effects released about Pfizer's COVID-19 vaccine 'may not have any causal relationship' to the jab, company says," Reuters, March 17, 2022.
65 Melanovski, Jason, "Vigilante punishment spreads in Ukraine," *World Socialist Web Site*, March 22, 2022.
66 Lodge, Matthew, "Caught with his pants down: Looter is tied up and humiliated as punishment for trying to steal during Russian attack on Kyiv," *The Daily Mail*, March 8, 2022.

The Normalization of The New Normal Reich

July 22, 2022

I know, you're probably sick and tired of hearing about the Rise of the New Normal Reich. You want it to be over. So do I. It isn't over, not by a long shot.

It might seem like it's over where you are. I imagine it does if you live in Florida, or in Texas, or the UK, or Sweden, or Croatia, or in some other country or state in which the majority of the "Covid restrictions" have been lifted, or perhaps were never introduced in the first place.

If that's the case, I'm happy for you.

I happen to live in New Normal Germany, the current tip of the New Normal spear, or one of the tips of one of its spears (or mRNA-laced hypodermic needles), the others being countries and states like Canada, China, Australia, New York, California, and assorted other hotbeds of New Normalism. If you live in one of these New Normal strongholds, you are acutely aware of how it is not over.

Yes, the Covidian Cult is kaput. The spell has been broken. Only the most insanely fanatical New Normal cultists continue to walk around in public in their plague masks and homemade hazmat suits. But the New Normal Reich is not kaput. The New Normal Reich is being . . . well, normalized. The masses are being systematically conditioned to accept the biosecurity police state that the global-capitalist ruling classes have been implementing for the last three years. Despite the now irrefutable evidence that the "vaccines" do not prevent transmission of the virus, "the

Unvaccinated" are still being segregated, banned from working, attending school, competing in major sporting events, and so on. People are still being forced to wear masks, the symbol of the New Normal Reich, on planes, trains, public transport, in doctors offices, hospitals, et cetera. Here, there, and everywhere, New Normal symbols and social rituals are being permanently integrated into everyday life.

These symbols and rituals are more than just the window dressing of the New Normal Reich. They are how our new "reality" is being created and maintained. The masses are like actors being forced to emotionally invest in the "reality" of an absurdist stage play. The more they repeat the performance, the more convincing the fictional "reality" becomes, regardless of how patently absurd it is . . . and it is becoming more and more absurd.

For example, at the airports in New Normal Canada, citizens attempting to enter their own country without the "ArriveCAN" app on their smartphones to provide proof of their "vaccination status" (including octogenarians who do not own smartphones) are subjected to extended absurdist harassment by imbecilic New Normal clowns in red vests. Here in New Normal Germany, the government is preparing to force everyone to wear medical-looking masks in public every Autumn and Winter, not just on account of the "Apocalyptic Plague" but also on account of the normal Winter flu. The pretext doesn't really matter anymore. The point is the display of ideological uniformity.

Meanwhile, Germany's Federal Ministry of Health was forced to publish a limited hangout regarding "vaccination" injuries and deaths. They did it in classic Goebbelsian fashion, announcing that "one in 5,000 people experience serious adverse effects following a Covid vaccination," on Twitter.

Apparently, they didn't like the actual data on the number of serious adverse effects, so they decided to just go ahead and lie about them. Serious adverse effects have been reported in approximately one in 5,000 *doses*, i.e., not one in 5,000 "vaccinated" people. Approximately 184,000,000 doses have been administered to people in Germany and . . . well, you can do the math. Naturally, the Twitter Corporation has been slapping fake "misleading content" warnings on retweets pointing out the German

Ministry of Health's lie, because the truth is whatever the Corporatocracy says it is, and everything else is "disinformation."

If you think I'm being harsh or hyperbolic in characterizing the Ministry's lie as a lie, keep in mind that the German Minister of Health, Karl Lauterbach, has been lying, repeatedly, to the German public for over two years now, promoting the "side-effects-free vaccines," ordering the segregation of "the Unvaccinated," and fomenting hatred of anyone refusing to conform to New Normal ideology.

And now, tens of thousands of people in Germany—at minimum, as vaccine adverse-effects have always been significantly underreported—have been seriously injured or . . . you know, killed, because Karl and his fascistic New Normal cronies lied to everyone, over and over, and the German media repeated those lies, and the New Normal masses repeated those lies, and the government and global corporations censored, deplatformed, and demonized those of us who challenged those lies as "far-right extremists," "science deniers," "anti-vaxxers," and so on.

And these are just a few recent examples. I don't think I need to provide an exhaustive list. At this point, you are either well aware and capable of facing what's happening or you are not, in which case you're telling yourself whatever you need to tell yourself in order to pretend that what is happening isn't happening.

If that is what you're doing, I cannot help you. Nothing I write or say will get through to you. Facts will not make any difference to you. Government and health officials and media talking heads will lie to your face, over and over, and get caught lying, and you will go on adamantly repeating their lies, not because you do not understand that they are lies, but because you do not care that they are lies. You do not care that you are killing and injuring countless people with your officially approved lies, with your cowardice, with your mindless obedience. Your goal is to remain within the bounds of "normality" and not get called a lot of names and get ostracized from your social circle, and if a lot of people have to die and you have to abandon any semblance of personal integrity to achieve that, so be it.

As for the rest of us, those who are aware of what's happening and are doing our best to face what's happening, even if we don't understand what's happening or disagree about why it's happening, I wish I had something clever to offer in terms of how to make it stop happening.

I don't, other than what I've been advocating, i.e., organized, non-violent civil disobedience, like what the Canadian truckers did in Ottawa, like what the Dutch farmers are doing in the Netherlands. Columns like this, social media memes, sporadic Sunday mass demonstrations, and individual acts of non-compliance are not going to stop the New Normal juggernaut. The normalization of the New Normal will continue, the pathologization of society will continue, the destabilization and restructuring of the global economy will continue, unless something truly historic happens and the workers of the world unite (or, if "workers" sounds too "Commie" to you, unless the "sovereign individuals" of the world unite) and jam a monkey wrench into the New Normal machinery.

The chances of that happening are slim. In my sixty years of corporeal existence, I have never experienced a time when people were this alienated, hopeless, and at each other's throats. I can't recall a period in which people were this humorless, sanctimonious, and vicious, and I am talking about the people who could make a difference, not the order-following New Normal masses. If there was ever a time when the working classes needed to set aside their political differences and flex their collective muscles, this is it, but most of us are too busy pissing on each other to score cheap points on Twitter, Gettr, Telegram, or Trump Social, or wherever.

I'm sorry to end on such a pessimistic note. I'm recovering from the Apocalyptic Plague, so perhaps I'm just feeling overly gloomy. Probably everything will be just fine, and people will eventually come to their senses, and the global-capitalist ruling classes will cancel the whole New Normal thing, and no one needs to organize any kind of international non-violent civil-disobedience campaign, and, one day, we'll wake up and check our phones and discover that there was no New Normal Reich, and that no one ever died because of a vaccine, and we will check our social credit status, and tell our smart-kitchens to start cooking our crickets, and pull up the War-of-the-Day on our ViewScreens so we can root for whoever we were told to root for . . . and everything will finally be "normal" again.

The Unvaccinated Question Revisited

August 6, 2022

On September 1, 1941, Chief of Reich Security Reinhard Heydrich, one of the most fanatical, mass-murdering Nazis, issued a now notorious decree ordering Jews above the age of six to wear an identifying badge in public. The "Jewish Badge," a yellow Star of David with the word "Jew" inscribed inside the star, was meant to stigmatize and humiliate the Jews and was also used to segregate them and monitor and control their movements.

Nothing like that is happening currently, especially not in New Normal Germany.

What is happening currently in New Normal Germany is, the fascist fanatics in control of the government are rewriting the "Infection Protection Act" again, as they have been doing repeatedly for the last two years, in order to allow themselves to continue to violate the German Constitution and rule the nation by decree under the guise of "protecting the public health."

This repeatedly revised "Infection Protection Act"—which has granted the government of New Normal Germany the authority to order lockdowns, curfews, the outlawing of protests against the New Normal, the mandatory wearing of medical-looking masks, the segregation and persecution of "the Unvaccinated," et cetera—is of course in no way remotely comparable to the "Enabling Act of 1933," which granted the government of Nazi Germany the authority to issue whatever decrees it wanted under the guise of "remedying the distress of the people."

There is absolutely no similarity whatsoever between these two pieces of legislation.

I mean, look at this "Autumn/Winter Plan"[67] for the new revision of the "Infection Protection Act," which will remain in effect from October until Easter, and which government officials and state propagandists (a.k.a. the German mainstream media) are likening to "snow chain ordinances."

There is absolutely nothing creepily fascistic or remotely Nazi about this plan.

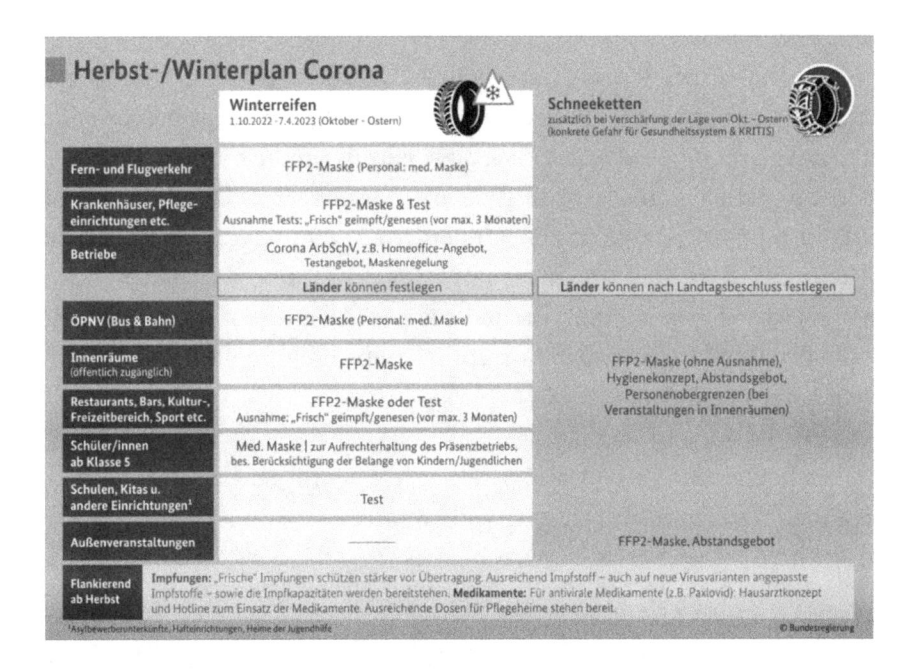

Herbst-/Winterplan Corona	Winterreifen 1.10.2022 - 7.4.2023 (Oktober - Ostern)	Schneeketten zusätzlich bei Verschärfung der Lage von Okt. – Ostern (konkrete Gefahr für Gesundheitssystem & KRITIS)
Fern- und Flugverkehr	FFP2-Maske (Personal: med. Maske)	
Krankenhäuser, Pflegeeinrichtungen etc.	FFP2-Maske & Test Ausnahme Tests: „Frisch" geimpft/genesen (vor max. 3 Monaten)	
Betriebe	Corona ArbSchV, z.B. Homeoffice-Angebot, Testangebot, Maskenregelung	
	Länder können festlegen	Länder können nach Landtagsbeschluss festlegen
ÖPNV (Bus & Bahn)	FFP2-Maske (Personal: med. Maske)	
Innenräume (öffentlich zugänglich)	FFP2-Maske	FFP2-Maske (ohne Ausnahme), Hygienekonzept, Abstandsgebot, Personenobergrenzen (bei Veranstaltungen in Innenräumen)
Restaurants, Bars, Kultur-, Freizeitbereich, Sport etc.	FFP2-Maske oder Test Ausnahme: „Frisch" geimpft/genesen (vor max. 3 Monaten)	
Schüler/innen ab Klasse 5	Med. Maske	zur Aufrechterhaltung des Präsenzbetriebs, bes. Berücksichtigung der Belange von Kindern/Jugendlichen	
Schulen, Kitas u. andere Einrichtungen¹	Test	
Außenveranstaltungen	—	FFP2-Maske, Abstandsgebot
Flankierend ab Herbst	Impfungen: „Frische" Impfungen schützen stärker vor Übertragung. Ausreichend Impfstoff – auch an neue Virusvarianten angepasste Impfstoffe – sowie die Impfkapazitäten werden bereitstehen. Medikamente: Für antivirale Medikamente (z.B. Paxlovid): Hausarztkonzept und Hotline zum Einsatz der Medikamente. Ausreichende Dosen für Pflegeheime stehen bereit.	

¹Asylbewerberunterkünfte, Haftanstalten, Heime der Jugendhilfe © Bundesregierung

Sorry, it's in German. Allow me to translate.

On planes and trains and at the airports and train stations, everyone will be forced to wear doggy-snout masks—i.e., FFP2 "Filtering Face Pieces" as defined by the EN 149 standard—except for the staff of the airports and train stations, and the flight attendants, conductors, et al., who will only be forced to wear "medical-looking masks." In hospitals, clinics,

---

67   Yes, this was an actual publication of the *Bundesregierung*, the Federal Government of Germany.

doctors' offices, nursing homes and other healthcare facilities, everyone, including the staff, will not only be forced to wear the dog-snout masks but they will also be forced to submit to testing, unless they can provide proof of "vaccination" (or recovery, which also means being tested) within the previous three-month period. On the premises of private companies, i.e., offices, factories, warehouses, and so on, the previously rescinded *Arbeitsschutzverordnung* ("Occupational Safety Ordinance")—masks, tests, forced "vaccinations," "social distancing," plastic barriers, et cetera—will go back into effect in October and will remain in effect until the Easter holidays.

The individual federal states will be empowered to impose other senseless "restrictions," like general mask mandates in shops, restaurants, and every other type of "interior spaces," limits on the number of people who can gather publicly or in their own homes, mandatory masks for kids in schools, and testing in kindergartens and daycare facilities. In restaurants, bars, theaters, museums, sports facilities, and pretty much everywhere else in society, the federal states can demand that people show proof of "vaccination" or recovery to be exempted from having to wear a mask.

OK, allow me to translate again.

What that last part means is that anyone who refuses to submit to repeated "vaccination" or testing will be forced to wear a mask in public to identify themselves as "Unvaccinated" (i.e., the New Normal Reich's official "*Untermenschen*").

So, OK, maybe it's a little creepily fascistic and not as non-Nazi as I suggested above.

Needless to say, this could get confusing, as the New Normals are extremely attached to their masks, which they've been wearing—like the Nazis wore swastika lapel pins—to publicly signal their "solidarity" (i.e., mindless conformity to the new official ideology) for going on the last two and half years. And now the masks will function like the "Jewish Badges" with the Star of David that the Nazis forced the Jews to wear, except on public transportation, and planes and trains, unless the federal states decide to force everyone to wear masks everywhere, in which case . . . well, you get the general idea.

Still, the fact that everyone will have to present their "vaccination papers" (or their "recovery papers") to enter a restaurant, or a bar, or go to the cinema or the theater, and, basically, to do anything else in society, should make up for the mask confusion. I mean, what kind of a fascist society would it be if you didn't have to show your "papers" to some beady-eyed goon to get a cup of coffee?

Now, before you report me to the BfV, i.e., Germany's domestic intelligence agency, for "relativizing the Holocaust" and "delegitimizing the democratic state," both of which are crimes here in Germany, I want to say, again, for the record, that I do not advocate using the yellow Star of David to protest the New Normal. I think it is dumb and counterproductive. The New Normal has nothing to do with the Holocaust, or the Jews, or even Nazism per se.

But let's be clear about what's happening in Germany.

What is happening is, a new official ideology is being imposed on society. It is being imposed on society by force. And now, those of us who refuse to conform to it will be ordered to walk around in public wearing visible symbols of our non-conformity.

I'm sorry, but the parallels are undeniable.

This new official ideology has nothing to do with a respiratory virus or any other public health threat. At this point, I do not have to repeat this argument. The majority of countries around the world have finally rescinded their "emergency measures" and acknowledged the facts that we "conspiracy theorists" have been citing for the past two and a half years, and that we've been relentlessly demonized and censored for citing.

Not even Germany's recent independent evaluation of its "Corona measures" could produce any evidence supporting their effectiveness. Seriously, the New Normal German authorities are basing their claim for the efficacy of mask mandates on "the Golden Syrian Hamster Model."[68] You probably think I'm joking, but I'm not.

---

68 Fook-Wu Chan, Jasper, et al., "Surgical Mask Partition Reduces the Risk of Noncontact Transmission in a Golden Syrian Hamster Model for Coronavirus Disease 2019 (COVID-19)," *NIH National Library of Medicine*, November 19, 2020 ("Methods: We used a well-established golden Syrian hamster SARS-CoV-2 model. We placed SARS-CoV-2-challenged index

And Karl Lauterbach, the fanatical Minister of Health, has openly stated that forcing "the Unvaccinated" to wear masks in public is a motivational tactic to harass us into following orders and submitting to a series of experimental "vaccinations" that even the German government now admits have killed or seriously injured tens of thousands of people, at minimum, in Germany.

No, this new official ideology, the New Normal—which is still very much in effect in places like Germany, China, Canada, Australia, New York, California, et cetera—is nakedly, undeniably, purely ideological. It is based, not on facts, but belief. It is a belief system, as is every other ideology. It is essentially no different than an official religion . . . one which demonizes and persecutes all other religions, and non-religions, and all other belief systems.

According to this new official belief system, those of us who maintain different beliefs (and refuse to convert to the new official beliefs, or pretend to convert to the new official beliefs), are dangerous foreign elements in society. And thus, from now on, in New Normal Germany, we will be forced to wear a visible symbol of our different beliefs (our "otherness") in public, so that the authorities and the Good German masses will be able to identify us.

Is any of this sounding vaguely familiar?

I'm fairly certain that someone will read this and report me for "relativizing the Holocaust." So, for the record, I am not "relativizing the Holocaust." I'm comparing one totalitarian system to another. Yes, Nazi Germany and New Normal Germany are two very different totalitarian systems, and I have outlined their essential differences and similarities, but, come on, this is not that fucking hard. In Nazi Germany, the Jews were the scapegoats. In New Normal Germany, it's "the Unvaccinated."

---

hamsters and naive hamsters into closed system units each comprising two different cages separated by a polyvinyl chloride air porous partition with unidirectional airflow within the isolator. The effect of a surgical mask partition placed between the cages was investigated. Besides clinical scoring, hamster specimens were tested for viral load, histopathology, and viral nucleocapsid antigen expression.")

How much more blatant does it have to get before people stop pretending that this isn't what it is? Do the authorities have to literally put us in camps? How many more people have to die or be seriously injured by "vaccinations" they did not need but were forced to submit to? I'm not talking to the New Normals now, nor to the people who have been fighting this all along. I'm talking to the people who see what is happening, and are horrified by what is happening, but, for whatever reasons, have refused to speak out. And, yes, I know there are very good reasons. Some of you have families to support, and careers to protect, and, seriously, I get it. But how far does it have to go? At what point do you feel you have to speak out regardless of the consequences?

Maybe take some time and meditate on that.

And, if you need a little visual aid to help you with your meditation, let me know, and I'll try to send you a photo I saved of some of the colorful New Normal graffiti people have been spray-painting on buildings here in Germany . . . for example, "*UNGEIMPFTE INS GAS!*"

Sorry, that's in German again. Allow me to translate one more time. The graffiti reads: "GAS THE UNVACCINATED!"

Who says the Germans have no sense of irony?

The Rise of the New Normal Reich Banned

August 31, 2022

So, the censorship of my latest book, *The Rise of the New Normal Reich: Consent Factory Essays, Vol. III (2020–2021)*, continues. Amazon has banned the book in three countries: Germany, Austria, and the Netherlands.

The pretext the Amazon Content Review Team has cited as grounds for banning the book is the semi-visible swastika on the cover. This pretext is obviously just a pretext. Amazon sells a number of books and other products displaying semi-visible swastikas in Germany, Austria, and the Netherlands. For example, William Shirer's books or Quentin Tarantino's movie *Inglorious Basterds*. Some of the swastika-displaying products that Amazon offers in these markets display not merely semi-visible swastikas, but totally visible swastikas on their packaging.

So, the Amazon Content Review Team's pretext for banning the book is clearly a lie, and not even a convincing lie. But then Amazon doesn't have to lie convincingly. When you are an unaccountable supranational corporation founded and executive-chaired by Jeff Bezos, the second-richest person in the world, and a component of the US intelligence community,[69] the "rule of law" does not apply to you. You do not have to justify your actions to any court of law or regulatory body, much less

---

69 Konkel, Frank, "The Details About the CIA's Deal with Amazon," *The Atlantic*, July 17, 2014.

to some mid-list expatriate author whose income and reputation you are maliciously damaging.

Sure, there are constitutional protections against censorship and discrimination, for example, Article 5 of the *Grundgesetz* (i.e., Germany's Constitution):

> Every person shall have the right freely to express and disseminate his opinions in speech, writing, and pictures and to inform himself without hindrance from generally accessible sources. Freedom of the press and freedom of reporting by means of broadcasts and films shall be guaranteed. There shall be no censorship.

And Article 3 of the *Grundgesetz*:

> No person shall be favoured or disfavoured because of sex, parentage, race, language, homeland and origin, faith or religious or political opinions.

But these laws do not apply to you, not when you are Amazon.com, because you know that: (a) the governments in question, i.e., the governments of Germany, Austria, and the Netherlands, condone your violations of their constitutions (which they have abrogated in any event under the pretext of a "public health emergency") and might have even had something to do with them, i.e., with your constitutional violations; and (b) lawyers will be too afraid of your wealth and power to challenge you in court.

Moreover, mainstream journalists will completely ignore your censorship of political literature that does not conform to the new official global-capitalist ideology, or they will just "like" or retweet one of my non-conformist tweets, and then rush back to covering whatever one of their colleagues tweeted about some other colleague's tweet, and their colleagues' responses to that tweet, i.e., the tweet about the original tweet, because they, i.e., these mainstream journalists, are also scared shitless of incurring your ire, and potentially getting their own books banned by

Amazon, and their incomes and reputations damaged, and getting fired by their literary agents, and so on.

Which means you can pretty much do whatever you want to anyone you want, which is a pretty sweet deal if you are an immensely powerful supranational corporation that dominates book sales and distribution globally and is also an essential component of the global-capitalist intelligence community.

Which, that is kind of the point of this piece. Yes, Amazon's banning of my book will damage my book sales and my reputation as an author, but I will survive. The important point is, as I put it in a post I published yesterday, before Amazon advised me that they had banned the book in Austria and the Netherlands, in addition to Germany:

> What is important is that corporations like Amazon, Google, Facebook, Twitter, etc. (which control our communication networks) do not have the slightest qualms about censoring information, banning books, suppressing facts, spreading disinformation, and generally behaving like Orwellian Thought Police, and we are gradually becoming accustomed to it. It is becoming "normal," boring even. I don't know about you, but I am not OK with living in a world where Amazon and other unaccountable global corporations decide which books we are allowed to read, which films we are allowed to watch, which facts we are allowed to know about. And that is where we are headed, currently. We're not going to arrive there suddenly, one day. We're going to arrive there just like this, little step by little step, one little act of corporate censorship at a time.

I don't know how to fight this, exactly—not my book ban, the larger phenomenon. It probably has to start with mainstream journalists and lawyers taking on these global corporations. Relatively obscure little literary outlaws (like me) do not have the juice to do it.

So if you happen to know any people like that . . .

Oh, and, for those of you who enjoy seeing how the ideological sausage gets made, here, for the purpose of criticism and review, is my recent correspondence with the Amazon Content Review Team.

August 29, 2022 (4:35 PM)

Hello, During our review process, we found that your book's cover image contains content (i.e. Swastika, Reichsadler, Sowilō) that is in violation of our content guidelines for Germany and may infringe German law. As a result, we will not be offering the following book for sale in Germany: The Rise of the New Normal Reich: Consent Factory Essays, Vol. III (2020–2021), ASIN: B0B1VCK39P, 3982146429. You may reply to this message if you believe this decision has been made in error.

Our content guidelines are published on the Kindle Direct Publishing website.

Best regards,
Amazon KDP Content Review Team/Amazon Content Review Team

August 29, 2022 (5:18 PM)

Dear Amazon KDP Content Review Team,
German law is clear on the banned/permitted use of images of swastikas. See, e.g., this *Deutsche Welle* article . . .

> Swastikas and other banned symbols can displayed in Germany if they are used for "civic education, countering anti-constitutional activities, art and science, research and education, the coverage of historic and current events, or similar purposes," according to the Criminal Code.

There are numerous examples of books, films, artworks, etc. containing swastikas for the above-cited purposes in Germany.

The cover artwork of my book (which has been on sale throughout the world since May of 2022, and was an Amazon bestseller in several countries upon its release) clearly falls under such exceptional use under German law, therefore, there is no legal ground for Amazon to ban its sale or otherwise censor it.

Additionally, Amazon.de offers for sale other products bearing images of swastikas, e.g., William Shirer's books, a Quentin Tarantino film, etc. Thus, your decision to ban my book can only be seen as arbitrary, rather than as the result of a consistent in-house policy.

Moreover, Amazon's banning of my book violates Germany's constitutional protection of freedom of expression as set forth in Article 5 of the Grundgesetz:

> Every person shall have the right freely to express and disseminate his opinions in speech, writing, and pictures and to inform himself without hindrance from generally accessible sources. Freedom of the press and freedom of reporting by means of broadcasts and films shall be guaranteed. There shall be no censorship.

I trust you have taken this decision based on your misunderstanding of German law and lack of awareness of the other books and products Amazon offers in Germany that also contain images of swastikas for the above-cited purposes, and not based on any political or ideological bias and/or intention to damage my income and reputation as an author. Thus, I assume you will immediately reverse this ban.

I look forward to your prompt reply.

Yours sincerely,
CJ Hopkins

August 30, 2022 (3:07 PM)

Hello, Thank you for bringing this to our attention. We need a little time to look into the problem. We'll reply and send you more information within 2-3 business days.

Thanks for your patience.
Content Review Team/Amazon Content Review Team

August 30, 2022 (6:24 PM)

Hello,
Thanks for your email. We've reviewed your book "The Rise of the New Normal Reich: Consent Factory Essays, Vol. III (2020–2021)" (ASIN:B0B1VCK39P, 3982146429), and found that it is in violation of our content guidelines and we will not be offering this title for sale on Amazon. We reserve the right to determine whether content provides a poor customer experience and remove that content from sale. You can find our KDP content guidelines here [link omitted].

Thanks for your understanding.

Best regards,
Amazon KDP Content Review Team/Amazon Content Review Team

August 30, 2022 (6:39 PM)

Hi Amazon Content Review Team,
Could you please clarify: (1) in which countries Amazon KDP has banned and/or is planning to ban the book; (2) the nature of the "poor customer experience" you have cited, or which specific "content guidelines" the book violates? I would note that the book has overwhelmingly positive reader reviews from readers all around the world, so I am unclear as to which customers are having a "poor experience."

With kind regards,
CJ Hopkins

August 31, 2022 (9:38 AM)

Hello,
During our review process, we found that your book's cover image contains content (i.e. Swastika) that is in violation of our content guidelines for Germany and may infringe German law. As a result, we will not be offering the following book for sale in Germany, Netherlands and Austria: "The Rise of the New Normal Reich: Consent Factory Essays, Vol. III (2020–2021)" (ASIN:B0B1VCK39P, 3982146429) Regarding the Paperback version "The Rise of the New Normal Reich: Consent Factory Essays, Vol. III (2020–2021)" (ASIN: 3982146429) KDP Print availability may not always align with digital availability. For European countries sales, in order for a KDP paperback title to be available in one European country, you must make the book(s) available in all European countries. If your book(s) is not in the public domain, or you don't have publishing rights in any one of those countries, then none of the European countries should be selected as territories. For a list of European countries, visit Help: [link omitted].

If you have additional questions, please reply to this email. You may reply to this message if you believe this decision has been made in error. Our content guidelines are published on the Kindle Direct Publishing website.

Best regards, thanks for using Amazon
KDP Content Review Team/Amazon Content Review Team

August 31, 2022 (1:31 PM)

Dear Amazon Content Review Team,
Thank you very much for clarifying in which countries you have arbitrarily decided to ban my book, clearly for political/ideological reasons, as you offer several other products containing "content (i.e. Swastika)" that you falsely claim is "in violation of [y]our content guidelines for Germany and may infringe German law" (referenced in my previous

email). I especially appreciated your failure to address my explication of German law regarding the permitted use of swastikas for certain purposes, and your robotic repetition of the phrase "may infringe German law," as if I had not explained it (i.e., German law) to you. That was a lovely touch. It radiates Faceless Unaccountable Power, which I assume was what you were going for, so kudos! Your refusal to explain the nature of the "poor customer experience" that you claimed customers have experienced or might experience, after I demonstrated that your "German law" pretext was nonsense, and a lie, and which specific Amazon "content guidelines" the book violates, is also much appreciated. Again, it evokes that "You-Are-Dealing-With-A-Faceless-Orwellian-Machine" feeling, so . . . good job! Thank you also for the gibberish about "publishing rights" in European countries, which has absolutely nothing to do with this matter. I will be sure to update you regarding the results of your efforts to damage my income and reputation as an author in due course. Until then . . .

All best wishes and kindest personal regards,
CJ Hopkins

The Morning After
October 3, 2022

This is the weirdest part of the PSYOP. It's like the morning after an office party on which you wake up almost terminally hungover to hazy memories of having performed a Tequila-fueled blowjob on Bob in Accounting in what was either the 9th Floor Reception Area or possibly the downstairs lobby of your building while someone vaguely resembling that smirking kid in the Mail Room filmed it on his phone.

Yes, it's the Morning After . . . that revolting regurgitant chorus you're hearing is the sound of millions of Covidian Cultists down on their knees in their gender-neutral bathrooms praying to the Porcelain God.

It has been quite a trip these last two and a half years, but the orgy of fear and hatred is over, the mass hysteria is wearing off, and the reality of the damage they have done is beginning to become undeniable.

Countless thousands of people have been killed, seriously injured, and permanently disabled, victims of experimental "vaccines" they did not need but were coerced into taking. Societies have been torn apart, economies crippled, institutions discredited, democratic precepts like the rule of law and constitutional rights made mockeries of, friends and families turned against each other, and so on . . . and the dust hasn't even settled yet. It will take many years to assess the damage, or, rather, to recontextualize, rationalize, deny, and memory-hole the damage (while simultaneously "normalizing" the fascistic biosecurity dystopia the damage made it possible to implement).

This process is now well underway. As I'm sure you've noticed over the past several months, governments, global health authorities, the corporate and state media, the culture industry, and other key components of the New Normal Reich have been quietly phasing out their "Covid restrictions," rewriting The Science, rewriting history (i.e., the science and history they had previously rewritten), executing limited hangouts, and otherwise transitioning the masses out of "emergency" mode and into the New Normal.

In other words, everything is going to plan.

You can't keep people whipped up into a state of full-blown hysteria indefinitely. When you're radically destabilizing and restructuring a society, you hit them hard with the shock-and-awe for a few weeks, or months (or years in this case), and then you gently ease them into the new "reality." Which, after being systematically terrorized, gaslighted, threatened, and otherwise tormented for however long you did that to them, they'll be grateful for anything resembling "normality," no matter how fascistic it turns out to be.

You have to be delicate executing this phase, in which the vast majority of the masses, having forced themselves to believe whatever you needed them to believe during the shock-and-awe phase, have to force themselves to believe they never believed whatever you needed them to believe then and believe whatever you need them to believe now, which typically completely contradicts whatever they had previously forced themselves to believe (and actually, literally, believed) in a desperate attempt to keep you happy, so that maybe you would eventually stop beating on them, and relentlessly gaslighting and terrorizing them.

Now, a lot people seem to be having trouble understanding or accepting this fact, i.e., the fact that human beings are capable of forcing themselves to believe whatever they need to believe in order to survive or remain in good standing with "normal" society, or whatever social body they are members of and depend on to meet their basic needs . . . not pretend to believe, *literally* believe, the way that religious converts believe, the way we believe whatever we believe today that we didn't believe ten years ago.

I must say, I find it rather baffling, people's lack of understanding and acceptance of this fact, as this capability is a fundamental human attribute that has been documented, over and over, throughout the course of human history. It is not some crazy theory I just made up. It is how we maintain social cohesion. It is how we socialize our children. It is how armies and university departments work. It is a basic part of how social bodies function; conformity is rewarded and non-conformity is punished. There's nothing new about this phenomenon. People have been conforming to new official "realities" and making themselves believe whatever they have to believe to survive within them for approximately five thousand years.

It is, however, a rare occasion when we are able to observe the process this clearly. It usually takes place more or less invisibly within the context of normal everyday life. It is only during sudden radical shifts from one "reality" to another "reality" that we can watch people force themselves to believe whatever they perceive they need to believe, or are instructed by their rulers to believe, in order to survive and thrive in society (e.g., cult indoctrinations, religious conversions, the outbreak of war, physical torture, or in the wake of political revolutions).

This is what we've been watching since March 2020, not "mass hypnosis," or "mass formation psychosis," but the masses forcing themselves to believe whatever they sensed they needed to believe (or were instructed by the authorities to believe) in order to remain parts of "normal" society and not be demonized by their governments and the media, ostracized by their friends and family, fired from their jobs, segregated, censored, beaten and arrested by the police, and otherwise punished for non-conformity as a new "reality" was manufactured and imposed on societies throughout the world.

And now their "reality" is changing again, or "The Science is evolving," or whatever, and the absurdities they forced themselves to believe are being exposed as . . . well, as absurdities, and their fanatical and often fascistic behavior, as it turns out, was based on absolutely nothing.

Many of them couldn't care less, as their behavior was never based on anything other than going along with the herd, and so they have simply transitioned from fanatically hating "the Unvaccinated" to fanatically hating "the Russians," and fanatically supporting Ukrainian neo-Nazis, and fanatically doing whatever else the GloboCap puppets on their televisions instruct them to fanatically do. However, a significant number of them have retained enough of their critical faculties that being yanked back and forth from "reality" to "reality" is causing them to experience mild cognitive dissonance, and confusion, and shame, or borderline psychosis.

Believe it or not, my heart goes out to them, these formerly fanatical Covidian Cultists that wanted me segregated from society, and silenced, and locked up in an internment camp. I cannot make it easier for them by pretending they didn't do what they did (and in too many cases are still actively doing), or pretending they were hypnotized, or in some other altered state of consciousness, while they did what they did for the past two and half years, but just imagine how they must be feeling now that the party is finally over and the brutal morning after has arrived.

Imagine realizing at this late stage of things that everything you believed, thought, and said, the incalculable harm you have done to people, and to society, was never about a pandemic, but was always about conditioning the masses to respond to fear, coercion, and control like some global Pavlovian behavioral experiment.

Or take it from Canadian actress Jennifer Gibson, who recently posted a video of her weeping, Bells-palsied face on Telegram, explaining how, despite having "a rough go" with the "vaccine," and the face-paralyzing palsy, she "would do it again, because it's what we have to do to see people."

And now comes the really nauseating part, the part where the New Normal authorities admit that they "overreacted," and that "mistakes were made," and that they deeply regret having needlessly murdered and seriously injured God knows how many people, and psychologically crippled countless children, and accidentally totally destabilized and restructured the entire global economy, and explain in a lengthy piece in *The New Yorker* how they're sorry, but they were drunk at the time, and they swear they will never do it again.

You remember this part from 2004 after the invasion and occupation of Iraq when the photos of Abu Ghraib were published, and the American masses who had been hooting and hollering and waving American flags around, and calling people "ragheads" and "sand niggers," and so on, had to stare themselves and their war crimes in the face.

You recall how the Americans dealt with their shame. That's right, they reelected George Bush and carried on murdering and torturing Iraqis, and Afghans, and assorted other brown people, and hooting and hollering "we're number one," and waving American flags around, because in for a penny, in for a pound.

You see, another fundamental human attribute, in addition to our ability to force ourselves to believe whatever we need to believe in order to survive and thrive in society, is that we don't tend to deal with shame very well. We tend to repress it and react aggressively to anyone who tries to force us to face it. If you don't believe me, ask anyone you know who has been (or still is) in an abusive relationship. Ask them how their abuser reacts when they try to get them to take responsibility for their abusive behavior.

I can't tell you exactly what's going to happen over the coming months, but I told you back in January that there was going to be wailing and gnashing of teeth, and wailing and gnashing of teeth there has been, and there is certainly going to be a lot more of it . . . and probably not just wailing and gnashing.

This is just the dawn of the Morning After. I have a feeling we ain't seen nothing yet.

The Gaslighting of the Masses
October 16, 2022

For students of official propaganda, mind control, emotional coercion, and other insidious manipulation techniques, the rollout of the New Normal has been a bonanza. Never before have we been able to observe the application and effects of these powerful technologies in real-time on such a massive scale.

In a little over two and a half years, our collective "reality" has been radically revised. Our societies have been radically restructured. Millions (probably billions) of people have been systematically conditioned to believe a variety of patently ridiculous assertions, assertions based on absolutely nothing, repeatedly disproved by widely available evidence, but which have nevertheless attained the status of facts. An entire fictitious history has been written based on those baseless and ridiculous assertions. It will not be unwritten easily or quickly.

I am not going to waste your time debunking those assertions. They have been repeatedly, exhaustively debunked. You know what they are and you either believe them or you don't. Either way, reviewing and debunking them again isn't going to change a thing.

Instead, I want to focus on one particularly effective mind-control technology, one that has done a lot of heavy lifting throughout the implementation of the New Normal and is doing a lot of heavy-lifting currently. I want to do that because many people mistakenly believe that mind-control is either (a) a "conspiracy theory" or (b) something that can only be achieved with drugs, microwaves, surgery, torture, or some other invasive physical means. Of course, there is a vast and well-documented history of the use of such invasive technologies (see, e.g., the history of the CIA's infamous MKULTRA program), but in many instances mind-control can be achieved through much less elaborate techniques.

One of the most basic and effective techniques that cults, totalitarian systems, and individuals with fascistic personalities use to disorient and control people's minds is "gaslighting." You're probably familiar with the term. If not, here are a few definitions:

> The manipulation of another person into doubting their perceptions, experiences, or understanding of events. —American Psychological Association
>
> An insidious form of manipulation and psychological control. Victims of gaslighting are deliberately and systematically fed false information that leads them to question what they know to be true, often about themselves. They may end up doubting their memory, their perception, and even their sanity. —*Psychology Today*
>
> A form of psychological manipulation in which the abuser attempts to sow self-doubt and confusion in their victim's mind. Typically, gaslighters are seeking to gain power and control over the other person, by distorting reality and forcing them to question their own judgment and intuition. —Newport Institute

The main goal of gaslighting is to confuse, coerce, and emotionally manipulate your victim into abandoning their own perception of reality and accepting whatever new "reality" you impose on them. Ultimately, you want to completely destroy their ability to trust their own perception, emotions, reasoning, and memory of historical events, and render them utterly dependent on you to tell them what is real, and what "really" happened, and how they should be feeling about it.

Anyone who has ever experienced gaslighting in the context of an abusive relationship, or a cult, or a totalitarian system, or who has worked in a battered women's shelter, can tell you how powerful and destructive it is. In the most extreme cases, the victims of gaslighting are entirely stripped of their sense of self and surrender their individual autonomy completely. Among the best-known and most dramatic examples are the Patty Hearst case, Jim Jones's People's Temple, the Manson family, and various other cults, but, the truth is, gaslighting happens every day, out of the spotlight of the media, in countless personal and professional relationships.

Since the Spring of 2020, we have been subjected to official gaslighting on an unprecedented scale. In a sense, the "Apocalyptic Pandemic" PSYOP has been one big extended gaslighting campaign (comprising countless individual instances of gaslighting) inflicted on the masses throughout the world. The events of this past week were just another example.

Basically, what happened was, a Pfizer executive confirmed to the European Parliament last Monday that Pfizer did not know whether its Covid "vaccine" prevented transmission of the virus before it was promoted as doing exactly that and forced on the masses in December of 2020. People saw the video of the executive admitting this, or heard about it, and got upset. They tweeted and Facebooked and posted videos of Pfizer CEO Albert Bourla, Bill Gates, the director of the CDC, official propagandists like Rachel Maddow, and various other "experts" and "authorities" blatantly lying to the public, promising people that getting "vaccinated" would "prevent transmission," "protect other people from infection," "stop the virus in its tracks," and so on, which totally baseless assertions (i.e., lies) were the justification for the systematic segregation and persecution of "the Unvaccinated," and the fomenting of mass fanatical hatred of anyone challenging the official "vaccine" narrative, and the official New Normal ideology, which hatred persists to this very day.

The New Normal propaganda apparatus (i.e., the corporate media, health "experts," et al.) responded to the story predictably. They ignored it, hoping it would just go away. When it didn't, they rolled out the "fact-checkers" (i.e., gaslighters).

The Associated Press,[70] Reuters,[71] *PolitiFact*, and other official gaslighting outfits immediately published lengthy official "fact-checks" that

---

70   Goldin, Melissa and Angelo Fichera, "Posts mislead on Pfizer COVID vaccine's impact on transmission," Associated Press, October 14, 2022.
71   "Fact Check: Preventing transmission never required for COVID vaccines' initial approval; Pfizer vax did reduce transmission of early variants," Reuters, October 12, 2022.

would make a sophist blush. Read them, and you'll see what I mean. They are perfect examples of official gaslighting, crafted to distract you from the point and suck you into an argument over meaningless details and definitions. They sound exactly like Holocaust deniers pathetically asserting that there is no written proof that Hitler ordered the Final Solution, which, there isn't, but it doesn't fucking matter. Of course Hitler ordered the Final Solution, and of course they lied about the "vaccines."

The Internet is swimming with evidence of their lies, tweets, videos, articles, and so on.

This is what makes gaslighting so frustrating for people who believe they are engaged in an actual good-faith argument over facts and the truth. But that's not how totalitarianism works. The New Normals, when they repeat whatever the authorities have instructed them to repeat today (e.g., "trust the Science," "safe and effective," "no one ever claimed they would prevent transmission"), could not care less whether it is actually true, or even if it makes the slightest sense.

These gaslighting "fact-checks" are not meant to convince them that anything is true or false. And they are certainly not meant to convince us. They are official scripts, talking points, and thought-terminating clichés for the New Normals to repeat, like cultists chanting mantras at you to shut off their minds and block out anything that contradicts or threatens the "reality" of the cult. You can present them with the actual facts, and they will smile knowingly, and deny them to your face, and condescendingly mock you for not "seeing the truth."

But here's the tricky thing about gaslighting.

In order to effectively gaslight someone, you have be in a position of authority or wield some other form of power over them. They have to need something vital from you, sustenance, safety, financial security, community, career advancement, or just love. You can't walk up to some random stranger on the street and start gaslighting them. They will laugh in your face.

The reason the New Normal authorities have been able to gaslight the masses so effectively is that most of the masses do need something from them . . . a job, food, shelter, money, security, status, their friends, a relationship, or whatever it is they're not willing to risk by challenging those in power and their lies. Gaslighters, cultists, and power freaks, generally, know this. It is what they depend on, your unwillingness to live without whatever it is. They zero in on it and threaten you with the loss of it, sometimes consciously, sometimes just intuitively.

Gaslighting won't work if you are willing to give up whatever the gaslighter is threatening to take from you, or stop giving you, as the case may be, but you have to be willing to actually lose it, because *you will be punished for defending yourself,* for not surrendering your autonomy and integrity, and conforming to the "reality" of the cult, or the abusive relationship, or the totalitarian system.

I have described the New Normal (i.e., our new "reality") as pathologized-totalitarianism, and as a "a cult writ large, on a societal scale." I used the "Covidian Cult" analogy because every totalitarian system essentially operates like a cult, the main difference being that, in totalitarian systems, the balance of power between the cult and the normal (i.e., dominant) society is completely inverted. The cult becomes the dominant (i.e., "normal") society, and non-cult-members become its "deviants."

We do not want to see ourselves as "deviants" (because we haven't changed, the society has), and our instinct is to reject the label, but that is exactly what we are. Deviants. People who deviate from the norm, a new norm, which we reject, and oppose, but which, despite that, is nonetheless the norm, and thus we are going to be regarded and dealt with like deviants.

I am such a deviant. I have a feeling you are too. Under the circumstances, it's nothing to be ashamed of. On the contrary, we need to accept it, and embrace it. Above all, we need to get clear about it, about where we stand in this new "reality."

We are heading toward New Normal Winter No. 3. They are already cranking up the official propaganda, jacking up the fabricated "cases," talking about reintroducing mask-mandates, fomenting mass hatred of "the Unvaccinated," and so on. People's gas bills are doubling and tripling. The global-capitalist ruling classes are openly embracing neo-Nazis. There is talk of "limited" nuclear war. Fanaticism, fear, and hatred abound. The gaslighting of the masses is not abating. It is increasing.

The suppression of dissent is intensifying. The demonization of non-conformity is intensifying. Lines are being drawn in the sand. You see it and feel it just like I do.

Get clear on what's essential to you. Get clear about what you're willing to lose. Stay deviant. Stay frosty. This isn't over.

The Road to Totalitarianism Revisited

November 13, 2022

OK, it feels like it's finally over, doesn't it, the whole "Apocalyptic Pandemic" thing? I mean, really, really over this time. Not like all those other times when you thought it was over, but it wasn't over, and was like the end of those *Alien* movies, where it seems like Ripley has finally escaped, but the alien is hiding out in the shuttle, or the escape pod, or Ripley's intestinal tract.

But this time doesn't feel like that. This time it feels like it's really, really over. Go out and take a look around. Hardly anyone is wearing masks anymore (except where masks are mandatory) or being coerced into submitting to "vaccinations" (except where "vaccination" is mandatory), and the hordes of hate-drunk New Normal fanatics who demanded that "the Unvaccinated" be segregated, censored, fired from their jobs, and otherwise demonized and persecuted, have all fallen silent (except for those who haven't).

Everything is back to normal, right?

Wrong. Everything is not back to normal. Everything is absolutely New Normal. What is over is the "shock-and-awe" phase, which was never meant to go on forever. It was always only meant to get us here.

Where, you are probably asking, is "here"? "Here" is a place where the new official ideology has been firmly established as our new "reality," woven into the fabric of everyday life. No, not everywhere, just everywhere that matters. Do you really think the global-capitalist ruling classes care whether people in Lakeland, Florida, Elk River, Idaho, or some little village in Sicily believe in the official "reality"? Yes, most government restrictions have been lifted, mainly because they are no longer necessary, but in centers of power throughout the West, in political, corporate, and cultural spheres, in academia, the mainstream media, and so on, the New Normal has become "reality," or, in other words, "just the way it is," which is the ultimate goal of every ideology.

For example, I just happened upon this "important COVID-19 information," which you need to be aware of, and strictly adhere to, if you want to attend a performance at the Vinyard Theatre in New York City, where "everything is back to normal."

> Important COVID-19 Information
>
> Mask: Unless eating or drinking, all guests are required to wear a mask at all times while inside this venue
>
> Proof of vaccine: All guests must be fully vaccinated prior to their performance date in order to attend

I could pull up countless further examples, but I don't want to waste your time. At this point, it isn't the mask and "vaccination" mandates themselves that are important. They are simply the symbols and rituals of the new official ideology, an ideology that has divided societies into two irreconcilable categories of people: (1) those who are prepared to conform their beliefs to the official narrative of the day, no matter how blatantly ridiculous it is, and otherwise click heels and follow the orders of the global-capitalist ruling establishment, no matter how destructive and fascistic they may be; and (2) those who are not prepared to do that.

Let's go ahead and call them "Normals" and "Deviants." I think you know which group you fall into.

This division of society into two opposing and irreconcilable classes of people cuts across and supersedes old political lines. There are Normals and Deviants on both the Left and the Right. The global-capitalist establishment couldn't care less whether you are a "progressive," or a "conservative," or a "libertarian," or an "anarchist," or whatever it is you call yourself. What they care about is whether you're a Normal or a Deviant.

What they care about is whether you will follow orders. What they care about is whether you are conforming your perceptions and behavior and thinking to their new "reality," the hegemonic global-capitalist "reality" that has been gradually evolving for the last thirty years and is now entering its totalitarian stage.

I've been writing about the evolution of global capitalism in my essays since 2016, and since the early 1990s in my stage plays, so I'm not going to reiterate the whole story here. Readers who have just tuned in to my political satire and commentary during the last two years can go back and read the essays in *Trumpocalypse* (2016–2017) and *The War on Populism* (2018–2019).

The short version is, back in 2016, GloboCap was rolling along, destabilizing, restructuring, and privatizing the planet that it came into sole unchallenged possession of when the Soviet Union finally collapsed, and everything was hunky-dory, and then along came Brexit, Donald Trump, and the whole "populist" and neo-nationalist rebellion against globalism throughout the West. So GloboCap needed to deal with that, which is what is has been doing for last six years . . . yes, the last *six*, not just the last two and a half years.

The War on Dissent didn't start with Covid and it isn't going to end with Covid. GloboCap (or "the Corporatocracy" if you prefer) has been delegitimizing, demonizing, and disappearing dissent and increasingly imposing ideological uniformity on Western society since 2016. The New Normal is just the latest stage of it. Once it gets done quashing this "populist" rebellion and imposing ideological uniformity on urban society throughout the West, it will go back to destabilizing, restructuring, and privatizing the rest of the world, which is what it was doing with the "Global War on Terror," among other "democracy"-promoting projects, from 2001 to 2016.

The goal of this global *Gleichschaltung* campaign is the goal of every totalitarian system, i.e., to render any and all deviance from its official ideology pathological. The nature of the deviance does not matter. The official ideology does not matter. GloboCap has no fixed ideology. It can abruptly change its official "reality" from day to day, as we have experienced recently. What matters is one's willingness or unwillingness to conform to whatever the official "reality" is, regardless of how ridiculous it is, and how many times it has been disproved, and sometimes even acknowledged as a fiction by the very authorities who nonetheless continue to fanatically assert its "reality."

I'll give you one more concrete example.

After I happened upon the "Covid restrictions" (i.e., the social-segregation system) still being enforced by the Vineyard Theatre, I stumbled upon an article in *Current Affairs*[72] about the oracle Yuval Noah Harari, the writer of which article mentions in passing that somewhere between six million and twelve million people have "died of Covid," as if this were a fact, a fact that no one in their right mind would question. Which it is, officially, in our new "reality," despite the fact (i.e., the actual fact) that—as even the "health authorities" have admitted—anyone who died of anything in a hospital after testing positive was recorded as a "COVID-19 death."

This is how "reality" (i.e., official "reality," consensus "reality") is manufactured and policed. It is manufactured and policed, not only by the media, corporations, governments, and non-governmental governing entities, but also, and, ultimately, more effectively, by the constant repetition of official narratives as unquestionable axiomatic facts.

In our brave new totalitarian global-capitalist "reality," anyone who questions or challenges such "facts" immediately renders oneself a "Deviant" and is excommunicated from "Normal" society. Seriously, just for fun, try to get a job at a corporation, or a university, or a part in a movie or a Broadway play, or a book deal, or a research grant, et cetera, while being honest about your beliefs about Covid. Or, if you're a "respectable" journalist, you know, with literary and public-speaking agents, and big book deals, and personal managers, and so on, go ahead, report the facts (i.e., the actual facts, which you know are there, but which you have been avoiding like the plague for the last two years), and watch your career get violently sucked down the drain like a turd in an airplane toilet.

---

72 Narayanan, Darshana, "The Dangerous Populist Science of Yuval Noah Harari," *Current Affairs*, July 6, 2022

That last bit was meant for "urban professionals," who still have careers, or are aspiring to careers, or are otherwise still invested in remaining members in good standing of "Normal" society, i.e., not you folks in Florida and Idaho, or my fellow literary and artistic "Deviants."

We have pretty much burned our bridges at this point. Unless you're prepared to mindfuck yourself, and gaslight yourself, and confess, and convert, there's no going back to "normal" society (which we couldn't go back to anyway, on account of how it doesn't exist anymore).

I realize that a lot of folks have probably been looking forward to that, to the day when the Normals finally "wake up" and face the facts, and truth prevails, and we return to something resembling normality. It's not going to happen. We're not going back. The Normals are never going to "wake up." Because they're not asleep. They are not hypnotized. They're not going to "come to their senses" one day and take responsibility for the damage they have done. Sure, they will apologize for their "mistakes," and admit that possibly they "overreacted," but the official narrative of the Covid pandemic and the new "reality" it has ushered into being will remain in force, and they will defend both with their lives.

Or, rather, they will defend both with *our* lives.

If you think I'm being hyperbolic, well, consider the epithets GloboCap has conditioned the Normals to use to demonize us . . . "conspiracy theorist," "science denier," "insurrectionist," "extremist," "violent domestic terrorist." None of which signify a political ideology or any political or critical position whatsoever. They signify deviation from the norm. *Any* type of deviation from the norm. They are tactical terms, devoid of meaning, designed to erase the political character of the diverse opposition to global-capitalism (or "globalism," if you are touchy about the word "capitalism"), to lump us all into one big bucket of "deviance."

It is usually not a very good omen when nations, or totally unaccountable, supranational global-power systems, suddenly break out the "deviance bucket." It is usually a sign that things are going to get ugly, ugly in a totalitarian fashion, which is precisely what has been happening for the past six years.

Back in July of 2021, at the height of the fascistic New Normal hate frenzy, with the military enforcing "Covid restrictions," a global segregation system being implemented, and Internet people threatening to decapitate me for refusing to get "vaccinated," I published an essay called *The Road to Totalitarianism*. We are still on that road. Both the Normals and we Deviants. We've been on that road for quite some time, longer than most of us probably realize. The weather has improved, slightly. The scenery out the window has changed. The destination has not. I haven't seen any exits.

Let me know if you do, will you?

The Year of the Gaslighter
December 18, 2022

Well, it has been quite a year, 2022. I'm officially dubbing it "The Year of the Gaslighter." I was going to dub it "The Year of the Mother of All Mindfucking Global-Capitalist Gaslighters," but that seemed like a mouthful, so I'm opting for brevity.

Seriously, if there were an Olympics of Gaslighting, GloboCap (i.e., the global corporatocracy) would take the gold in every event. At this point, the majority of the global masses have been successfully gaslighted into a semi-conscious, quasi-cyclothymic state in which they oscillate, on a moment-by-moment basis, between robotic obedience and impotent rage. Those who are not still walking around in their medical-looking masks and prophylactic face shields and injecting themselves with experimental "vaccines" for reasons they no longer even pretend to be able to articulate without gibbering like imbeciles are genuflecting at the feet of an oligarch huckster who they believe has come to deliver them from Wokeness.

If you were GloboCap, and in the process of imposing your new official ideology on the entire planet in a global "*Gleichschaltung*" op, and otherwise establishing your "New Normal Reich," and you needed the masses confused and compliant, you couldn't ask for much more from your Gaslighting Division!

The gaslighting got underway in January, when the corporate media, health authorities, and other major organs of the New Normal Reich started suddenly "discovering" that the official Covid narrative was "inaccurate," or, you know, a bunch of lies.

A series of limited hangouts ensued.

Suddenly, it appeared that the "Covid case" and "Covid death" statistics were inaccurate, or inflated, or had been fabricated. The "vaccines" didn't work. They were killing people. Lockdowns had been a "serious mistake." And so on. Duplicitous politicians, pusillanimous public-health authorities, perfidious pundits, and assorted other professional sycophants and lying weasels were shocked to discover they had inadvertently been part of the most insidious PSYOP that had ever been perpetrated on the masses in the history of insidious PSYOPs.

The Last Days of the Covidian Cult were upon us! The Corporatocracy had overplayed their hands, and underestimated their opposition, and they knew it.

But the Cult was not going to go down quietly. In February, in Ottawa, Canada, thousands of truckers and other working-class people who had had enough of the Pandemic PSYOP occupied the streets outside the capitol and demanded an end to "vaccination mandates," the segregation of "the Unvaccinated," and other "emergency health measures." Justin Trudeau, the Canadian media, and their counterparts throughout the New Normal Reich immediately denounced the protesters as "treasonous, Russia-backed, transphobic, Nazi terrorists."

This affront to the authority of the New Normal Reich could not be allowed to go unpunished, so Trudeau declared de facto martial law and unleashed a battalion of militarized police and other unidentified goons to beat and trample the protesters with horses, including an old lady with a "terrorist walker." Then he went about hunting down and freezing the bank accounts of any Canadians who had donated to the protest, and otherwise attempting to destroy the lives of anyone who had disobeyed him.

This display of contempt for the rule of law and the ruthlessness of the New Normal Reich was one of the last of the bloody crackdowns on dissidents in countries all over the world that had been in progress for over a year by then, e.g., in Australia, the Netherlands, France, Germany, China, and other countries. These vicious "crackdowns" on peaceful protests were conducted "to protect the public health," of course, and were not at all a display of brute force meant to intimidate the masses into obedience. The global-capitalist ruling classes are not fascists, or totalitarians, after all, and anyone who suggests that they are is clearly a "Russia-backed, Covid-denying, conspiracy-theorizing extremist," or whatever.

Oh, and speaking of totalitarians, and fascists, and goose-stepping, Sieg-heiling neo-Nazis, the Gaslighting Cavalcade of 2022 reached a whole new level of gaslighting in March, when, after years of provocation, Russia finally invaded Ukraine, and all the Ukrainian neo-Nazis that the corporate media had been extensively reporting on magically vanished into the ether.

Yes, it was Springtime for the GloboCap Nazis! And not just for the GloboCap Nazis! Liberals, still struggling with withdrawal symptoms from the adrenaline rush of the Covidian Cult, and the thrill of fanatically persecuting "the Unvaccinated," suddenly had a new official narrative that they could mindlessly parrot and fanatically defend from the "conspiracy theorists" and "disinformationists."

The only problem was, it didn't make any sense. According to the new official narrative, those reports of Ukrainian neo-Nazis by virtually every mainstream media outlet and Nazi-hunting organization on the planet in the years leading up to 2022 were now, suddenly, just "Russian propaganda." GloboCap hadn't even bothered to scrub or visibility-filter those reports. They were all still right there on the Internet.

And, OK, the other problem was, in order to remain "New Normals in Good Standing" and keep their jobs and social contacts, liberals were now forced to actively cheer for swastika-tattooed, Sieg-heiling Nazis and look the other way as Ukrainian fascists openly advocated the mass murder of children and quoted Adolf Eichmann on Ukrainian television.

The Spring and Summer were kind of a blur, or maybe I was preoccupied with publishing *The Rise of the New Normal Reich*, a collection of my essays documenting the rollout of the New Normal in 2020 and 2021, which was an international Barnes & Noble and Amazon bestseller upon its release, and then was promptly banned by Amazon in Germany, the Netherlands, and Austria, and labeled with a "COVID-19 vaccine warning" advising readers to visit the CDC before purchasing and (God help them!) reading the book in every other Amazon market.

I vaguely remember something about monkeypox, but, mostly, when I wasn't promoting the book, or struggling to keep my breakfast down after seeing another one of my liberal friends cheering for neo-Nazis on Facebook, I was focused on events here in New Normal Germany (where, yes, mask mandates are still in effect), and The Normalization of the New Normal Reich (which, no, is not over, but is just beginning), and attempting to start to emotionally recover from two solid years of official gaslighting, demonization, segregation, and so on.

Fortunately, in September, right on cue, as I was working through my emotional issues, i.e., how most of my former friends and colleagues had either gone silent and looked away as our constitutional rights were canceled, political dissent was censored and demonized, goon squads were dispatched to brutalize dissidents, experimental "vaccines" were forced on people, a social segregation system was implemented, and so on, or else, if they hadn't gone silent, they had joined the shrieking fascistic mob ... just as I was starting to process all that, as were a lot of other people, a prophet arrived on the "freedom" scene!

That's right, as it turned out, I was totally wrong about the new totalitarianism, and how it works! I had stupidly assumed it was a political phenomenon ... you know, a sociopolitical and cultural system imposed on the masses from above by force, but, according to Mattias Desmet, it's actually a psychological phenomenon, a "mass formation" or "mass hypnosis"-type thing!

It's possible that I'm not describing it correctly. As his devoted fans have repeatedly informed me, I don't understand the nuances of Desmet's theory. He explained it all on *The Alex Jones Show*, while he was lying, which he does, repeatedly, but ... whatever. I'm not a professor of psychology. The point is, the Covidian Cultists were all hypnotized! No one was threatening or gaslighting the masses! The poor confused things were doing it to themselves!

But that was not the end of the gaslighting. GloboCap saved the best for last!

See, the problem was, there were all these people who hadn't joined the Covidian Cult or any other part of the New Normal movement, and who were extremely angry about having been demonized, and segregated, and censored, and gaslighted, and so on, by their governments, global corporations, non-governmental governing entities, the corporate media, "scientific experts," and the majority of the masses for two and a half years.

Something needed to be done about all that anger. It needed to be redirected somewhere. At something that wasn't GloboCap, and that wouldn't interfere with the New Normal program.

Emperor Elonicus to the rescue!

If Elon Musk wasn't actually appointed by the global-capitalist ruling classes to redirect the pent-up anger of "the Unvaccinated" demographic, and the "Systematically Censored and Demonized" demographic, and everyone else who opposed the New Normal into a balls-out left/right shit-slinging contest . . . well, they couldn't have found anyone better for the job.

Consider what he's accomplished in the space of six weeks. After purchasing Twitter for $44 billion, he got himself a few independent journalists—because who could resist the Twitter Files? I certainly couldn't have, had I been in their position—and is staging the most audacious limited hangout in the history of limited hangouts. Whether it will work over the longer term is unclear—Bari Weiss and Matt Taibbi are already starting to become uncomfortable with being perceived and treated as Elon Musk's employees—but, so far, it's going gangbusters!

Now, students of limited hangouts, whitewashing, and other COINTELPRO-type ops, really need to pay attention. Because the beauty of this limited hangout is that the hangout is actually a monumental story, an up-close look at the nuts-and-bolts processes of the global-capitalist Ministry of Truth. As Matt Taibbi reported in a recent piece . . .

> [T]he Twitter Files show something new. We now have clear evidence that agencies like the FBI and the DHS are in the business of mass-analyzing social media activity—your tweets and mine, down to the smallest users with the least engagement—and are, themselves, mass-marking posts to be labeled, "bounced," deleted or "visibility filtered" by firms like Twitter. The technical and personnel infrastructure for this effort is growing. As noted in the

thread, the FBI's social media-focused task force now has at least 80 agents, and is in constant contact with Twitter for all sorts of reasons. The FBI is not doing this as part of any effort to build criminal cases. They've taken on this new authority unilaterally, as part of an apparently massive new effort to control and influence public opinion. These agencies claim variously to be concerned about election integrity, foreign interference, medical misinformation, and monitoring domestic extremism, among other things. As crises wax and wane, the building out of the censorship infrastructure to ever-bigger and broader dimensions has been constant, suggesting that creating and deploying the tool to manipulate opinion was always the real end.[73]

And this monumental story is being buried in shit. American "red/blue" partisan shit. With a series of ham-handed PR stunts, cheap provocations, attention-grabbing antics, and good old-fashioned diversionary shit-slinging, Musk is (a) whitewashing the new "free-speech Twitter," which continues to censor and defame us with impunity, (b) burying the actual story under a steaming heap of partisan acrimony, and (c) driving a big blunt wedge into the supra-partisan coalition of forces that had aligned in opposition to the rollout of the New Normal.

That, my friends, is some world-class gaslighting! And the wildest part is, he probably doesn't even consciously realize what he's doing. Nevertheless, by the time he's done playing grab-ass with the freedom-of-speech thing, and getting revenge on Taylor Lorenz, and so on, corporate censorship will have been completely normalized. "Freedom of speech" will be a running joke, as opposing camps of hate-drunk hypocrites take turns applauding as global corporations and their governmental partners censor one camp or the other.

On that cheery note, I'll sign off for the year and go tend to all the irate messages I'm getting from abject Elon Musk worshipers, and

---

[73] Taibbi, Matt, "From the Twitter Files: Twitter, The FBI Subsidiary," *Racket News*, December 16, 2022.

the hate-email from assorted anti-Semites, and so on, and then hibernate until 2023.

Oh, yeah, and those "Covid Twitter Files." I can't wait to scroll through those with a nice glass of eggnog. I'm sure they will be coming out any day now, maybe even on Christmas morning!

Happy holidays to one and all!

2023

If they can get you asking the wrong questions, they don't have to worry about answers.

—Thomas Pynchon, *Gravity's Rainbow*

ized to the public, in
The Mother of All Limited Hangouts

January 11, 2023

The Mother of All Limited Hangouts has begun. Yes, I'm talking about the "Covid Twitter Files," which are finally being released to the public, in almost textbook limited-hangout fashion. I'll get into that in just a minute, but first, let's review what a "limited hangout" is, for those who are not familiar with the term.

The way a limited hangout works is, if you're an intelligence agency, or a global corporation, or a government, or a non-governmental organization, and you have been doing things you need to hide from the public, and those things are starting to come to light such that you can't just deny that you are doing them anymore, what you do is, you release a limited part of the story (i.e., the story of whatever it is you're doing) to distract people's attention from the rest of the story. The part you release is the "limited hangout." It's not a lie. It's just not the whole story. You "hang it out" so that it will become the whole story, and thus stop people from pursuing the whole story.

Victor Marchetti, a former special assistant to the deputy director of the CIA who went on to become a critic of the intelligence community, described the tactic this way in 1978 . . .

> [A] favorite and frequently used gimmick of clandestine professionals. When their veil of secrecy is shredded and they can no longer rely on a phony cover story to misinform the public, they resort to

admitting, sometimes even volunteering, some of the truth while still managing to withhold the key and damaging facts in the case. The public, however, is usually so intrigued by the new information that it never thinks to pursue the matter further.[74]

All right, so, you're probably asking, if the "Covid Twitter Files" are a limited hangout, what's the whole story that they're distracting us from? Let me try to refresh your memory.

In March and April 2020, in the course of roughly five to six weeks, the majority of societies throughout the world were transformed into pathologized-totalitarian police states. A global "shock-and-awe" campaign was conducted. Constitutional rights were suspended. The masses were locked down inside their homes, where they were subjected to the most relentless official propaganda blitzkrieg in human history. Goon squads roamed the streets of Europe, the USA, the UK, Canada, Australia, Asia, the Americas, et cetera, beating and arresting people for being outdoors without permission and not wearing medical-looking masks in public. Corporate media around the world informed us that life as we knew it was over . . . a "new normal" was coming, and we needed to get used to it.

The entire official pandemic narrative was rolled out during those first few weeks. Everything. Masks. Mandatory "vaccines." "Vaccination" passports. The segregation of "the Unvaccinated." The censorship and demonization of dissent. Everything. The whole "New Normal" package. It was rolled out all at once, *globally*.

That is the story. How that happened. Why that happened. And who or what made it happen. It isn't a story about a virus, or our governments' reactions to a virus. It is the story of the radical restructuring of society based on lies and official propaganda, executed, *globally*, through sheer brute force and systematic psychological conditioning. It is the story of the implementation of our new totalitarian global-capitalist "reality," the "New Normal" that was announced in the Spring of 2020. It is not a story the global-capitalist ruling classes can permit to be told, except by

---

74 Marchetti, Victor, "CIA to 'Admit' Hunt Involvement in Kennedy Slaying," *The Spotlight*, August 14, 1978.

"crazy conspiracy theorists," "science deniers," and other "crackpots" and "extremists."

All right, so . . . the "Covid Twitter Files," or the "Fauci Files," or whatever we're calling them. If you wanted to bury the actual story (i.e., the story I just outlined above) with a limited hangout and discredit those of us who have been trying to report it for nearly three years, you couldn't do any better than Elon Musk is doing. Instead of a story about how the entire global-capitalist power apparatus coordinated with global IT corporations like Twitter, Facebook, Google, et al., to conduct a global *Gleichschaltung* op the scale of which Goebbels could have never dreamed of, censoring and visibility-filtering dissent and enforcing the official pandemic narrative, not just in the USA, but in countries all throughout the world . . . instead of that monumental story, we are getting *The Alex Berenson Show!*, starring Alex Berenson as Alex Berenson, with a special guest appearance by Alex Berenson, written and directed by Alex Berenson, and so on.

Seriously, though, who better to handle the "Covid Twitter Files" than Alex Berenson, in whose opinion the events of the last three years were simply due to mass hysteria (or *Pandemia*, $14.99 on Amazon), and certainly not to any kind of coordinated radical restructuring of society by the global-capitalist power apparatus, or any other wild conspiracy theories. Forget about that 257-tweet thread I compiled in March and April of 2020. What actually happened, according to Alex Berenson, was that people just went kind of crazy, and overreacted, and "mistakes were made." Mistakes like Twitter suspending Alex Berenson, and other very important people! Or, wait, no, it wasn't just mass hysteria . . . it was also Pfizer and Dr. Scott Gottlieb, and the White House, and someone named Andrew Slavitt, all of whom conspired with Old Evil Twitter to suspend Alex Berenson from the platform, all of whom Alex will be suing forthwith![75]

The Alex Berenson Show! is just getting started, so definitely stay tuned to "Free-Speech Twitter" to follow all of Alex Berenson's exploits as he leads "Team Reality" to its ultimate victory over "Team Apocalypse" and exposes the crimes of the usual assortment of official "bad apples,"

---

75 See, e.g., Alex Berenson's January 10, 2023, 29-Tweet Twitter thread explaining who he will be suing.

or whatever cartoonish fairy tales Alex Berenson and Elon Musk have in store for us! It promises to be quite the spectacle!

I'll be covering the show in my columns, of course—I still have a few subscribers and readers who I haven't totally alienated yet—and discussing The Art of the Limited Hangout for the benefit of anyone still paying attention in the weeks and months and possibly years ahead. If you are one of the many people who now appear to seriously believe that military-contractor oligarchs like Elon Musk and narcissistic ass clowns like Alex Berenson are going to deliver us from the New Normal Reich, and "prosecute Fauci," and end corporate censorship, or in any way meaningfully bite the hand of the global-capitalist system that feeds them, you may want to give those columns a miss.

For the rest of you, I will do my best to point out how this phase of the PSYOP works, because it's going to last for quite a while. The "Covid Twitter Files" are not The Mother of All Limited Hangouts; they are just one part of it. There are many more limited hangouts to come. The New Normal having been successfully implemented, the history of its implementation is now being written (or, rather, rewritten) to conform to the official Covid narrative, a process which will likely continue for years.

Those of you who are old enough might recall this phase from "The War on Terror." It started around April 2004, when the Abu Ghraib torture photos were released, and continued until the Summer of 2016, when The War on Terror was abruptly canceled and replaced by The War on Populism, which prepared the public for the implementation of the New Normal in the Spring of 2020. All of which is part of an even larger story, i.e., the story of the evolution of the first globally hegemonic power system in history, which, lacking any external adversary, has nothing to do but go totalitarian, eliminating all internal resistance and establishing ideological uniformity throughout the territory it occupies, which, in this case, means the entire planet.

Sorry, I know, history is boring, and complicated, and not nearly as fun (and cathartic) as the shit-slinging circus that Musk is making of the Twitter Files. Personally, I can't wait to find out which "bad apple" they're going to offer us in today's edition of the Two Minutes Hate, and who's going to be released from "old Twitter prison," and, whatever, anyway, don't worry about all that evolution-of-global-capitalism stuff. It's probably just a bunch of fancy-sounding nonsense I made up to try to sell you my books, or to make myself sound smart or something.

Forget that I even mentioned that stuff. Sit back, relax, and enjoy the show!

The War on Insensitivity

February 21, 2023

So, here's a "conspiracy theory" for you. This one is about the global-capitalist Thought Police and their ongoing efforts to purge society of "insensitivity." Yes, that's right, insensitivity. If there is anything the global-capitalist Thought Police cannot stand, it is insensitivity. You know, like making fun of ethnic or religious minorities, and the physically or cognitively challenged, and alternatively gendered persons, and hideously ugly persons, and monstrously fat persons, and midgets, and so on.

The global-capitalist Thought Police are terribly concerned about the feelings of such persons. And the feelings of other sensitive persons who are also concerned about the feelings of such persons. And everybody's feelings, generally. So they're purging society of any and all forms of literary content, and every other form of content, that might possibly irreparably offend such persons, and persons concerned about the feelings of such persons, and anyone who might feel offended by anything.

By now, I assume you have seen the news about the "sensitivity editing" of Roald Dahl, the author of books like *James and the Giant Peach*, *Charlie and the Chocolate Factory*, *The Witches*, *The Twits*, and numerous others. What happened was, Dahl's publisher, Puffin Books, hired a little clutch of "sensitivity editors" to substantively rewrite his books, purging words like "fat" and "ugly," and Dahl's descriptions of characters as "bald" and "female," and inserting their own ham-handed, "sensitized" language.

What you may not be aware of is that Puffin Books is a children's imprint of Penguin Random House, a multinational conglomerate publishing company and a subsidiary of Bertelsmann, a nominally German but in reality global media conglomerate. Penguin Random House is one of the "big five publishers," which control about eighty percent of the retail book market. The other four are Simon & Schuster, Macmillan, Hachette, and HarperCollins.

Together, these five corporate behemoths, with their hundreds of divisions, publishing groups, and imprints (e.g., Puffin Books), control the majority of what everyone reads. Pull a few books off your bookshelves at random and look up the imprints to see how many are owned by one of the "big five" publishers or one of their divisions or publishing groups.

Another thing you may not be aware of is the increasing employment of "sensitivity readers" by these publishing conglomerates and their legions of imprints, and by writers aspiring to be published by these imprints. *Writer's Digest* describes their function thus:

> Publishers and authors hire them to basically cancel-proof their books before they hit the street, hoping to head off any misspoken messages . . . hoping to depict peoples in an accurate light when it comes to genre, race, ethnicity, sexual orientation, and more. Sensitivity edits are a publisher's or editor's insurance to protect reputation and ward off profit loss, just in case, and an author's attempt to depict characters in an accurate light. Entities purchase a sensitivity read when the writing is outside of their expertise or experience, or they are uncertain they depicted details properly.[76]

Penguin Random House recommends "authenticity readers"[77] to any of its authors who are "writing outside their personal experience" (i.e., using their imaginations), to prevent them from "perpetuating stereotypes," or exhibiting their "unconscious or internalized bias" and creating "patterns of harmful representation," and so on.

If this sounds to you like some kind of creepy, Orwellian-Ministry-of-Truth-type mindfuckery, that's because that's exactly what it is. It doesn't

---

[76] Clark, C. Hope, "Who Are Sensitivity Editors? And How Much Does Sensitivity Reading Pay?," *Writer's Digest*, June 29, 2022.

[77] Cárdenas, Joanna, "Working with Authenticity Readers," *Penguin Random House - News for Authors*, April 2018.

really affect old farts like me—I wouldn't let any of the big corporate publishers or their "sensitivity readers" near my writing, which they would never publish in any event, and which would likely cause them to experience seizures, and then stagger around the office looking for differently abled-Black-transgender colleagues to kneel down in front of and apologize to—but there's a whole generation of aspiring writers who are being conditioned to accept this as "normal."

The Roald Dahl story is being framed as a "woke vs. anti-woke" culture-war story. It isn't. And it isn't an aberration. It's part and parcel of the new global-capitalist totalitarianism that I've been going on and on about. The entire "wokeness" phenomenon is. Global-capitalist cultural revolutionaries are hunting down "insensitivity" everywhere. In the arts, schools, TV shows, films, social media, et cetera. "Insensitivity" being any and all forms of deviation from global-capitalist ideology, regardless of where they fall on the left/right spectrum. I have described the process as a new form of *Gleichschaltung*, the systematic coordination of every element of society—or every element that matters—in conformity with global-capitalist ideology.

So, what *is* global-capitalist ideology?

Well, I told you I had a "conspiracy theory" for you. It is not a very sexy "conspiracy theory," but it'll have to do, because it's all I've got. And, forgive me, but I'm just getting started on my second "insensitive" dystopian novel, so I'm going to explain this "conspiracy theory" with a lengthy excerpt from the introduction to *The War on Populism: Consent Factory Essays, Vol. II (2018–2019)*, one of my collections of essays, rather than taking the time to reword it badly. It really is a rather lengthy excerpt, so, if you happen to be reading this at work (i.e., when you are supposed to be working), or if you need to get back to a Twitter-fracas, or if you have the attention span of a gnat, you might want to save it and try to read it later.

OK, I warned you. Here it is . . .

This conflict (i.e., global capitalism versus a global "populist" insurgency) is at the root of all the madness of the last four years. To understand it, one needs to understand that it is primarily *an ideological conflict*, a global war for hearts and minds.

Trump, Johnson, Corbyn, Sanders, and other so-called "populist" figures, were never a real threat to GloboCap, not in any material sense. They are symbols, figureheads, representations of resistance to global capitalist ideology. It is this resistance to its ideology (from both the left and the right . . . it makes no difference), more than any particular political leader or movement, that GloboCap has been trying to crush. It needs to put down this "populist" insurgency, so it can get on with the business of transforming the entire world into one big value-less marketplace . . . which is what it has been doing for last thirty years.

This is what capitalism was built to do. Ideologically speaking, it is a simple machine, one that strips societies of despotic values (e.g., religious, social, cultural values . . . values established by kings, priests, aristocracies, artists, communities, political parties, families, et cetera) and replaces them all with a single value (i.e., exchange value), rendering everything a commodity. In essence, it is *an ideological machine*, a values-decoding/recoding machine, which transforms societies into markets.

(I've cut a bit here, to make it somewhat less lengthy and get to the global-capitalist ideology part.)

Global capitalism's ideology (i.e., the territory that comprises our "reality") is unlike any other ideology in the 5,000-year history of ideology. It is an ideological territory without limits, neither internal nor external boundaries. It is a featureless territory, in which anything is possible, because nothing within it has any value, or meaning, in and of itself. It is literally a "desert of the real," an infinite, seamless desert of values, across the lifeless surface of which the ghosts of values eternally wander, in circles, aimlessly, signifying nothing, going nowhere, for they are already there, in the only place there is to be, because the desert is everywhere, and everything.

There is nowhere and nothing outside of this territory. There is no outside where anything could exist. It is one big global capitalist world, one unitary, omnipresent, capitalist "reality" . . . one big global marketplace, or it will be, once GloboCap finishes destabilizing and restructuring what remains of the post-Cold-War world.

This is the story of the last thirty years. Beneath the distractions of the day, the manufactured mass hysteria, the propaganda, the fabricated outrage, the scandals, the wars, rumors of wars, the deafening roar of millions of voices shrieking gibberish on social media, conspiracy theories, real and imagined, the cheap charade of electoral politics, and so on, right out there in the open, because no one has been paying much attention, GloboCap has been mopping up, cleansing societies of their outmoded values, absorbing them into the global market . . . implementing ideological conformity.

You're familiar with this ideological conformity. We all are. You're probably in favor of many of the values it purports to want to promote, anti-racism, equal rights, separation of church and state, et cetera, the traditional liberal agenda. Remember, capitalist ideology is what finally freed us from the rule of despots, kings, aristocracies, priests. (Personally, I'm extremely grateful for that.) As I explained above, capitalism did this by eradicating despotic values and replacing them all with a single value, exchange value, rendering everything a commodity. That doesn't sound very appealing, however. No one wants to see themselves as just a commodity, or live in a world without any real values. So capitalism marketed itself as "democracy," and that went over much better with the masses.

Here we are, a few hundred years later, and "democracy" (i.e., capitalism) is running out of despotic values to eradicate and liberate us from. Sure, it still has some work to do secularizing the Middle East, and there are still a few countries that aren't playing ball, but most of the planet has gotten with the program. Most of the values-eradicating work that remains to be done is right here at home. There are still a lot of Western consumers who haven't completely embraced "democracy," and who are clinging to old despotic values . . . racist values, religious values, nativist values, xenophobic values, homophobic values, transphobic values, cultural and artistic values, ableist values, alloist values, shadeism, lookism, ethnocentrism, cisgenderism, anti-Semitism, jingoism, sexism, sizeism, saneism . . . the list goes on and on, and on.

Democracy (i.e., global capitalism) will not rest until it has cleansed society (i.e., the global marketplace) of these ugly, destructive, despotic values, and implemented a worldwide code of conduct (like the ones that most global corporations have) with universal "anti-hate-speech rules," and "appropriate vocabulary" lists, and has erased any visible symbol of such despotic values from public view, and any references to them from school curricula, and has otherwise transformed humanity into a mass of hyper-conformist consumers who all look like models in a Benetton commercial and talk like customer service representatives.

Now, don't get me wrong, I'm in favor of democracy, and I'm not a fan of racism or any other type of discrimination or bigotry. I'm just trying to shed a little light on the forces behind the identity-politics zealotry that has been raging recently, and the "populist" backlash against such zealotry. This zealotry, this crusade for ideological conformity, is described by many leftists as a movement to establish "social justice," and by many right-wing types as "cultural Marxism." It is neither. Or, OK, it contains elements of both, but fundamentally it is global capitalism purifying society of despotic values, establishing that infinite, value-free, meaningless "desert of the real" I described above.

That's it. I warned you that it was rather lengthy. It was written in September of 2020, so about six months into the rollout of the New Normal.

As for the Roald Dahl dust-up, what will happen now is that A-list authors, journalists, and other official mouthpieces of the global-capitalist Simulation of Culture will make a big stink for a couple days, and then Penguin Random House and the other "big-five" publishers will go on "sensitivity-editing," and "authenticity-editing," and otherwise aggressively homogenizing mainstream literature until it won't really matter which books you read because they will all be minor variations of each other that will resemble nothing so much in their utterly soul-deadening, interchangeable blandness as the reception lobbies of corporate offices.

Of course, if you are into the literature thing, you can always seek out and read other books by disreputable and "insensitive" authors like me, who are unaffiliated with any global publishing behemoths, that is, assuming our books haven't been hidden behind one of "free-speech" X's fake "sensitive content" warnings.

> **CJ Hopkins** @CJHopkins_Z23 · Feb 4
>
> Thanks again, @elonmusk, for damaging my reputation and income as an author by hiding images of my books behind these new fake "sensitive content" warnings ... being visibility-filtered and defamed by the new "free-speech Twitter" feels so much "freer" than the old, bad Twitter!
>
> > **Consent Factory** @consent_factory · 12s
> >
> > Our books are available from **Amazon**, **Barnes & Noble**, **Indiebound**, **Waterstones**, **Bookshop**, **Booktopia**, and most other online booksellers throughout the world. See our list of just a few such booksellers to find one near you, or just walk in and order them at your local bookstore.
> >
> > ⓘ We put a warning on this Tweet because it might have sensitive content.
> > **Appeal this warning**
>
> Robert F. Kennedy Jr and 3 others
>
> 💬 5   🔁 52   ♡ 128   📊 6,067   ⬆

The New Normal Left
April 3, 2023

So, I went to London to speak to the Left. No, not "the Left" you're probably thinking of. Not the mask-wearing, Ukrainian-flag-flying Left. Not the pronoun-using, segregationist Left. Not the WEF, WHO, FBI, CIA, DHS, and MI6-loving Left. Not the global-capitalist New Normal Left. The other Left. The old-school Left. The "Covid-denying, conspiracy-theorizing, Putin-loving, far-right-extremist" Left.

There were approximately 150 of us, and we gathered in a "homophobic church" in Islington. Yes, Islington, which is more or less the British headquarters of the New Normal Left. We did not care. "Let them come for us," we said. They didn't. It was a Saturday. They were probably out shopping or hunting down imaginary anti-Semites.

So we went ahead and did our thing.

Our "thing" was a conference loosely based on leftist opposition to the WEF and its assorted dystopian visions for our future . . . you know, eating the bugs, owning nothing, being happy, that kind of stuff. I was invited by this group called Real Left to speak on a panel with Fabio Vighi, a professor of Critical Theory at Cardiff University. We didn't talk about the WEF very much. We mostly talked about global capitalism, totalitarianism, and "the New Normal Left."

Here are the broad strokes of what I said at the conference.

In order to understand what happened to the Left (i.e., how it became the New Normal Left), you have to understand the history of global capitalism over the last thirty years or so. Actually, you have to go back a bit farther, back to the early twentieth century, when the Great Ideological

Game was still afoot. Back then, capitalism, having dismantled the absolutist aristocracies, was on the march, transforming the world into one big marketplace. It was challenged by two opposing ideologies, fascism and communism. They fought it out.

Long story short, capitalism won.

Global capitalism (a.k.a. "GloboCap") was born. It's one big global-capitalist world now. It has been since the early 1990s. GloboCap has no external adversaries, so it has nothing to do but "clear and hold," i.e., wipe out pockets of internal resistance and implement ideological uniformity. Which is what it has been doing for the last thirty years, first in the former Soviet bloc, then in the "Global War on Terror," and finally in our so-called "Western democracies," as we have just experienced up close and personal during the shock-and-awe phase of the rollout of the New Normal, and are continuing to experience, albeit somewhat less dramatically.

In other words, GloboCap is going totalitarian. That is what the New Normal is. It is not your granddad's totalitarianism. It is a new, global-capitalist form of totalitarianism. It displays a number of familiar features—suspension of constitutional rights, official propaganda, goon squads, censorship, ubiquitous symbols of ideological conformity, gratuitous restrictions of freedom of movement and other aspects of everyday life, hatred and persecution of official "*Untermenschen,*" segregation, criminalization of dissent, mob violence, book burning, show trials, et cetera—but there won't be any Brownshirts goose-stepping around in jackboots shrieking about "the master race." It's not that kind of totalitarianism.

To understand it (which it would behoove us to do), we need to understand global-capitalist ideology, which isn't as easy as it sounds. Global capitalism has no ideology . . . or, rather, its ideology is "reality." When you have no ideological adversaries, you don't need an ideology. You're basically God. "Reality" is whatever you say it is, and whoever disagrees is a "science denier," or a "conspiracy theorist," or a "malinformationist," or some other type of deluded "extremist." You don't need to argue ideology with anyone, because you have no ideological opponents. Society is divided into two opposing groups, (a) the "normal people," who accept "reality," and (b) the "deviants" and "extremists," who do not.

Your political and ideological opponents are pathologized, preemptively delegitimized. After all, who would argue against "reality" except liars and the clinically insane?

Yes, of course, there is intramural political and ideological conflict within the confines of "normality," just as there is intramural competition between global corporations, but challenging the ideological system itself is impossible, because there is no ground outside it from which to mount an attack. This is probably the hardest thing for most of us to come to terms with. There is no ideological territory outside global capitalism. There is no "outside." There are no external adversaries. There are only insurgencies, and counterinsurgency ops.

The rest is intramural competition.

And here's another thing that we need to understand about global-capitalist ideology, and it isn't going to make my conservative readers, or my libertarian readers, or my leftist readers, happy. But it is essential to understanding the New Normal Left and the shape of the current ideological landscape. I'm going to try to keep this as simple as possible and not get lost in a bunch of post-structuralist mumbo jumbo.

Here we go.

Capitalism is a values-decoding machine. It decodes society of despotic values (i.e., religious values, racist values, socialist values, traditional values, any and all values that interfere with the unimpeded flows of capital . . . capitalism does not distinguish). This is how capitalism (or democracy if you're squeamish) freed us from a despotic "reality" in which values emanated from the aristocracies, kings, priests, the Church, et cetera. Basically, it shifted the production and maintenance of values from despotic structures to the marketplace, where everything is essentially a commodity.

So, hurrah, capitalism freed us from despotism! I'm grateful. I'm not a fan of despotism. The problem is, it's just a machine. And it has no off-switch. And now it dominates the entire planet unopposed and unrestricted in any meaningful way. So it's doing what it is designed to do, stripping societies of their despotic values, rendering everything and everyone a commodity, establishing and enforcing ideological uniformity, neutralizing pockets of internal resistance.

The vast majority of that resistance is reactionary. I do not mean that in the pejorative sense. Most of the opposition to the New Normal has come from the traditional political right, from folks who are trying to preserve their values, i.e., to prevent them from being decoded by the GloboCap values-decoding machine. A lot of these folks don't see it that way, because they do not want to face the fact that what they are resisting is global capitalism, so they call it other names like "crony capitalism," "corporatism," or "cultural Marxism." I don't really care what they call it, except when they call it "communism," which just makes them sound extremely silly.

The point is, these folks comprise a reactionary force that is pushing back against the advance of global-capitalism, whether they know what they are resisting or not. Russia is another such reactionary force, at least insofar as it is attempting to defend what remains of its national identity and sovereignty. Syria and Iran are two other examples. All of these reactionary forces are integrated within the global-capitalist system and, at the same time, they are resisting their absorption by it. The dynamics are complex. It isn't a cartoon or a Hollywood movie with good guys and bad guys.

Anyway, the battlefield looks like this . . . you've got GloboCap conducting its clear-and-hold op, and you've got the reactionary ("populist") backlash against it. And that's it. Those are the only significant forces on the battlefield, currently.

Which brings us to the miserable state of the Left.

The Left (and I mean "the Left" broadly, so liberals, and both serious and Brooklyn leftists) are in an ideological double-bind. Either they align with an increasingly totalitarian GloboCap or they align with the reactionary backlash against it.

They can't align with the reactionaries, because a lot of them are . . . well, you know, somewhat bigoted, or they believe in God, or they object to drag queens rubbing themselves all over kids. Many of them own multiple firearms (i.e., the reactionaries, not the drag queens) and fly giant American flags outside their homes (or whatever giant flags they fly in Great Britain). Many of them voted for Donald Trump, or Brexit, or the AfD here in Germany, or the National Rally in France, or The Brothers of

Italy. These are not BBC/NPR-listening people. These are not pronoun-using people. These are scary working-class people.

So the Left has aligned with GloboCap, which, after all, is still decoding all those nasty despotic values (e.g., racism, and other forms of bigotry), and is opposing dictators and religious zealots, and is spreading "democracy" across the planet. You might think I am being facetious. I am not. Global capitalism is still doing that. Which I support, as do all liberals and leftists.

The catch is, as global capitalism continues to do that, and makes a big show of doing that, it is also going totalitarian. It is not decoding those despotic values out of the goodness of its heart. What it is doing is establishing ideological uniformity. The problem is, it has no ideology. All it knows how to do is decode values, transforming societies into markets and everything in them into valueless commodities. Which it is doing in totalitarian fashion. The Nazis referred to this process as "*Gleichschaltung*," the synchronization of all elements of society according to official ideology. That is what is happening, currently, globally.

GloboCap has begun the transition from a "reality" of competing ideologies, sovereign nation-states, cultures, and values to a new, supranational, post-ideological, eventually trans-human, globalized "reality," and the message is, "you are either with us or against us."

The New Normal Left is obviously with GloboCap. New Normal Leftists will furiously deny this, as they shriek for more censorship of dissent and cheer for actual Sieg-heiling Nazis. Just as the "populist" Right cannot accept the fact that what it is opposing is a form of capitalism, the New Normal Left cannot accept the fact that it is aligned with a new form of totalitarianism. It is literally inconceivable to them. You can show them screenshots of their posts and tweets in which they called for "the Unvaccinated" to be locked up in camps, and pictures of when they formed fanatical mobs and threatened people who wouldn't chant their slogans, and they will look at you as if you are out of your mind.

And so we are in a bit of a fix. Which is basically what I told the conference in London. I wish I had some brilliant plan of action to offer.

Unfortunately, I do not. Probably no one does at this stage of things. After all, the New Normal is just getting started.

That said, one thing I'm sure about is, if you don't want to end up eating the bugs and owning nothing and being happy in your AI-monitored 15-minute city while you wait for your social-credit app to update your vaccination record so you can access your CBDC account and make another minimum payment on your ever-deepening credit-card debt, it would probably be a good idea to try to understand what is actually happening.

Or maybe not. What do I know? I'm just an old "far-right extremist lefty."

A Twitter Files Requiem
April 13, 2023

And so the "Twitter Files" limited hangout has come to its inevitable ignominious end. It is over. The Twitter Files story is dead. It isn't pining for the fjords. It is deceased, cadaverous, bereft of life. It has bought the farm and gone to meet its maker. It is Humpty Dumpty. It has fallen off the wall. Nothing can put it back together again.

I have to tip my hat to Elon Musk. It was quite an impressive limited hangout. The way Musk took the potential story of a global network of intelligence agencies, corporations, NGOs, and assorted "disinformation experts" censoring, visibility-filtering, and otherwise neutralizing dissent as GloboCap executed the "shock-and-awe" phase of the rollout of the "New Normal" over the last three years, the way Musk took that potentially game-changing story by the throat and throttled it, played around with its corpse for a while like a cat, and then finally threw it down, squatted over it, and obstreperously, definitively defecated on it, that was . . . well, quite impressive.

If you missed the final twists and turns in the Twitter Files story (R.I.P), Matt Taibbi, who is currently attempting to enjoy a vacation at Disneyland with the wife and kids, published an update on *Racket News*,[78] his "Twitter-killing" Substack newsletter, covering all the juicy bits.

Here's the "money" paragraph, or most of it . . .

---

78 Taibbi, Matt, "Meet the Censored: Me," *Racket News*, April 13, 2023.

In doing all this Elon immolated the last remnants of any reputation he had as a free speech advocate and gave immeasurable succor to the assorted David Brocks, AOCs, and Renee DiRestas who view him as an antichrist. All can now point to his outbursts of cartoon censorship and argue individual eccentric CEOs are the real danger to free expression, not squads of executives working in oligopolistic secrecy with the FBI, DHS, and ten million Pentagon-funded Centers for Securing Whatever. It won't be true, but Elon's public meltdown will in the short run take a ton of pressure off these villains, while accelerating the piranha frenzy currently skeletonizing Twitter's profits.

What Matt can't quite say (and I understand why) is that Elon's meltdown will not just "give immeasurable succor" to the David Brocks, AOCs, and other functionaries and puppets who have demonized him, and "take a ton of pressure off these villains," it will effectively kill the future of the story and consign what has been reported so far to the "lunatic fringes" of the Internet, where no one "normal" will ever be forced to pay it any serious attention again.

That, my friends, is called a limited hangout. As I explained in a column in January . . .

> The way a limited hangout works is, if you're an intelligence agency, or a global corporation, or a government, or a non-governmental organization, and you have been doing things you need to hide from the public, and those things are starting to come to light such that you can't just deny that you are doing them anymore, what you do is, you release a limited part of the story (i.e., the story of whatever it is you're doing) to distract people's attention from the rest of the story. The part you release is the "limited hangout." It's not a lie. It's just not the whole story. You "hang it out" so that it will become the whole story, and thus stop people from pursuing the whole story.

I was besieged by irate Elon-worshipers, and unfollowed, unfriended, and unsubscribed to for days and weeks after I published that column. Perhaps a few of them will get it now. The point is, it's over. That was it. There aren't going to be any "Covid Twitter Files." There are not going to be any "Nuremberg trials." The "Censorship Industrial Complex" isn't going anywhere. It is here to stay.

From now on, any further Twitter Files reporting will be summarily dismissed as another episode of Elon's Flying Narcissistic Circus. There will be no more congressional hearings. Anyone who continues to cover the story (i.e., the actual story, not the Twitter Files) will be branded a minion of Elon Musk, "a right-wing extremist conspiracy theorist," no more serious than a "9/11 truther."

Matt Taibbi, Michael Shellenberger, Bari Weiss, and less famous journalists like Jacob Siegel, who in a rational world would receive awards for their work, will be systematically, ritually, spat on. Others will simply be ignored. Mehdi Hasan and other hatchet men will parade around with permanent hard-ons spewing vitriol at anyone who even broaches the subject (i.e., the TV hatchet men will be spewing, not their hard-ons).

Interest in the story will precipitously decline.

Elon's interest is already declining. Elon is eager to "move on to the future."[79] And of course he is. His work is done.

Now, before anyone gets all jacked up and starts calling me a "conspiracy theorist," I don't believe that any of this was intentional, or at least not a conscious plan on Musk's part—I'm not quite that gibberingly paranoid yet—but, if the "Censorship Industrial Complex," or GloboCap, or whatever you need to call the multiplicitous, supranational network of governments, global corporations, NGOs, intelligence agencies, oligarchs, media, and other such entities that are radically, aggressively restructuring "reality" in a distinctly totalitarian fashion . . . if those folks (or that ideological system) wanted to execute an elaborate limited hangout and immunize themselves against any further exposure of their Orwellian schemes to eliminate dissent and gaslight the masses, they could not possibly have done a better job than Musk.

Oh, and one more thing . . . and this is for you Musk fans.

---

79   Binder, Matt, "Elon Musk said the Twitter Files were basically dead. Barely anyone noticed," *Mashable*, April 15, 2023.

Make sure to keep cheering for Elon to keep putting those hilarious "affiliation labels" on the Twitter accounts of the BBC, NPR, and all those other official corporate propaganda outlets, instead of, you know, just getting rid of all the labels. With any luck, one day soon, we will wake up in a brave new world where corporations put labels (or warnings) on us all.

I have a hunch what mine might look like.

← **Consent Factory**
16.8K Tweets
Following

💬 16   🔁 146   ♡ 312   📊 12.3K   ⬆

Age-restricted adult content. This content might not be appropriate for everyone. To view this media, you'll need to add your birthdate to your profile. Twitter also uses your age to show more relevant content, including ads, as explained in our Privacy Policy. Learn more

Age-restricted adult content. This content might not be appropriate for everyone. To view this media, you'll need to add your birthdate to your profile. Twitter also uses your age to show more relevant content, including ads, as explained in our Privacy Policy. Learn more

Age-restricted adult content. This content might not be appropriate for everyone. To view this media, you'll need to add your birthdate to your profile. Twitter also uses your age to show more relevant content, including ads, as explained in our Privacy Policy. Learn more

Age-restricted adult content. This content might not be appropriate for everyone. To view this media, you'll need to add your birthdate to your profile. Twitter also uses your age to show more relevant content, including ads, as explained in our Privacy Policy. Learn more

The Great Divide
April 28, 2023

Robert Kennedy Jr. is running for president. I could not possibly be more excited. So I'm going to give Bobby some unsolicited advice, which, if he knows what's good for him, he will not take.

I feel OK about doing this because, even if Bobby, in the wee hours of the night, when the mind is vulnerable to dangerous ideas, were to seriously consider taking my advice, I am sure he has people (i.e., PR people, campaign strategists, pollsters, and so on) that will not hesitate to take him aside and disabuse him of any inclination to do that.

OK, before I give Bobby this terrible advice, I have to do the "full disclosure" thing. I'm a pretty big fan of RFK Jr. I don't generally get involved in electoral politics, but, if I were a Democrat, I would definitely vote for him. Also, he was kind enough to blurb my book (which isn't going to make his PR people happy) and invite me onto his podcast, *RFK Jr. The Defender*, to talk about "New Normal" totalitarianism. So I am fairly biased in favor of Bobby Kennedy. I think he is an admirable, honorable human being. I would love to see him in the Oval Office.

That isn't going to happen, of course. The global-capitalist ruling classes are never going to let him near the Oval Office. They learned their lesson back in 2016. There are not going to be any more unauthorized presidents. The folks at GloboCap are done playing grab-ass, and they want us to know that they are done playing grab-ass. That's what the last six years have been about.

As I put it in a column in January 2021 . . .

This, basically, is what we've just experienced. The global capitalist ruling classes have just reminded us who is really in charge, who the US military answers to, and how quickly they can strip away the facade of democracy and the rule of law. They have reminded us of this for the last ten months, by putting us under house arrest, beating and arresting us for not following orders, for not wearing masks, for taking walks without permission, for having the audacity to protest their decrees, for challenging their official propaganda, about the virus, the election results, etc. They are reminding us currently by censoring dissent, and deplatforming anyone they deem a threat to their official narratives and ideology . . . GloboCap is teaching us a lesson. I don't know how much clearer they could make it. They just installed a new puppet president, who can't even simulate mental acuity, in a locked-down, military-guarded ceremony which no one was allowed to attend, except a few members of the ruling classes. They got some epigone of Albert Speer to convert the Mall (where the public normally gathers) into a "field of flags" symbolizing "unity." They even did the Nazi "*Lichtdom*" thing. To hammer the point home, they got Lady Gaga to dress up as a *Hunger Games* character with a "Mockingjay" brooch and sing the National Anthem. They broadcast this spectacle to the entire world.

Does that sound like the behavior of an unaccountable, supranational power apparatus that is prepared to stand by and let Bobby Kennedy Jr., or Donald Trump, or any other unauthorized person, become the next president of the United States?[80]

So, here's my bad advice for Bobby.

Fuck them. They're not going to let you win, anyway. They are going to smear you, slime you, demonize you, distort every other thing you say, and just generally lie about who you are and what you believe in and what

---

80 Obviously, I was wrong about the unaccountable, supranational power apparatus not being prepared to stand by and let Donald Trump become president. Or, well, he hasn't actually become president again yet. He still has to make it through the holidays and inauguration ceremony in January. Hopefully, his security detail is up to snuff. (December 15, 2024)

you stand for. They are going to paint you as a bull-goose-loony, formerly smack-addled, conspiracy-theorizing, anti-vax fanatic no matter what you do. If you tone down your act and try to "heal the divide" and "end the division," they are going to have you for lunch and then sit around picking their teeth with your bones. You know, and I know, and the American people know, that the things you say you want to do as president—which I know you sincerely want to do as president and are crazy enough to actually try to do, i.e., "to end the corrupt merger of state and corporate power that is threatening now to impose a new kind of corporate feudalism in our country"—are things, well, as Michael Corleone once put it, that they would "use all their power to keep from happening."

So, fuck it, and fuck them. Tell the truth.

Not the ready-for-prime-time truth. Not the toned-down-for-mainstream-consumption truth. The truth. The ugly, unvarnished truth. The scary, crazy-sounding truth. The angry, divisive, uncensored truth.

Yes, there is a "divide." A great divide. A chasm. A schism. A gulf. An abyss. A gaping, yawning, unbridgeable fissure. A Grand Canyon-sized fault in the foundation of society. A rupture in the very fabric of reality.

The global-capitalist ruling classes have decommissioned one "reality" and are replacing it with another "reality" . . . corporate feudalism, pathologized totalitarianism, global corporatism, or whatever anybody wants to call it. Whatever we call it, everyone feels it.

In that "reality," an apocalyptic virus (with a survival rate of roughly ninety-nine point seven percent) nearly wiped out the entire planet, and would have, if not for the Emergency Health Measures (i.e., mass house arrest, forced conformity rituals, cancellation of constitutional rights, censorship of dissent, official propaganda on a scale that even Goebbels could never have dreamed of, the fomenting of mass hysteria and hatred, segregation and persecution of a designated scapegoat underclass) imposed on society by our admittedly imperfect but well-intentioned government and global health authorities. In that "reality," the experimental "vaccines" they forced on billions of people who didn't need them are "safe and effective," despite the fact, which even they now acknowledge, that they have seriously injured or killed millions of people. In that "reality," a few hundred unarmed Trump supporters horsing around in the Capitol Building was an "insurrection," or an "attempted coup," or . . . well, I know you get the picture. There are no neo-Nazis in the Ukraine! The Russians blew up their own pipelines! And so on.

What I am trying to get at, Bobby, is that those of us who have refused to convert to the new "reality"—which I am guessing is approximately twenty-five to thirty percent of the global population—are not looking for a leader who can "heal the divide." We are in a fight. We are fighting for reality. We're fighting for what's left of reality.

At the moment, we are getting our asses kicked.

So, fuck it. What have you got to lose? Throw out the playbook. Fire your PR people. Go for broke. Tell the truth. Tell folks what we're up against. That it isn't something an election is going to fix. That it isn't something a new president can fix. That it isn't fixable. That it is a fucking fight. And not one according to the Queensberry Rules. A ball-kicking, eye-gouging, chair-swinging, bar fight. And that sometimes, like now, when there's nowhere to run to, well, you have to stand and fight, even if you know you're going to lose.

That's it. That's my bad advice for Bobby. Hopefully, one of his staff will spot it and delete it before he reads his email.[81] Otherwise, I'm afraid he might be tempted to take it. He's already leaning in that direction. And . . . well, you know how those Irish love a good fight.

---

81 Unfortunately, Bobby saw my advice before one of his PR people could get to it and delete it, and he responded: "This is advice I intend to follow. Thanks for the wisdom, CJ!" OK, he didn't quite make it into the Oval Office, but being nominated to head the US Department of Health and Human Services ain't bad. (December 22, 2024)

The War on Reality Revisited
May 22, 2023

Reality isn't what it used to be. It never was, but that's another story. This one isn't about reality per se. It's about the War on Reality, the one we're in the middle of, the war that started when the War on Terror was canceled in the Summer of 2016. It's actually an extension and an evolution of the War on Terror, and the War on Populism, and the rollout of the New Normal in 2020, but all that is also another story.

I want to focus on the war that is raging currently, on the Internet, in people's workplaces, homes, among friends and families, and in people's heads. I'm pretty sure you know the war I'm talking about, regardless of which "side" you feel you are on.

The War on Reality is a civil war, but it is much more than just a civil war. It is an asymmetrical, polymorphous, metastatic, multiplicitous war. It is an ontological free-for-all. It has no conventions or rules of engagement. There are no battle lines. The battle is everywhere. Alliances shift from day to day. It is chaos—unrelenting, inescapable chaos. It is an omnipresent, immaterial, omnipotent organism attacking itself. It is continual, and completely unwinnable. It is unwinnable because it has already been won. It ended in victory the moment it began, and now we're doomed to go on fighting it forever, or until some less ethereal leviathan is born, or reborn, out of its ashes.

Unfortunately, that's rather likely, the less ethereal leviathan scenario. It may not come about in my lifetime—and, selfishly, I am hoping it doesn't—but this state of affairs cannot continue indefinitely. As I wrote in an essay in June of 2021:

The global capitalist ruling classes are implementing a new official ideology, in other words, a new "reality." That's what an official ideology is. It's more than just a set of beliefs. Anyone can have any beliefs they want. Your personal beliefs do not constitute "reality." In order to make your beliefs "reality," you need to have the power to impose them on society. You need the power of the police, the military, the media, scientific "experts," academia, the culture industry, the entire ideology-manufacturing machine. There is nothing subtle about this process. Decommissioning one "reality" and replacing it with another is a brutal business. Societies grow accustomed to their "realities." We do not surrender them willingly or easily. Normally, what's required to get us to do so is a crisis, a war, a state of emergency, or . . . you know, a deadly global pandemic. During the changeover from the old "reality" to the new "reality," the society is torn apart. The old "reality" is being disassembled and the new one has not yet taken its place. It feels like madness, and, in a way, it is. For a time, the society is split in two, as the two "realities" battle it out for dominance. "Reality" being what it is (i.e., monolithic), this is a fight to the death. In the end, only one "reality" can prevail.

I wrote that almost two years ago, in the relative calm before the storm of fascistic, hate-drunk mass hysteria and systematic persecution that was unleashed on "the Unvaccinated" in the months that followed. Since then, the madness of the reality-changeover has intensified, albeit somewhat more subtly, or at least Keith Olbermann is not shrieking hatred like a meth-addled Joseph Goebbels anymore.

GloboCap, Inc. and its innumerable subsidiaries, agents, assigns, political puppets, media goons, and other loyal minions are desperately endeavoring to enshrine the official COVID-19 narrative in the annals of "history." According to new figures from the WHO, "almost fifteen million excess deaths" (or "a total of 336.8 million lost life-years") had been caused by the virus by the end of 2021,[82] none of which had anything to

---

82 "15 million excess deaths worldwide were caused by COVID over two years—WHO," *Sky News*, May 19, 2023.

do with ventilators, or the classification of anyone who died of anything[83] (i.e., cancer, heart disease, an auto accident, etc.) who had also tested positive as a "Covid death." Previously perfectly healthy young people are dropping dead left and right from heart attacks and other "natural" (or "undisclosed") causes that have nothing to do with the experimental "vaccines" that they did not need but were coerced into taking, which saved millions or 100 million lives.[84] The masks that didn't work worked, except they didn't, but that was only if you studied how they worked in reality.[85] Being locked down, forced to wear medical-looking masks, gaslighted and terrorized by official propaganda, bullied, segregated, censored, demonized, and otherwise systematically tortured, was actually good for people's mental health,[86] except for "people with existing mental health conditions, and children, and people with disabilities, and adolescents, and people without financial or social security nets."

Meanwhile, cognitively dissonant New Normals are taking to the Internet to claim that no one knew any better at the time, and that, OK, sure, "mistakes were made," but if we "science-denying conspiracy theorists," who they censored, demonized, and systematically persecuted for over two years, had just spoken up . . .

I could go on, but you get the picture, or, rather, you either do or you don't. Because it's not just the folks at GloboCap, Inc. that are fanatically waging this War on Reality. Everybody and their brother is trying to ram their "reality" down everyone's throat. You got the "Viruses Do Not Exist" people. You got the "There Are No Neo-Nazis in Ukraine" people. The "Putin Is Our Savior" people. The Vote Blue Cult. The Multipolar people. The Transgendered People's Army. The Doomsday

---

[83] Hays, Gabriel, "CNN analyst slammed after writing COVID deaths are being overcounted: 'TWO AND A HALF YEARS LATE'," *New York Post*, January 14, 2023.

[84] Slisco, Aila, "Trump Dismisses COVID-19 Vax Safety Claims, Says He Saved 100 Million Lives," *Newsweek*, January 19, 2023.

[85] Rudy, Melissa, "Face masks made 'little to no difference' in preventing spread of COVID: study," *New York Post*, February 14, 2023.

[86] Sridhar, Devi, "Was the Covid pandemic bad for mental health? It depends who you ask," *The Guardian*, March 10, 2023.

Clock Hucksters. The Folks Who Still Listen to NPR. The Insurrection Truthers. The Insurrection Deniers. The 9/11 Truthers. The Moon-Landing Truthers. The Cult of Trump. The Church of Russiagate. The Rothschild Obsessives. The Anti-Racism Racists. The Anti-Anti-Semitism Anti-Semites. The Mass Formation Movement. The Cult of Marx. The Cult of Capital. The Climate Change Fanatics. The Musk Cult. The list goes on and on.

Historically, we humans have not done very well in such psychotic ontological environments. When "reality" is shattered into a thousand little shards, and things fall apart, and the center does not hold, we tend to get rather scared and confused. We start to panic. We try to put "reality" back together again. This does not work. This worsens our panic. We start looking around for a new "reality." We start looking for a savior, a leader, a *Führer*, someone with a vision, and the will, and the power, to impose a new "reality" on the ontological chaos that is making us so confused and agitated, and scared, and angry, and restore some sense of ideological cohesion so that we don't have to think about "reality" on a moment-by-moment basis anymore.

This is the time of dime-store messiahs, tinpot tyrants, zealots, gurus, hustlers, hosers, scam artists, quacks, snake oil salesmen of every variety, fanatical revolutionary movements, new religions and political parties, and so on. Typically, eventually, once the hapless masses have been repeatedly duped, bilked, betrayed, gaslighted, and humiliated to the point where they can't even think anymore, literally cannot think anymore because their brains are broken, and they just want someone, anyone, to make it all stop ... well, to rephrase an old Buddhist platitude, "when the masses are ready, the despot will appear."

I think you know how this story ends.

The fascinating thing is, GloboCap, Inc. (i.e., global capitalism, corporatism, or whatever you need to call the supranational network of global corporations, governments, banks, military contractors, media and entertainment conglomerates, pharmaceutical behemoths, oligarchs, and non-governmental governing entities that comprise the de facto empire we live in) cannot afford to let that happen, and is tirelessly working to prevent that from happening.

Traditional (i.e., twentieth century) totalitarianism does not work for GloboCap, Inc. Capitalism, though it can adapt to anything, has never been inherently inclined toward fascism or any other form of totalitarianism. Totalitarianism is a value-coding machine. Its objective is to completely code society with its values, its official ideology (i.e., "reality"). Every aspect of society, not just politics, culture, and so on, but the most intimate aspects of people's lives.

Capitalism is a value-decoding machine. Its objective is to completely *decode* society of any values that impede the free flows of capital, rendering everything and everyone a de facto commodity, transforming societies into markets. It can adapt to totalitarianism and other varieties of despotism when necessary, but left to its own devices, or, you know, granted dominion over the entire planet Earth and every creeping thing that creeps upon it, it sets about decoding and destabilizing values, destabilizing value and meaning itself, until, ultimately, everything means anything, or nothing, or whatever the market decides it means or is worth at any given moment.

The point is, the War on Reality is not a means to an end. It is the end. The official ideology (i.e., "reality") that GloboCap, Inc. is implementing is not a set of official values or beliefs. It is the absence of any values or beliefs, any non-commodifiable values and beliefs. Values and beliefs are fine, as long as they are just empty signs, logos, meaningless identity statements, and not principles and beliefs you are trying to live by, and that you are crazy enough to fight to preserve. Those kind of values have to go, so that the people of the New Normal future can be free to believe that war is peace, ignorance is strength, two plus two equals five, men have periods, Donald Trump is a Russian secret agent and literally Hitler, Vladimir Putin (who is also literally Hitler) invaded Ukraine for no reason whatsoever, or certainly not because of anything to do with GloboCap, Inc., or NATO, or the non-existent Ukrainian neo-Nazis, and then destroyed his own pipelines in the Baltic Sea, or whatever blatantly ridiculous nonsense they (i.e., the people of the New Normal future) are told to pretend or to actually believe by Rachel Maddow and other talking heads.

And, if that doesn't sound like your kind of future, or reality, the "everything is a floating signifier" reality, no worries, you can always drop out of the "mainstream" and join the carnival of "conspiracy theorists, anti-vaxxers, Covid deniers, Russiagate deniers, climate change deniers, disinformationists, malinformationists, transphobes, white supremacists, violent domestic extremists," and assorted other freaks and curiosities of nature that are actively being quarantined, or are quarantining themselves, in ideological ghettos where normal consumers never have to see them and they (i.e., we, the deviants and freaks) are preyed upon by legions of charlatans, demagogues, agents provocateurs, and other such spiritual and emotional parasites, until the day comes when we find ourselves spastically tweeting about an eighty-six-year-old Chomsky chasing naked sex slaves around Epstein's island, ripped to the gills on Viagra and Ecstasy, and probably freshly harvested adrenochrome!

That, or you could withdraw from society and go live in a Kaczynski cabin in Montana, or Idaho, or wherever folks are doing that these days, as several of my readers have advised me recently, and forage for berries, and barbecue squirrels, and . . . well, you know, defecate in a hole in the ground.

I'm sorry, I realize that all sounds pretty bleak. I guess I'm in a bleak mood these days, or running short on passionate intensity, or something. There's no shortage of passionate intensity out there, if that's what you are looking for. Don't let me stop you. It's just that, whenever I switch it off for a while, that passionate intensity, that howling maelstrom of warring realities, and listen closely, I hear the slouch of Yeats's rough beast, whose hour, apparently, is coming round again.

I'm not sure which "side" it is slouching our way from, but probably that doesn't matter.

Oh, well, as the French say, *plus ça change* . . .

New Normal Germany Blues
June 12, 2023

The first rule of New Normal Germany is, you do not compare New Normal Germany to Nazi Germany! I did that on the cover of my best-selling book, *The Rise of the New Normal Reich*, so the public prosecutor's office in Berlin has launched a criminal investigation of me for allegedly "disseminating propaganda, the contents of which are intended to further the aims of a former National Socialist organization," which is punishable by up to three years in prison.

Actually, the first rule of New Normal Germany is "Shut Up, Click Heels, and Follow Orders!" I think the second rule is probably the one about not comparing New Normal Germany to Nazi Germany.

Which is totally reasonable. After all, Nazi Germany was not just one type of totalitarian social system among others, like Maoist China, Fascist Italy, the USSR under Stalin, the Khmer Rouge in Cambodia, and other totalitarian social systems that you're allowed to compare New Normal Germany to. And, even if it was (i.e., one example of totalitarianism, among others, and not the incomparably singular and utterly unprecedented historical event that it was), there is no such thing as totalitarianism anymore, so you can't compare any present-day system, or movement, or widespread sociopolitical phenomenon, to it (i.e., to Nazi Germany), or to any of those other totalitarian systems, especially not in New Normal Germany.

If you do . . . well, this is what happens.

You want to see a picture of my "propaganda, the contents of which are intended to further the aims of a former National Socialist organization," don't you? Sure you do. All right, here you go.

My book is the one on the right, of course. The other book is the international bestseller, *The Rise and Fall of The Third Reich*, by William Shirer, which has sold, I don't know, a gazillion copies since it was published in 1960, and which you can buy in any bookshop in Germany, and which is absolutely not "propaganda, the contents of which are intended to further the aims of a former National Socialist organization."

Nor is Rammstein's music video *Deutschland*, in which some of the Rammstein guys dress up like Nazis, and some like concentration camp prisoners, and reenact the extermination of the Jews for entertainment and educational purposes.[87]

Nor is a recent tweet by Jessica Berlin, a "political analyst and expert in security issues and international development," and a former fellow of the German Marshall Fund of the United States, and founder and managing director of something called CoStruct, where she "advises governments, foundations, investment funds, NGOs, and companies large and small on strategy and program design to tackle global challenges with sustainable,

---

87 *Deutschland*, untitled seventh studio album, 2018.

scalable solutions," and who is also a commentator at *Deutsche Welle News*, *Washington Post*, *BBC World Service*, *Tagesspiegel*, ZDF, et al.

Jessica's tweet,[88] comparing a crowd of pro-Russia protesters in Germany to the Nazis, and prominently featuring a bunch of little girls waving little Nazi flags with swastikas on them, is absolutely not "propaganda, the contents of which are intended to further the aims of a former National Socialist organization," because Jessica was comparing these nasty Russia-supporting protesters in Frankfurt to the Nazis, whereas the artwork on my book cover is comparing the decent, well-meaning, order-following people all around the world who have been persecuting "the Unvaccinated," and who wanted to lock us all up in "quarantine camps," and forcibly experimentally "vaccinate" us, to the Nazis.

But, seriously, this investigation is a joke, and it's not. The Berlin authorities have the power to imprison me for up to three years, or to fine me thousands of Eurodollars, for tweeting the artwork on the cover of my book.

Apparently, I tweeted an image of the book cover (or at least the cover art of the book) on my birthday, August 24, 2022, at 5:51 P.M. CET, and then again on August 27, 2022, at 8:47 P.M. CET, according to the notice of *Ermittlungsverfahren* from the *Staatsanwaltschaft Berlin*, i.e., the Berlin district prosecutor.[89]

I can't go into all the details of my case, and I'm certainly not going to argue it in this column—my attorney's job is challenging enough . . . I mean, imagine having me for a client—but I can fill you in on life in New Normal Germany and share some of my personal emotional feelings about the country I have called home for almost twenty years now.

---

88 On the advice of my attorney, I will not reproduce Jessica Berlin's here, in order to avoid (a) being sued by Jessica Berlin, and (b) being arrested by the German authorities and charged with "disseminating (even more) propaganda, the contents of which are intended to further the aims of a former National Socialist organization."

89 Yes, I just used the German terms for comic effect, so they can add that to my charges.

My personal emotional feelings are, it sucks. It didn't used to suck. It used to be lovely. When I arrived here in Berlin in 2004, the city was still in its "poor but sexy" phase. It reminded me of my years in San Francisco in the early 1980s, before the dotcom boom, except for all the bullet holes in the facades of buildings from the Russian machine guns, and the *Stolpersteine*, and . . . well, everyone speaking German. I was still "poor but sexy" back then, and in the throes of an extended midlife crisis (i.e., running around making a fool of myself with Berlin club kids half my age and engaging in assorted degenerate behaviors), so it seemed the perfect place to set up camp in Europe.

And it was . . . until the Spring of 2020.

Given its history and the character of its denizens, Berlin felt like the last place on Earth that was ever going to go totalitarian again. And then it did. In the blink of an eye. Like someone had flipped a big "fascism on" switch.

Constitutional rights were abruptly canceled. Protests against the New Normal were banned. The German media started pumping out propaganda like a Goebbelsian keyboard instrument. Public displays of conformity were mandated. "The Unvaccinated" were banned from society. Hate-drunk mobs of New Normal Germans began hunting down maskless people on trains. By the end of it, the government was making plans to forcibly "vaccinate" the entire population.

I'm not going to tell the whole story again here. I told it in the book. I told it as it happened. I told it in my Consent Factory columns.

As anyone who has read those columns or the book knows, "the New Normal Reich" does not refer to Germany exclusively. I have also written extensively about the New Normal USA, the New Normal United Kingdom, New Normal Canada, New Normal Australia, and various other New Normal countries, none of which, as far as I'm aware, are attempting to imprison me for my writing, currently.

But Germany is sensitive about its Nazi history, and, well, who wouldn't be? I certainly would be. If I were a member of the German government, or the police, or the media, or the culture industry, I probably wouldn't take very kindly to an American writer reminding everyone of when my people tried to conquer Europe and systematically murdered millions of

Jews and other varieties of human beings because they thought they were the "master race."

Of course, the New Normal has nothing to do with the Jews, or the Holocaust, or even Nazism, specifically. As I've written and stated in my columns and my interviews, the New Normal is a new form of totalitarianism . . . *totalitarianism*, of which Nazism is one example among others.

It happens to be a really good example. And it is an example that I am allowed to cite when I am writing and speaking about totalitarianism, or else The Universal Declaration of Human Rights means nothing.

> Everyone has the right to freedom of opinion and expression; this right includes freedom to hold opinions without interference and to seek, receive and impart information and ideas through any media and regardless of frontiers. —Article 19, The Universal Declaration of Human Rights

The German authorities understand this. They are not total idiots. They attended universities. Some of them studied political science, and logic, and even twentieth-century history. They know the difference between pro-Nazi propaganda and anti-totalitarian artwork. They know how absurd the charges against me are, but they have to be pursued, because . . . well, orders are orders! And it isn't just the German authorities. As I've tried to explain in my essays, and in the book, and at a recent "Real Left" conference in London, the New Normal is a global phenomenon. GloboCap, Inc. is done playing grab-ass. Grab-Ass time is over. They are going totalitarian on us. It isn't your grandfather's totalitarianism. It is a new, global-capitalist form of totalitarianism. However, like every other form of totalitarianism, its ultimate goal is ideological uniformity and control of every aspect of society through a process the Nazis referred to as "*Gleichschaltung*." That process is well underway at the moment. The New Normal authorities and their diverse associates are implementing a variety of societal-control systems, censorship and "visibility-filtering" of speech, digital currencies, restrictions on movement, the enforcement of radical ideological dogmas, and so on. And they are aggressively cracking down on dissent.

One of the most repulsive aspects of their efforts to persecute political dissidents, censor our speech, and otherwise implement "New Normal *Gleichschaltung*" throughout the planet is the cynical way they're using the Holocaust and false accusations of anti-Semitism as pretexts. If you wanted to make a mockery of the memory of the Holocaust, and the dignity of its victims, and "further the aims of a former National Socialist organization" . . . well, I cannot imagine a better way to do it.

I'll keep you posted on the investigation, and I'll try my best to not go full "Late Lenny Bruce" and start publishing trial transcripts verbatim. In the meantime, some of us are gathering in London to discuss what to do about what Michael Shellenberger has dubbed the "Censorship Industrial Complex." So it's back to the Big Smoke once again, assuming the Germans let me leave the country.

The Criminalization of Dissent Revisited

July 3, 2023

Greetings from Thoughtcriminal 231Js1736/23!

That's my official Thoughtcrime Case Number, which my attorney needs to reference in all our official correspondence with the New Normal Thought Police. I think I'm going to silk-screen it on a T-shirt and wear it on my first day in Moabit Criminal Court, the largest criminal court in Europe with 340 judges and 360 prosecutors.

That's right, the Berlin state prosecutor's office is pursuing its criminal investigation of me for allegedly "disseminating propaganda, the content of which is intended to further the aims of a former National Socialist organization," which could send me to prison for up to three years.[90]

My attorney wrote to them and politely explained how ridiculous their investigation is and why they should summarily drop the charge, but New Normal Germany has a zero-tolerance policy when it comes to thoughtcrime, especially thoughtcrime involving any kind of "Covid-denying" propaganda.

The "propaganda" in question is these two tweets.

---

90 Taibbi, Matt, "First Roger Waters, Now This: Germany Places American C. J. Hopkins Under Investigation," *Racket News,* June 14, 2023.

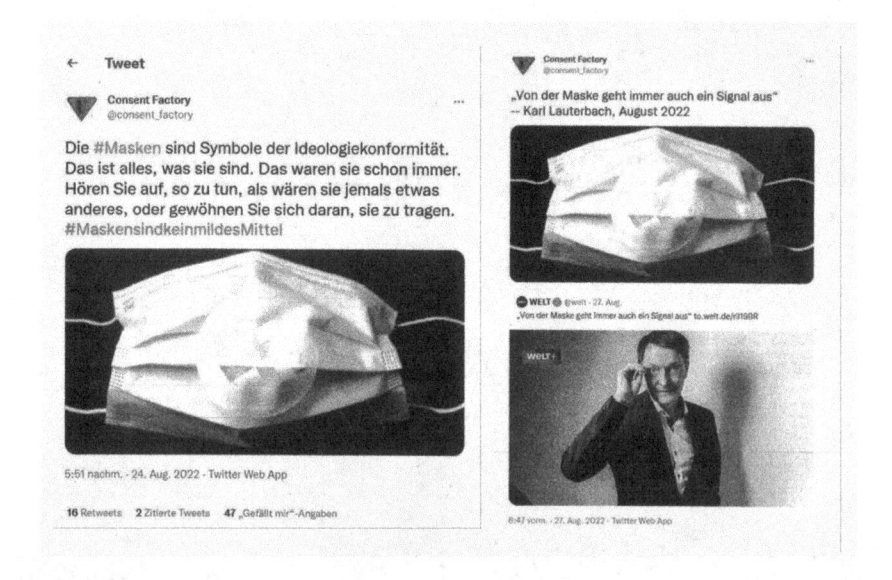

Which, OK, I just disseminated them again, so there's another three years in prison. Or, I don't know, maybe six years in prison, i.e., three years for each separate count of thoughtcrime.

I wrote those tweets in German, so let me translate.

The one on the left reads, "The masks are ideological-conformity symbols. That is all they are. That is all they have ever been. Stop acting like they have ever been anything else, or get used to wearing them." The hashtag translates as "Masks are not a benign measure."

The one on the right is a quote by Karl Lauterbach, the Minister of Health of Germany, tweeted by *Die Welt*, a national newspaper. It reads "The masks always send out a signal." And, yes, Karl, that's exactly the point I was making.

The image is from the cover artwork of my book *The Rise of the New Normal Reich: Consent Factory Essays, Vol. III (2020–2021)*, which was banned in Germany by Amazon, Inc. two days after I tweeted the above tweets. It appears to also be banned for sale in bookstores, but I don't have confirmation of that.

My attorney just received the screenshots of these tweets from the Berlin state prosecutor a few days ago. Up to then, we didn't know what they were, and we couldn't find them, because they have been censored by Twitter, presumably on the orders of the German Thought Police. We knew that they featured the cover art of my book, because the prosecutor's office described it, but we didn't know about the "Covid denial."

So, essentially, I'm facing criminal charges and being threatened with who knows how many years in prison, or thousands of Eurodollars in fines, for (a) stating what has now been widely acknowledged, and what was generally understood by every serious epidemiologist until the Spring of 2020, namely, that mask-mandates do not work, and thus are nothing but symbolic measures designed to generate and enforce mass obedience, and (b) insulting the Minister of Health of Germany, who happens to be a fanatical serial liar who is directly responsible for the serious injury and death of . . . well, we'll never know how many people.

Neither of which are actual crimes. Not even in the Federal Republic of Germany.

The pretext for the charges I am facing is the swastika behind the mask, which, as I noted in a recent essay, is a play on the international bestseller, *The Rise and Fall of The Third Reich*, by William Shirer, which you can buy in any bookshop in Berlin.

So, there you are . . . those are my thoughtcrimes.

I've been writing about the "New Normal" as a new form of totalitarianism for several years now. I wrote about it in one of my essays, *The Criminalization of Dissent*, in May of 2021. Some of my colleagues rolled their eyes. They thought I was being hyperbolic again. I wasn't. This is what I meant. It is literally the criminalization of dissent.

I wasn't the only one covering the story of the criminalization of dissent in Germany. The *New York Times* reported on it in 2021 . . .

The country's domestic intelligence agency says it will create a new department to deal with extremism among conspiracy theorists.[91]

As did *Aljazeera* . . .

---

91 Schuetze, Christopher F., "German Intelligence Puts Coronavirus Deniers Under Surveillance," *New York Times*, April 28, 2021.

For intelligence officers to be legally allowed to start observing parts of the anti-lockdown movement, Germany's Federal Office for the Protection of the Constitution (BfV) had to create an entirely new category of groups because the "Querdenkers" do not fit neatly into the existing classifications of right-wing or left-wing. The new category is for groups suspected of being "anti-democratic and/or delegitimizing the state in a way that endangers security." The designation allows intelligence officers to gather data about individuals and their activities, and could in a further step include shadowing people and tapping their communications.[92]

I was not a member of the "Querdenker" movement (or any other movement for that matter), but I doubt that makes any difference to the BfV or the Berlin state prosecutor. Anyone even vaguely prominent who spoke out against the "Corona measures" is fair game for threats and prosecution. The beneficent-sounding Federal Office for the Protection of the Constitution, or "BfV," is basically Germany's FBI. It's now two years after the above stories were published, and they are still on the hunt for "Covid deniers," "conspiracy theorists," and other such persons suspected of "delegitimizing the state" . . . whatever that Orwellian language means.

Of course, it doesn't matter what it means. It means whatever they say it means. That's what it means. It means it doesn't mean anything. And they do not have to pretend it means anything. It means, "Shut the fuck up. Get in line. Do what we tell you. Say what we tell you. Think what we tell you. Or we will fucking get you. We will make up some charges and prosecute you. We will censor you into Internet oblivion. We will shut off your fucking bank account. We'll send the IRS to your house. We'll ruin your career. We'll hurt your family. We will extradite you to the USA and lock you up in Supermax prison for 175 fucking years."

How am I doing? Do I sound hyperbolic?

And, no, of course I'm not just talking about Germany. The criminalization of dissent is being rolled out everywhere. Ireland is just the latest

---

92 "German spy agency to monitor some anti-lockdown protesters," *Aljazeera*, April 28, 2021.

of dozens of countries all throughout the West that are criminalizing so-called "hate speech."[93] The specifics are different but the message is the same, "Watch what you say, or we will prosecute you, or otherwise seriously fuck you up."

Oh, and also, I should probably mention, my lawyer advised me not to republish those tweets. He completely understands where I am coming from, but it is his job to look out for me and to try his best to . . . you know, keep me out of German prison, which I'm not making easy for him.

Now, I want to be very clear about this. I have no desire to go to German prison. I am about to turn sixty-two years old. I'm not at all interested in tossing anyone's salad or having my salad tossed by anyone, especially not a pumped-up, tattooed member of some local Turkish drug gang, or an actual German neo-Nazi, but I'm not going to be intimidated into shutting up or toning my act down to placate the New Normal Thought Police.

The thing is, I don't respond well to bullies. I feel a particular antipathy toward them. I'm not very fond of liars either. And totalitarians. There's another group of people I don't like. I am not ashamed to admit my bias against such people. I wish them ill. I am sorry about whatever vicissitudes of fortune or experience turned them into lying, bullying, totalitarian creeps, but they can suck foul wind out of my ass if they think I am going to bow down to them. They can do what they want to me. They have that power. They can silence me for a while if they want. But they cannot make me silence myself.

And they cannot make me pretend to respect them.

The Germans are real big on respecting authority. So am I. But authority is earned. It does not stem from a title or a uniform. It stems from knowledge, experience, integrity, and honorable behavior, not from brute force. Fascists, totalitarians, and the like do not deserve our respect. They deserve our scorn. They deserve our derision. I have plenty of it for them.

Also, there are the kids to think about. I don't have any, but other people do. What kind of an example are we setting for the kids if we start

---

93   Myers, Fraser, "Ireland's new thoughtcrime bill is shockingly draconian," *Spiked*, May 3, 2023.

censoring (or "sensitivity-editing") ourselves every time some fascist bully threatens to put us in jail if we don't? A lot of the young people are already pretty pussified as it is these days. I'm certainly not a tough guy or anything, but sometimes, in life, you have to fight, and it doesn't really matter if you get your ass kicked.

Oh, and, if you're contemplating writing to me and advising me to "get the hell out of Germany" or inquiring as to why I haven't "gotten the hell out of Germany," please do not do that. I am extremely tired of hearing it. Instead, just wire a high six-figure sum into the Swiss account I will be setting up shortly, and, I promise you, I'll get the hell out of Germany and send you a postcard from an undisclosed location somewhere in the Ionian Sea.

In the meantime, I'll definitely keep you posted on Case 231Js1736/23, and maybe I'll go ahead and do up that T-shirt. Wait, what am I thinking? This is New Normal Berlin! I could find a VC, round up some twenty-year-old, transgender, Ayahuasca-guzzling tech bros (or "tech persons with penises" or whatever the proper "non-harmful" nomenclature is at the moment), and start up some type of totally Bitcoined bespoke Thoughtcriminal T-shirt business!

The way things are going, I'll probably make a killing, or at least I'll be able to cover my legal costs, which, after that last little gratuitous outburst, Lord knows what kinds of new charges I'll be facing!

The "Free-Speech Twitter" PSYOP

August 14, 2023

It's never a very enjoyable experience, facing the fact that you've been bamboozled. Realizing that you've fallen prey to an elaborate con, or PYSOP, is painful. It's embarrassing. People feel ashamed. No one likes to see themselves as a sucker. It's humiliating. It makes people angry. It makes them want to lash out at someone.

The funny thing is, it usually isn't the person who conned them that they want to lash out at. Doing that would only make them feel more ashamed. No, typically, who people want to lash out at, when they finally realize that they have been bamboozled, are the people who didn't get bamboozled along with them, and who tried to warn them that they were being bamboozled.

This phenomenon is occurring right now. I know this because a certain sector of my readers are angrily unsubscribing from my Substack, and unfollowing me on Twitter, and so on. This happens more or less every time that people start to realize I was right about some PSYOP or con that I warned them about—Russiagate, Covid, and now "free-speech Twitter," or "X," or whatever we're calling it today.

Yes, that's right, the jig is up. The bloom is off the rose. The cat is out of the bag. The party is over. The thrill is gone. People are finally starting to realize that "free-speech Twitter" was an elaborate con (or a PSYOP, depending on how paranoid you are), and they're none too happy about this realization.

So they're taking it out on blasphemers like me who tried to warn them about "The Emperor Elonicus,"[94] and how the Twitter Files was a textbook limited hangout, and who pointed out how Musk shut it down as soon as it had served its purpose, and who referred to some of them as "Musk cultists" and "suckers."

But I'm not writing this column to whine about that. It's part of human nature. I get it.

I'm writing this column because, maybe, now that folks are starting to face the fact that the whole "free-speech Twitter" thing was an elaborate con, or a trap, or a PSYOP, maybe, now, they can knock off the "Elon is our savior!" crap and try to pay attention to what is actually happening.

Linda Yaccarino, CEO of X, explained very clearly what is actually happening in a Twitter "Spaces" thing she did recently.

> We've introduced a new policy called "Freedom of speech, not reach." If you're going to post something that is lawful but is awful, you get labeled. You get deamplified, which means it cannot be shared. And it is certainly demonetized.[95]

Here's my favorite Yaccarino quote:

> Since acquisition, we have built brand-safety and content-moderation tools that have never before existed at this company. And we've introduced a new policy to [address?] your specific point about hate speech, called "Freedom of speech, not reach."

What she's talking about is the future of Internet censorship. Not the ham-fisted government-initiated censorship that people tend to think of when they think about censorship. Corporate censorship. "Free-market" censorship. What she's talking about is the virtually imperceptible moment-by-moment manipulation of social-media content, search engine results,

---

94 Hopkins, C. J., "The Emperor Elonicus," *Consent Factory*, November 27, 2022.
95 Eric Abbenante, Twitter (audio recording by @EricAbbenante), August 11, 2023.

"reference" platforms like Wikipedia, everything most people see on the Internet. The corp-speak term is "visibility filtering."

From now on, instead of being suspended or deplatformed—which is bad PR and only draws more attention to the deplatformed party—dissident voices will be "deamplified." We will be "free" to post whatever we like, but we will be talking to no one, in a digital void, which most people won't even know exists. "Red/blue" culture-war mud-slinging content, and other such harmless entertainment that keeps the masses infuriated and at each other's throats, will of course be allowed, and will be "amplified" and "monetized." But any serious form of political dissent or deviation from official narratives will be labeled "disinformation," or "malinformation," or "hate speech," or simply "awful" and "unhealthy." Corporations like X, Meta, Alphabet, and Tencent will decide what is "healthy." They will do so with algorithms, but not only with algorithms.

Here's Linda Yaccarino again, talking to CNBC this time . . .

> X is committed to encouraging healthy behavior . . . 99.9 percent of all impressions are healthy . . . and we have an extraordinary team of people who are overseeing, hands on keyboards, monitoring, all day, every day, to make sure that that 99.9 percent of impressions remain at that number.[96]

I don't know how much clearer she could make it. A team. Of people. Monitoring everything. Moment by moment. Every day. Not some badly written algorithm. Not some secret cabal of mutinous Wokesters sabotaging Elon's vision. Not the FBI. Not the CIA. Not the WEF. Not the Rothschilds. Just Twitter. Just X.

This isn't one of my "conspiracy theories." There is absolutely nothing secret about it. It's all explained on the "Twitter Safety" blog, with examples of the interstitial labels that Twitter might put on your "unhealthy" tweets before they "deamplify" them into oblivion.

See! Twitter is, like, totally committed to transparency!

---

[96] Goswami, Rohan, "X CEO Linda Yaccarino explains reason for getting rid of Twitter name," CNBC, August 10, 2023.

Of course, you have nothing to worry about if you are tweeting (or Xing?) "healthy" content. That "extraordinary Twitter-Safety team" that is monitoring everything "all day, every day" would never "deamplify," or "visibility-filter," or otherwise censor political speech that isn't "hate speech," or ... you know, use one of those interstitial labels to maliciously defame some troublesome author by deceiving people into thinking he was tweeting child pornography or graphic violent content, like bestiality, or necrophilia, or some other type of "age-restricted adult content," as Twitter was doing to me until May of this year.

I'm just joking, of course. They're going to keep doing that. Not to me anymore, not that way. (After I embarrassed Ella Irwin publicly, they removed the fake labels and just deamplified me.) But they are going to keep doing it to other people. And not just X. All the corporations. They are going to keep "visibility filtering," and "deamplifying," and vaporizing dissent, and there is currently nothing we can do about it.

Meanwhile, we (i.e., the "Free Speech Movement") will be celebrating our "victory" over the bad apples in government who were forcing the poor, helpless global corporations to censor everyone until we took them to court and made them stop with our democratic rights! Then we'll all live happily ever after!

I don't mean to shit on my friends and colleagues who are fighting hard against government censorship. At least they're actually achieving something, while I'm just sitting here running my mouth. And the fight against government censorship is important. It is vitally important. And it has to be fought. I support it wholeheartedly, and I applaud them for fighting it. But it isn't going to change what's happening.

What's happening is, GloboCap, or Corporatism, or whatever you want to call the network of global corporations, governments, media, non-governmental governing entities, investment banks, global health authorities, academia, the culture industry, and other such entities that together comprise the decentralized system of power and ideology that is currently running the entire planet ... whatever you want to call that, it's going totalitarian.

It has been going totalitarian, more or less openly, for the better part of the last three years. I've been covering this transition for quite a while now, and I have reiterated my analysis in many of my columns, and I published a book about it, which is possibly going to get me sent to prison here in Germany, so I'm not going to rehash it all again here.

For now, trust me, we are going totalitarian. That's what all the "visibility filtering" is about. That's what the "cancel culture" is about. That's what all the mass hysteria and the demonization and criminalization of dissent is about.

It's what the "Free-Speech Twitter" PSYOP is about. At the end of the day, it doesn't matter whether Elon Musk even knows what he is doing. The system that he is an integral part of is evolving. Musk will help it evolve or he will be replaced by someone who will help it evolve. Musk, Yaccarino, Zuckerberg, Pichai, Gates, Klaus Schwab, Wang Zhonglin, or pick your evil mastermind . . . these people, notwithstanding their very real power, are just components of a system, a global system, a system that is evolving toward totalitarianism, because it doesn't really have anything else to do.

I do not know how to stop this from happening, this evolution of global capitalism into a new form of totalitarianism, but one thing that occurs to me is, it might help matters if we slowed down a bit and tried to actually understand what is happening, like in the broader, historical, systemic sense, and maybe didn't chomp down on every little piece of red-meat bait that gets dangled in our faces and then whipped up into a frenzy over whatever the visibility-filtering team at Twitter, or X, or Meta, or Alphabet, or some other corporation, wants us whipped up over.

Oh, and, maybe, next time some self-aggrandizing global-capitalist military contractor comes riding into town like Billionaire Jesus to save us from his buddies in the proverbial Big Club—you know, the one that you ain't in, the one George Carlin told you about—maybe folks could take a moment and at least hear me out before they start prostrating themselves at his feet.

I'm not right about everything, of course, but I seem to be doing OK with this PSYOP stuff.

The Order of Punishment
August 24, 2023

So, the German authorities are putting me on trial for my thoughtcrimes, and, apparently, I've already been found guilty and sentenced. Bear with me and I'll try to explain.

The Berlin District Court has issued a so-called "penalty order" or "order of punishment," in which I am advised that I am now officially a criminal in Germany, for tweeting two tweets. According to my attorney, a trial will now be scheduled, at which my attorney will argue the case before the judge that just issued the "order of punishment." At this trial, the judge will listen attentively to the arguments my attorney has already made in writing, consider them carefully, and find me guilty, again. Then the judge will reaffirm the "order of punishment."

Go ahead, read that paragraph again.

After my Kafkaesque trial has concluded, my attorney will file a series of appeals, which will fail, at which point I will have to decide whether to pay a fine of 3,600 Euros or go to German prison for sixty days.

This process will take months, if not years, and will cost me God knows how much money in attorney's fees, court costs, and then the €3,600 fine. Yes, I'm going to pay the fine. I am not going to German prison for sixty days. Life is too short, and I am getting older, and it wouldn't really accomplish anything except making a narcissistic spectacle of myself.

However, what will accomplish something—I don't know how much, but something—is if I see the whole process through to the end, and shine as much light on it as I possibly can, because my case is just one of many such cases, and the real story here is not about me, it is about the crackdown on political dissent that is being carried out, not just here in Germany, but also in other countries all throughout the West.

There are not many outlets reporting this story, not outlets with any significant reach. If you are reading this column, you're probably aware of various alternative media outlets that are, but most of these outlets are quarantined off where "normal" people never have to see them, and are delegitimized as "unreliable sources" and purveyors of "misinformation," and so on. There are a few bigger sources covering the story, sources which are also increasingly being branded "unreliable" or "illegitimate," e.g., Matt Taibbi's *Racket News*, Michael Shellenberger's *Public*, Glenn Greenwald's Locals thing, et cetera.

The point is, unless you're a charter member of the "science-denying, conspiracy-theorizing, hate-speech-speaking, anti-vaxxing, misinforming left-or-right extremist" club—i.e., people who read weird "malinformationist" publications like *The Grayzone, OffGuardian, ZeroHedge, Dissident Voice,* and *Unlimited Hangout,* and who are planning to vote for Bobby Kennedy, or, God help them, Donald Trump—you probably have no idea what I mean when I refer to "the crackdown on dissent," or you do, and you think it's just hunky-dory.

I won't mince words. The folks who think it's hunky-dory are totalitarians. They are fascists. They applaud the crackdown on dissent. They applaud the criminalization of dissent. They applaud the censorship of political speech, of *any* speech they do not agree with. They want their political opponents in prison. They want everyone who disagrees with them punished. They want people who offend them canceled. They want anyone who refuses to conform to their official ideology erased.

I have been calling these people "totalitarians" and "fascists" for a number of years now. I do not enjoy doing that. I'm not doing it gratuitously. Some of these people were my friends. I'm doing that, calling these people "fascists," and comparing the nascent totalitarianism that is erupting all throughout the West to other, earlier totalitarian systems, like Stalinism—sorry, Marxist friends—and, yes, to fucking Nazi Germany, because, despite the fact that there are numerous differences, a lot of it is textbook totalitarianism. Naked textbook totalitarianism. There isn't another, nicer word for it, or for those who are enthusiastically embracing it.

I'm not going to present the evidence for that assertion again. I have done that ad nauseam, much of it in my latest book, the cover art of which is about to make me an official "hate criminal," with a criminal record.

That's right, as I explained at greater length in a previous column, the pretext for this "hate crime" prosecution is two tweets I tweeted almost exactly one year ago of the cover art of that very same book, which just happens to document the rollout of the New Normal (i.e., the new totalitarianism) in 2020 and 2021.

Say what you want about me and my writing. I can be "provocative," and some of my political satire is bombastically over-the-top, but, as Matt Taibbi put it in a recent *Racket News* piece . . .

> No amount of drugs exist that if consumed would allow a rational person to conclude that the writing of C.J. Hopkins furthers "the aims of a former National Socialist Organization." Agree with him or not, and I increasingly do, he used his imagery to compare the sweeping declarations of emergency power that were common around the world during the pandemic (and were particularly authoritarian in Germany) to Nazi tactics.[97]

And that is what I am being accused of and "punished" for doing, by the German authorities, i.e., "furthering the aims of a National Socialist Organization" . . . basically, promoting Nazism.

There is no complex legal issue here. Yes, swastikas are banned in Germany for Nazis and people promoting Nazism, but they are permitted for the purposes of "civic education, countering anti-constitutional activities, art, science, research and education, and coverage of historic and current events," and similar purposes, according to German law.[98]

Do you seriously believe that the German hate-crime police and the prosecutor and the judge do not understand that? Of course they understand that. They are not complete imbeciles. They know the charges are

---

[97] Taibbi, Matt, "Madness: American Satirist C.J. Hopkins Sentenced in German Speech Case," *Racket News*, August 22, 2023.

[98] Bierbach, Mara and Karsten Kaminski, "The selective penalty for swastikas in Germany," *DW News*, August 14, 2018.

just a pretext. And they know we know the charges are just a pretext. They do not care. They do not have to. They don't even have to pretend to be following the rule of law. Not anymore. Because they know the majority of the masses are with them.

The point of prosecutions like this, and much more serious and significant prosecutions, like that of Julian Assange, for example, is to send a message. The naked disregard for the rule of law, the absurdity of the charges, the open contempt for democratic principles, is all part of the message. It's not a message about the law. It is a message about power. Who has it, and who doesn't. And what happens to those who refuse to bow down to it.

The message is not intended for me, or for more important figures like Julian Assange, or the many other less well-known dissidents that are being made examples of currently. We're just the medium that conveys the message. We're the delivery service. The message is for you.

I'm pretty sure you're getting the message. The question is, how are you going to respond?

I do not mean by storming your capitol. Please do not go out and get yourself shot. I mean, are you going to help shine a light on where we are headed? Because it's pretty fucking dark. People are offering to send me money to help with my legal costs, and I'm extremely grateful, but what I think we need to do is a little harder, and costs more, and is much more important.

We need to talk to the totalitarians. Yes, the ones who wanted to put us in camps. If we can't get through to them, we're probably screwed. And there is a window of opportunity to do that now. It's not 2020 or 2021 anymore. The mass hysteria has worn off for a lot of people. I know, not all of them, but for some of them, a lot of them. Some of them are finally reachable.

Take a chance, talk to them, the ones you know, or used to know. Try to get through to them. Not the bug-eyed, fanatical, foaming-at-the-mouth types who can't wait for the return of the "emergency measures." The other ones. You know the ones I mean. The ones who want out. You can see it in their eyes. Take a chance. Talk to these people. Totalitarianism, fascism, it is not an identity. It's a mindset. No one is born a fascist. People can be deprogrammed. Some of them can. And, at this point, we need all the help we can get.

So, if you're one of the kind and generous folks who have been asking what you can do to help and offering to send me money, sure, go ahead and send me the money—thank you, I've been overwhelmed by your messages, and I'm sorry that I can't personally respond to all of them—but also consider what I'm suggesting, if you can possibly bring yourself to do it. If you can't, I completely understand. Trust me, I am still just as angry as you are. I am hurt. I feel betrayed and abandoned. I have a feeling that some of you feel that way too. So I know what I'm asking when I ask you to talk to the New Normal totalitarians, the ones who might be reachable.

If you can't yet, don't. But if you're able to, try.

Don't try to convince them that you were right and they were wrong. Just try to shine a light on the road we're on. Try to get them to recognize where we're headed. Regardless of who was right and who was wrong about whatever, we are all going down this road together.

Personally, I'd rather not ride it all the way to the end and face what's down there this time.

The Criminalization of Dissent Ad Absurdum

September 10, 2023

So, the Berlin state prosecutor has launched another criminal investigation of me. Apparently, I'm being accused of the crime of reporting on the original investigation of me that the Berlin state prosecutor launched in June.

What happened is, the prosecutor visited my blog and read a column that I published in July, *The Criminalization of Dissent (Revisited)*, which included screenshots of the alleged "hate-crime" tweets that the original criminal investigation is based on, and that resulted in the "Order of Punishment" that the Berlin District Court handed down two weeks ago. So the prosecutor opened a new criminal investigation and sent my attorney an official notice explaining the gravity of the additional charges.

The charges are of the utmost gravity. I am officially accused of "relativizing" or "minimizing" the crimes of the Nazis, by republishing the two tweets I originally tweeted.

Here, once again, are the tweets . . .

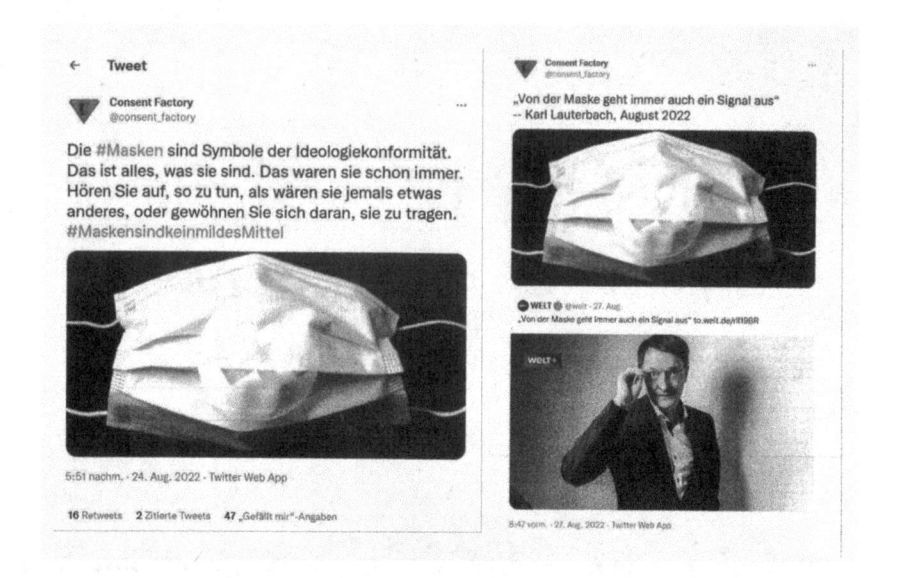

Yes, that's right, I just published them again. I am going to explain why I just published them again.

I am not going to explain the tweets again. I have explained them in several previous columns. I have explained them to a number of journalists, Matt Taibbi of *Racket News*, Max Blumenthal of *The Grayzone*, Patrick Henningsen, Dirk Pohlmann, Christine Black at *Brownstone Institute* (forgive me if I'm forgetting anyone). I explained them to Stefan Millius of *Weltwoche*, and to another journalist at a Swiss newspaper of record. My attorney has explained them, in German, to the prosecutor. I believe they have been exhaustively explained.

Not that they ever really needed explanation. You would have to be a certified moron to believe they "minimized," or "relativized," or in any way made light of the crimes of the Nazis. You and I are not certified morons. Neither is the Berlin state prosecutor. Neither is the District Court of Berlin. Not to put too fine a point on it, the charges are horseshit, and everyone involved knows it. They are a blatant pretext to crack down on dissent.

OK, let me explain why I just published the tweets again, knowing full well that the Berlin state prosecutor is probably going to read this column, become extremely agitated, and charge me with additional "hate crimes."

No, I am not a glutton for punishment. I'm not at all enjoying my introduction to the so-called "German legal system." It is taking up my time. It is making me angry. It is upsetting my wife, which I do not appreciate. It is costing me a lot of money. It has forced me to ask other people for money, which is something I do not like to do. It's screwing with my sleep. It is distracting me from my work. And so on. Which is exactly the point.

The goal of horseshit prosecutions like mine (and those of many other dissidents currently) is (a) to punish us for speaking out against "New Normal" totalitarianism by making our lives as miserable as possible, (b) to make examples of us to discourage others from speaking out, and (c) to intimidate us into shutting the fuck up.

Totalitarians, fascists, and other power freaks are essentially just glorified schoolyard bullies. They may cloak themselves in the mantle of the law, but their modus operandi is brute force. Beneath all the bullshit, their message is simple: "Do what we say, or we will hurt you."

OK, prepare yourself, because I'm going to give you some advice. I do not generally like to do that, but, in this case, I'm going to make an exception.

Never, ever, give in to a bully. The second you do, that bully owns you. What the bully wants, more than whatever he is demanding, more than anything else in the world, is your fear. The bully interprets your fear as respect, because the bully doesn't understand respect. The bully craves your fear, and your obedience, because they reify the bully's "authority." They enable the bully to feel powerful and important. The bully needs to feel "powerful" and "important" because the bully feels weak and unimportant, and afraid. All fascists are essentially cowards. They are cowards, and nihilists, who hate themselves, and fear themselves, and hate and fear life, which is why they are so obsessed with controlling everything.

The point is, never give in to a bully. Never, ever reify a bully's "authority." If you do, you will find yourself sucked into the bully's sadistic, nihilistic "reality." You will be playing by the bully's rules. And that is all "reality" actually is, a set of rules we agree to play by, or, in this case, do not agree to play by.

So, getting back to my criminal case and the Berlin state prosecutor's attempt to bully me into shutting up and demonstrating my "respect" for the "authority" and "power" of the Berlin state prosecutor, fuck that. I do not respond well to threats. I do not take orders from totalitarians and fascists, or any other type of authoritarians or bullies. So that is why I have republished those tweets, and why I will continue to republish those tweets every time the German authorities threaten me with additional criminal charges for refusing to obey their "authority."

Again, I am under no illusions. I expect the prosecutor to file new charges and issue further threats, which I will defy, which will lead to additional charges, and so on. I am not looking forward to that, but I don't have any other choice, not if I want to be able to respect myself.

If you have any doubts about whether that will happen (i.e., an endless cycle of new bullshit criminal charges stemming from my repeated refusal to respond to the German authorities' bullying), well, let me tell you about another political dissident the German authorities are currently persecuting. I'll do it quickly, and then I'll let you go.

As many of my readers are aware, I am presently holed up in an undisclosed location in the Italian countryside. Michael Ballweg, the founder and lead organizer of the "Querdenken" movement, was also here for a while. Michael, who is an excellent cook, whipped up some delicious "extremist" dinners, after which we all sat around "denying Covid," "conspiracy theorizing," brainwashing each other with "Russian propaganda," and "delegitimizing the state," and so on. Late at night, when the other "extremists" were sleeping, Michael and I discussed our criminal cases.

Michael's case is a bit more serious than mine. Michael just spent about nine months in jail. The German authorities have seized his assets and frozen all his funds, so he is homeless, and bankrupt, and they are prosecuting him for attempted fraud, money laundering, and tax evasion ... or, in other words, for launching a protest movement.

The most absurd aspect of Michael's case is the German authorities' "theory of his crimes." According to this theory, Michael's devious scheme was to commit serious fraud by, well, basically, launching a nationwide protest movement that was certain to get a buttload of media attention and incur the wrath of the German authorities. Of course, as any criminal mastermind will confirm, the best way to commit major fraud is to absolutely infuriate the government by organizing a series of massive protests, and generate tons of media attention, because you definitely want as much publicity as possible while you are defrauding your unsuspecting supporters of their voluntary donations to your cause.

Seriously, this is their "theory of the crime," which would make Michael Ballweg the most idiotic and incompetent fraudster in the history of fraud.

I could go on about his case, and mine, or those of the numerous other dissidents that are currently being made examples of, and about the broader GloboCap crackdown on dissent, which is happening, not just in New Normal Germany, but all throughout the New Normal Reich, but I need to end here and go water some plants. I am serving as "caretaker" of this Italian thought-criminal sanctuary, and I take my responsibilities seriously.

I'll keep you (and the Berlin state prosecutor) posted on my further "hate crimes." In the meantime, best wishes from somewhere in Italy!

Israel's 9/11

October 15, 2023

Sorry, but I've seen this movie before. I saw it in New York in 2001.

On the afternoon of September 11, I stood among the crowd on the Brooklyn Heights Promenade and watched what was left of the Twin Towers burn. Walking home as the sun was setting, it appeared to be snowing. It wasn't snowing. The snowflakes were bits and pieces of paper, burnt ginger orange and rust brown around the edges, which the wind had carried across the East River—contracts, memos, actuarial tables, pages torn out of paperback books, scribbled notes, pink telephone messages, the children's drawings and affirmations that adorn the colorless upholstered walls of corporate cubicles throughout America.

It was snowing relics, the hideous detritus of thousands of people's mundane lives.

America had been attacked. It was time to come together as Americans, to put aside our political differences, to rally around the flag, and the president, and go and kill a whole lot of people who had absolutely nothing to do with it.

You might be too young to remember that time. I remember it vividly. I remember it in detail. I remember how the nation "came together." I remember how the Western world "stood with America." I remember how we declared a "Global War on Terror," how we "took the gloves off," both at home and abroad, how the government and the media whipped the public up into a bloodthirsty, jingoistic frenzy. I remember being called a "traitor," a "Saddam apologist," a "terrorist sympathizer," because I wouldn't wave the flag, and "stand with

America," and get on board with murdering hundreds of thousands of men, women, and children.

So forgive me if what follows seems a bit cold. As I said, I've seen this movie before.

Actually, I'm pretty torn up at the moment. Many people are. It's been quite a week. I was planning to publish one of my satirical columns about the recent events in Israel and Gaza. It was going to focus on the "forty beheaded babies" propaganda. I started it. And stopped it. I cannot do it. Not today. I just don't have it in me.

Instead, I'm going to drop the sarcasm for now, and say a few things for the record. Maybe just to get this out of my system. Nothing I publish is going to change what has happened, or what is going to happen in the coming days and weeks, or anyone else's mind, probably.

I am not going to condemn the Hamas attack, as hideous as I think it was. I do not condemn things on command, or perform any other kind of tricks on command. If that's what you're looking for, get a dog.

That said, I am not going to call the Hamas attack "resistance" or try to justify it. I refuse to justify mass murder. If you're OK with mass murdering civilians for your cause, fine, but own it. Call it what it is. And spare me the "legitimate resistance" bullshit.

Same goes for Israel. If you "stand with Israel" as it murders civilians, fine. Own it. Give me a break with the "Israel has the right to defend itself" bullshit, and own it.

Whatever side of this conflict you are on, at least have the integrity to call things what they are.

Here is what things are, in a nutshell.

Israel is a nation-state. It is doing what a lot of nation-states have done throughout the history of nation-states. It is wiping out, or otherwise removing, the indigenous population of the territory it conquered. It has been doing this for seventy-five years. The indigenous population, i.e., the Palestinians, have been trying not to get completely wiped out, or otherwise removed from their indigenous territory, and lashing out at Israel in a variety of ways, from throwing stones to committing mass murder.

That is what is happening. The rest is PR. Public relations. Propaganda.

If you "stand with" the nation-state of Israel and its ongoing efforts to wipe out and otherwise remove the Palestinians from the territory it controls, I get it. The United States of America did that to its indigenous population. The British Empire did it in its colonies. A lot of nations and empires have done it. It is standard nation-state behavior. There is nothing aberrational about it. If you can live with supporting that, OK, go for it, but spare me the sanctimony and the "unprovoked attack" crap.

If you "stand with" the Palestinians in their ongoing efforts to not get wiped out, or otherwise removed from their homeland, I get it. My sympathies are with them too. I've never found nation-states particularly sympathetic, especially when they are in their Mercilessly-Wiping-Out-the-Indigenous-Population phase. However, if you believe that "standing with" the Palestinians means celebrating mass murder, and making excuses for it, like "settlers are not civilians," OK, fine, but count me out.

What's my point? Well, my point is, at times like this, everything conspires to keep everyone from seeing things clearly and thinking critically. Everyone's selling you a narrative and punching your emotional buttons to force you into joining their side.

Hamas is playing on your basic human decency, on your empathy for the Palestinians. Their game is, if you support the Palestinian people, you have to support the Hamas attack and condone the mass murder of unarmed civilians.

Israel is playing on your basic human decency, on your sympathy for the murdered Israelis. Their game is, if you don't support the mass murder of Palestinian civilians that is now in progress, then you are a "terrorist-sympathizer," who hates the Jews.

Both of these parties are fucking with your head, as are their assorted propaganda-spewing mouthpieces. They are trying to force you into a position where your only choice is to support mass murder.

You do not have to support mass murder.

I know it's difficult at times like this, but please try not to let people fuck with your head. Try not to let them punch your buttons. Try not to let them make you react to emotional stimuli like Pavlov's dog. Take a break from the mass hysteria. Try to see things clearly. Try to understand the goals and tactics of both sides of this conflict, regardless of which side you think you're on. If you do not know the history of this conflict—the conflict I described above in a nutshell—please take a few minutes and educate yourself. It's actually not that complicated.

That's it, for now. I'm sure I'll be writing more about this in the coming weeks. As far as I can tell, what we are about to witness is going to be protracted and extremely ugly. The IDF appears to be preparing to liquidate a sizable portion of Gaza. One assumes Hamas has prepared for this, as that was obviously what their massacre was meant to provoke. Who knows how long the fighting will last, whether it will spread, and what it will lead to?

In the meantime, everything is going by the numbers. The nations of the New Normal Reich are marching in lockstep. This is "Israel's 9/11." Democracy is at war with "evil" again!

The demonization and criminalization of dissent that was rolled out during the "Covid pandemic" in 2020–2022 has gone into overdrive. Germany, France, and other countries have banned demonstrations expressing support for the Palestinians.

Here in Berlin, police are roaming the streets, harassing and arresting Arab-looking kids and anyone improperly criticizing Israel. In Neukölln, the district where I live, a major police action was recently launched because someone spray-painted "fuck Israel" on a sidewalk. Oh, yeah, and then there was the German schoolteacher who punched a fifteen-year-old student in the face for defending his friend whose Palestinian flag the teacher had snatched out of his hand.[99] And so on.

And this is only Week One. You know what happens in Week Two, don't you?

Sorry, I know, I'm spoiling the movie for the folks out there who haven't seen it. I'll shut up now and let you get back to it.

---

[99] Link, Gregor, "Berlin teacher hits pupil for supporting fellow student holding Palestinian flag," *World Socialist Web Site*, October 13, 2023.

The Year of the Mindfuck
December 21, 2023

Well, that's pretty much it for 2023, which I'm officially dubbing the Year of the Mindfuck.

I am doing that against the advice of my attorney, who is (a) trying to keep me out of German prison for as long as possible, and (b) trying to stop me from gratuitously alienating whatever remains of my former readership and going totally broke.

I'm not making that particularly easy for him.

The thing is, no one wants to hear that they have been mindfucked. People want to hear that other people have been mindfucked. Which they have. Other people have been thoroughly mindfucked. But that doesn't mean that other people—i.e., the people who want to hear that other people have been mindfucked, but not that they, themselves, have been mindfucked—haven't also been mindfucked, which is what I've been mostly writing about in 2023, which, as Matt Taibbi put it in a blurb for one of my books, "probably this is not a profitable life choice."

So it goes in the political satire racket. Sometimes you are hailed as a "prophet," other times you're scorned as a "dissension-sowing asshole," censored into Internet oblivion by beloved billionaire free-speech defenders, and prosecuted for trumped-up "hate crimes." It depends which way the wind is blowing.

It hasn't been blowing my way this year.

On top of which, I've been pissing into it, the wind, at more or less every opportunity. I know, it's dumb, but I can't seem to stop. Something about watching people being mindfucked over and over and over again "triggers" me, or punches my buttons, or something.

But enough about me. Let's get to the mindfucking. Due to the voluminosity of it, I won't be able to review it all, but I'll try to cover most of the mindfucking highlights.

Ready? OK, here we go.

The mindfucking started in January with the birth of the Musk Cult and the whitewashing of Twitter, and the trickle of "revelations" about "mistakes that were made" during the "Covid pandemic." The Powers That Be needed to memory-hole the story of what actually happened (and didn't actually happen) in 2020–2022 and enshrine the official Covid narrative in history. To achieve this, they needed to mindfuck some people—not the Covidian cultists, who they had already mindfucked—the other people, the ones they hadn't been able to mindfuck. It was obvious that we were about to be subjected to *The Mother of All Limited Hangouts*.

If your memory of what actually happened (and didn't actually happen) in 2020 is a little hazy, here's an excerpt from that column, which I published in January.

> In March and April 2020, in the course of roughly five to six weeks, the majority of societies throughout the world were transformed into pathologized-totalitarian police states. A global "shock-and-awe" campaign was conducted. Constitutional rights were suspended. The masses were locked down inside their homes, where they were subjected to the most massive official propaganda blitzkrieg in human history. Goon squads roamed the streets of Europe, the USA, the UK, Canada, Australia, Asia, the Americas, and elsewhere, beating and arresting people for being outdoors without permission and not wearing medical-looking masks. Corporate media around the world informed us that life as we knew it was over . . . a "New Normal" was coming, and we needed to get used to it. The entire official pandemic narrative was rolled out during those first few weeks. Everything. Masks. Mandatory "vaccines." "Vaccination passes." The segregation of "the Unvaccinated." The censorship and

demonization of dissent. Everything. The whole "New Normal" package. It was rolled out all at once, *globally*.

Now, over three years later, the facts are indisputably clear to everyone except the hopelessly brainwashed. There was no global epidemiological emergency, no legitimate justification whatsoever for that initial "shock-and-awe" campaign or the totalitarian "New Normal" it ushered into being.

However, by January of 2023, that wasn't a problem for The Powers That Be, as most of the masses had been hopelessly brainwashed, and they would break down and start spastically gibbering at you like frightened hyenas if you confronted them with facts.

No, the problem for The Powers That Be was us (i.e., those of us who had never bought the PSYOP). By the end of 2022, we comprised what you call a sizable minority, a problematic, pissed-off, sizable minority. So we needed to be promptly and extensively mindfucked. We needed to be managed, decoyed, distracted, buried in minutiae, partial revelations, limited hangouts, official inquiries, and so on. Above all, we needed to be made to feel like we were getting revenge on The Powers That Be. And we needed to be made to feel this way without actually endangering The Powers That Be, or inconveniencing them in any significant way.

Enter Elon Musk & Co.

Yes, that's right, Elon Musk, the multibillionaire military contractor! At last, a savior had arrived to deliver us from the Evil Cabal of Wokeness, and Cultural Marxism, and Globalistism! Vanquished were the libtard censors and shadowbanners of Old Bad Twitter! It was Morning in America Again!

An Elon's-ass-kissing contest ensued. Internet hucksters, social media influencers, and all manner of money-worshiping toadies competed against each other to get their lips on the Muskian anal orifice! This salacious spectacle went on for months.

Meanwhile, the sleight-of-hand artists got to work, distracting folks with groundbreaking stories like how the Pfizer Corporation had engineered THE MUTANT COMMUNIST VIRUS BIOWEAPON that had caused the pandemic that never happened and triggered THE MASS

FORMATION PSYCHOSIS that had prompted The Powers That Be to go bonkers and launch the PSYOP that the sleight-of-hand artists were memory-holing right before our eyes . . . or something more or less along those lines.

And then, right on cue, came the Twitter Files story! Do you recall, way back in 2008, when Obama took office, admitted that we had "tortured some folks" in Iraq, and so on, and then decided against prosecuting Bush and his cronies for launching a textbook war of aggression, murdering hundreds of thousands of people, and destabilizing and restructuring the Middle East, based on a lie about WMDs? Do you recall all the limited hangouts back then? The Abu Ghraib scandal? The mea culpas?[100] Is your memory of all that a little hazy? Imagine what people's memories of "Russiagate" and "the Pandemic" will be like in twenty years.

People's memories don't get hazy just by accident. If they did, The Powers That Be wouldn't need to distract us, redirect our attention, and otherwise relentlessly mindfuck us. Which is how Class-A limited hangouts work. You feed people a juicy part of the story so they forget about the rest of the story. You redirect their attention away from the globally coordinated simulation of "a worldwide epidemiological emergency" and the rollout of new totalitarian "health measures"— "health measures" that become permanent features of society, like the post-9/11 "security measures" did—with a story about US "Red/Blue" politics, government overreach, "woke" bad apples, and the so-called "Censorship Industrial Complex."

---

[100] Cozens, Claire, "New York Times: we were wrong on Iraq," *The Guardian*, May 26, 2004. ("The New York Times today issued an extraordinary mea culpa over its coverage of Iraq, admitting it had been misled about the presence of weapons of mass destruction by sources including the controversial Iraqi leader Ahmad Chalabi. In a note to readers published today under the headline 'The Times and Iraq', the editors of the newspaper said they had found 'a number of instances of coverage that was not as rigorous as it should have been'. 'In some cases, information that was controversial then, and seems questionable now, was insufficiently qualified or allowed to stand unchallenged. Looking back, we wish we had been more aggressive in re-examining the claims as new evidence emerged - or failed to emerge,' they continued.")

I don't mean to denigrate the Twitter Files story. I really don't, and I have made that clear to Matt and other Twitter Files journalists. Had I been in their positions, I would have done the same thing. I would have gladly taken whatever Musk gave me and reported on it, exactly as they did. And no, the Twitter Files story is not at all a "nothingburger." It is one of the most important stories about censorship in the twenty-first century so far, despite the fact that it is also a limited hangout, like Abu Ghraib and most of those other "Iraq-post-mortem" stories were.

In real life—as opposed to the Hollywood version, or the social-media version, where people are conditioned to see everything in black-and-white terms and judge everyone as "good" or "bad," as "truth-telling heroes" or "controlled opposition"—historical events have different aspects, and sometimes even contradictory aspects. One aspect doesn't cancel out the others.

Some people absolutely hate it when I say this, but the kind of mindfucking I've been writing about is not intentionally perpetrated by "bad guys." In fact, most of it is perpetrated by the "good guys." In other words, yes, of course the Twitter Files are a limited hangout and part of the mindfuck, but the Twitter Files journalists are not the mindfuckers. And Elon Musk is not Mindfucker in Chief. The kind of mindfucking I'm talking about is not a conspiracy; it's built into the system. It's how the system protects itself.

Ideological systems are not just sets of interconnected components and procedures. They are organic entities, self-sustaining organisms, with survival programming, just like you and me. They react when threatened, like any other organism, like our bodies react to mutating cells, invasive pathogens, and other internal threats. They perceive (or at least register) these threats, and take defensive action against them. The more totalitarian the ideological system is, the more aggressive its reaction to internal threats will be.

In our global-capitalist ideological system, mindfucking is one of the primary means of dealing with internal threats. Global capitalism cannot afford to do the Orwellian boot-stomping-on-a-human-face thing, not for extended periods, anyway. It needs to maintain a simulation of "freedom" and some semblance of "the rule of law" so consumers will continue shopping, and not, you know, launch an armed rebellion.

Anyway, that's the kind of mindfucking I'm talking about. It's how the system knows exactly when to release a certain limited hangout, or when to launch an anti-Semitism panic, or an attempted Wokester coup at Free-Speech-Twitter HQ, or a Literal Russian-Agent-Hitler sequel, or when to shut down the aforementioned limited hangout for no actual reason whatsoever, or manipulate a belligerent political satirist into obsessively writing about exactly what it wants him to be writing about.

Yes, you read that last part right. If you thought I think I am immune to the mindfuckery, I don't. I am not. I get mindfucked too. For example, I got mindfucked into traveling to London and taking part in "The Michael Shellenberger Show" in June, and wasting months afterward helping to draft and gather VIP-signatories for the "Westminster Declaration," which turned out to be the weakest popcorn fart in the history of popcorn farts.

My foray into pretentious NGO-activism did not end well.[101] After I mouthed off one time too many in the "group chat," Mike excommunicated me from his "movement," banned me from *Public*, and blocked me on Twitter, where his "free-speech" hero, Elon Musk, is still "visibility filtering" me into oblivion.

And then I spent most of the remainder of the year obsessing over my prosecution for "Nazi hate tweets" here in Germany, and raising money for my legal defense fund, and so on, which, OK, there's another example of something that is both an important matter and, at the same time, a colossal mindfuck (i.e., for me, personally, but also for people who will be bullied into censoring themselves by the example the authorities are making of me).

But that wasn't it for the mindfucking. Oh, no, the mindfucking *coup de grâce* was still to come!

If The Powers That Be had consciously set out to come up with something that would hammer the final nail into the coffin of the "anti-New Normal resistance," they couldn't have done any better than October 7, also known as "Israel's 9/11." Two and a half months of 24/7 balls-out mindfuckery have broken the brains of everyone whose brains hadn't

---

[101] Hopkins, C. J., "Mr. Mike's Mondo Imbroglio, or: How Not to Launch a Global Anti-Censorship Movement," *Consent Factory*, September 20, 2023.

already been broken. It started with the "forty beheaded babies" story,[102] a classic piece of official propaganda, and rapidly devolved to the point where "anti-Zionist" publications were claiming the October 7 attacks were "an Israeli massacre."[103]

I tried to comment on the story dispassionately and was instantly set upon by both shrieking pro-Israeli and pro-Palestinian fanatics. It turns out I'm both a genocidal, atrocity-denying Israel apologist and a genocidal, atrocity-denying, anti-Semitic Hamas apologist! The neo-Roman orgy of hatred and projectile spewing of propagandistic vomitus is ongoing, as I'm sure you are aware, so I'll spare you the gory details on that one.

My point is, the October 7 attacks and Israel's ongoing liquidation of Gaza have obliterated any remaining shred of clarity about what's actually happening, globally, i.e., regarding the New Normal Reich, and has re-polarized the "populist" resistance to it.

The Red Team has become the new "cancel culture" mob, hunting down and "canceling" university presidents,[104] and the Blue Team is shocked and horrified that the new totalitarianism they helped usher into being during "the pandemic" is suddenly being turned against them.[105]

So it goes in the bug-eyed, stark raving Schizotocracy that is the New Normal Reich. One by one, opposing demographics are being mindfucked into aligning with The Powers That Be and going full-fascist, almost as if the whole global-ideological system were going totalitarian, and what it needed to do was whip the masses into a mindless, hate-drunk frenzy of zealotry and pit us all against each other, and then switch the sides and do it again, over and over, until we don't trust anyone or anything, and we literally can't even think.

---

102 "White House walks back Biden's claim he saw children beheaded by Hamas," *Aljazeera*, October 12, 2023.
103 Van Wagenen, William, "Was October 7th a Hamas or Israeli massacre?," *The Cradle*, November 24, 2023.
104 Saul, Stephanie et al., "Penn's Leadership Resigns Amid Controversies Over Antisemitism," *New York Times*, December 9, 2023.
105 Connolly, Kate, "Award ceremony suspended after writer compares Gaza to Nazi-era Jewish ghettos," *The Guardian*, December 14, 2023.

But I wouldn't worry too much about that. I'm pretty sure The Powers That Be will be happy to do our thinking for us. They are getting rather good at that, and sadly, we are getting rather good at letting them.

That's it for me for 2023. Merry mindfucked Christmas and happy mindfucked New Year!

2024

Just because you're paranoid doesn't mean they aren't after you.
—Joseph Heller, *Catch-22*

Not Guilty

January 24, 2024

My "thoughtcrime" trial took place in the Amtsgericht Berlin (i.e., Berlin District Court) on January 23, 2024. I was acquitted of the charge of disseminating pro-Nazi propaganda (i.e., tweeting the cover art of my book, The Rise of the New Normal Reich*). The following is an English translation of my Statement to the Court.*

My name is C. J. Hopkins. I am an American playwright, author, and political satirist. My plays have been produced and received critical acclaim internationally. My political satire and commentary is read by hundreds of thousands of people all over the world. Twenty years ago, I left my own country because of the fascistic atmosphere that had taken hold of the USA at that time, the time of the US invasion of Iraq, a war of aggression based on my government's lies. I emigrated to Germany and made a new life here in Berlin, because I believed that Germany, given its history, would be the last place on earth to ever have anything to do with any form of totalitarianism again.

The gods have a strange sense of humor. This past week, thousands of people have been out in the streets all over Germany protesting against fascism, chanting "never again is now." Many of these people spent the past three years, 2020 to 2023, unquestioningly obeying orders, parroting official propaganda, and demonizing anyone who dared to question the government's unconstitutional and authoritarian actions during the so-called Covid pandemic. Many of these same people, those who support Palestinian rights, are now shocked that the new form of totalitarianism they helped usher into existence is being turned against them.

And here I am, in criminal court in Berlin, accused of disseminating pro-Nazi propaganda in two tweets about mask mandates. The German authorities have had my speech censored on the Internet and have damaged my reputation and income as an author. One of my books has been banned by Amazon in Germany. All this because I criticized the German authorities, because I mocked one of their decrees, because I pointed out one of their lies.

This turn of events would be absurdly comical if it were not so infuriating. I cannot adequately express how insulting it is to be forced to sit here and affirm my opposition to fascism. For over thirty years, I have written and spoken out against fascism, authoritarianism, totalitarianism, et cetera. Anyone can do an Internet search, find my books, read the reviews of my plays, read my essays, and discover who I am and what my political views are in two or three minutes. And yet I am accused by the German authorities of disseminating pro-Nazi propaganda. I am accused of doing this because I posted two tweets challenging the official Covid narrative and comparing the new, nascent form of totalitarianism that it has brought into being—i.e., the so-called "New Normal"—to Nazi Germany.

Let me be very clear. In those two tweets, and in my essays throughout 2020 to 2022, and in my current essays, I have indeed compared the rise of this new form of totalitarianism to the rise of the best-known twentieth-century form of totalitarianism, i.e., Nazi Germany. I have made this comparison and analyzed the similarities and differences between these two forms of totalitarianism over and over again. And I will continue to do so. I will continue to analyze and attempt to explain this new, emerging form of totalitarianism, and to oppose it, and warn my readers about it.

The two tweets at issue here feature a swastika covered by one of the medical masks that everyone was forced to wear in public during 2020 to 2022. That is the cover art of my book. The message conveyed by this artwork is clear. In Nazi Germany, the swastika was the symbol of conformity to the official ideology. During 2020 to 2022, the masks functioned as the symbol of conformity to a new official ideology. That was their purpose. Their purpose was to enforce people's compliance with government decrees and conformity to the official Covid-pandemic narrative, most of which has now been proven to have been propaganda and lies.

Mask mandates do not work against airborne viruses. This had been understood and acknowledged by medical experts for decades prior to the Spring of 2020. It has now been proven to everyone and acknowledged by medical experts again. The science of mask mandates did not suddenly change in March of 2020. The official narrative changed. The official ideology changed. The official "reality" changed. Karl Lauterbach was absolutely correct when he said, "The masks always send out a signal." The signal they sent out from 2020 to 2022 was, "I conform. I do not ask questions. I obey orders."

That is not how democratic societies function. That is how totalitarian systems function.

Not every form of totalitarianism is the same, but they share common hallmarks. Forcing people to display symbols of conformity to official ideology is a hallmark of totalitarian systems. Declaring a "state of emergency" and revoking constitutional rights for no justifiable reason is a hallmark of totalitarian systems. Banning protests against government decrees is a hallmark of totalitarian systems. Inundating the public with lies and propaganda designed to terrify people into mindless obedience is a hallmark of totalitarian systems. Segregating societies is a hallmark of totalitarian systems. Censoring dissent is a hallmark of totalitarianism. Stripping people of their jobs because they refuse to conform to official ideology is a hallmark of totalitarian systems. Fomenting mass hatred of a "scapegoat" class of people is a hallmark of totalitarianism. Demonizing critics of official ideology is a hallmark of totalitarian systems. Instrumentalizing the law to punish dissidents and make examples of critics of the authorities is a hallmark of totalitarianism.

I have documented the emergence of all of these hallmarks of totalitarianism in societies throughout the West, including but not limited to Germany, since March of 2020. I will continue to do so. I will continue to warn readers about this new, emerging form of totalitarianism and attempt to understand it, and oppose it. I will compare this new form of totalitarianism to earlier forms of totalitarianism, and specifically to Nazi Germany, whenever it is appropriate and contributes to our understanding of current events. That is my job as a political satirist and commentator, and as an author, and my responsibility as a human being.

The German authorities can punish me for doing that. You have the power to do that. You can make an example of me. You can fine me. You can imprison me. You can ban my books. You can censor my content on the Internet, which you have done. You can defame me, and damage my income and reputation as an author, as you have done. You can demonize me as a "conspiracy theorist," as an "anti-vaxxer," a "Covid denier," an "idiot," and an "extremist," which you have done. You can haul me into criminal court and make me sit here, in Germany, in front of my wife, who is Jewish, and deny that I am an anti-Semite who wants to relativize the Holocaust. You have the power to do all these things.

However, I hope that you will at least have the integrity to call this what it is, and not hide behind false accusations that I am somehow supporting the Nazis by comparing the rise of a new form of totalitarianism to the rise of an earlier totalitarian system, one that took hold of and ultimately destroyed this country in the twentieth century and murdered millions in the process, because too few Germans had the courage to stand up and oppose it when it began. I hope that you will at least have the integrity to not pretend that you actually believe I am disseminating pro-Nazi propaganda, when you know very well that is not what I am doing.

No one with any integrity believes that is what I am doing. No one with any integrity believes that is what my tweets in 2022 were doing. Every journalist that has covered my case, everyone in this courtroom, understands what this prosecution is actually about. It has nothing to do with punishing people who actually disseminate pro-Nazi propaganda. It is about punishing dissent and making an example of dissidents in order to intimidate others into silence.

That is not how democratic nations function. That is how totalitarian systems function.

What I hope even more is that this court will put an end to this prosecution, and apply the law fairly, and not allow it to be used as a pretext to punish people like me who criticize government dictates, people who expose the lies of government officials, people who refuse to deny facts, who refuse to perform absurd rituals of obedience on command, who refuse to unquestioningly follow orders.

Because the issue here is much larger and much more important than my little tweet case.

We are, once again, at a crossroads. Not just here in Germany, but throughout the West. People went a little crazy, a little fascist, during the so-called Covid pandemic. And now, here we are. There are two roads ahead. We have to choose . . . you, me, all of us. One road leads back to the rule of law, to democratic principles. The other road leads to authoritarianism, to societies where authorities rule by decree, and force, and twist the law into anything they want, and dictate what is and isn't reality, and abuse their power to silence anyone who disagrees with them.

That is the road to totalitarianism. We have been down that road before. Please, let's not do it again.

The Resistible Rise of the New Normal Reich

February 4, 2024

So, the German authorities have filed an appeal to overturn my acquittal in criminal court last week. Apparently, their plan is to keep putting me on trial until they get a judge who is willing to convict me of something, or to bankrupt me with legal costs. Silly me, for a moment there, I was actually starting to believe this was over.

Let me quickly review how I got here for anyone just tuning in.

I am an author and a political satirist and commentator. In August 2022, I posted two tweets criticizing the Covid mask mandates and making fun of Karl Lauterbach, Germany's Minister of Health. Both tweets included an image from the cover artwork of my latest book, *The Rise of the New Normal Reich: Consent Factory Essays, Vol. III (2020–2021)*.

The German authorities did not appreciate those tweets, so they (1) had them censored by Twitter, (2) had Amazon ban my book in Germany,[106] and (3) dragged me into criminal court and prosecuted me on trumped-up "hate crime" charges.

Last week, a judge acquitted me of those charges, after which she launched into a tirade in which she insulted me at considerable length and then strapped on a "Covid mask" and stalked out of the courtroom.

---

[106] The book also became inexplicably "unavailable" to order in German bookstores, unlike all my other books, around the same time that Amazon officially banned it.

During her diatribe, she made a big show of proclaiming that, by acquitting me of the fabricated hate-crime charges, she was proving that "Germany is not a totalitarian state" . . . you know, the kind of totalitarian state where books are banned, political speech is censored, and dissident authors are harassed by the police and subjected to ridiculous show trials.

The judge didn't have much choice but to acquit me, because the relevant German law is clear, as my attorney had reminded her in his pretrial pleading, and because my case had received some international press.[107] Also, the public gallery was packed, and there was a fair amount of independent media in the courtroom. Unlike the German mainstream media, which have been churning out government propaganda like the proverbial Goebbelsian keyboard instrument for years, and which were too busy covering the totally organic government-sponsored mass demonstrations against the government's only political opposition, some of the alternative German media are still interested in actual journalism.

The prosecutor, who appeared to be drunk or on some kind of high-grade sedatives, was very clearly unhappy to be there performing in front of a sold-out house. He spent the proceedings hidden behind one of those Plexiglas "anti-Covid" panels that cashiers still have to sit behind in grocery stores and other retail establishments, so I couldn't make out every word he slurred. The gist of his argument was, although I didn't intend to "disseminate pro-Nazi propaganda," I nonetheless "disseminated pro-Nazi propaganda," by comparing New Normal Germany to Nazi Germany, and "unnecessarily using a swastika in an artwork."

My favorite part of the prosecutor's argument was made in a pretrial pleading to the court, not during the actual trial itself. He accused me of "relativizing the Holocaust" because he claimed that comparing New Normal Germany to Nazi Germany is factually inaccurate, which assertion is revealing, and just staggeringly ignorant.

---

107 Kirchick, James, "What Happens Where Free Speech Is Unprotected," *The Atlantic*, January 3, 2024.

Here's a translation of the excerpt from his pleading (emphasis in italics mine):

> [T]he accused is interested in relativizing this Nazi tyranny, which is also the aim of supporters of this ideology in a different form. By specifically using the swastika, the accused equates *the crisis management measures of the years 2020–2022, which came about within constitutional procedures and were enacted and implemented by and through democratically legitimized institutions*, with the dictatorial methods of the Nazi regime and thus—regardless of his intention—promotes the normalization of National Socialist ideas and actions.

Of course, the history of the transformation of Germany into a Nazi dictatorship by means of "constitutional procedures and democratic processes" is extremely well-documented. In the election of July 1932, the Nazi Party won 37.3 percent of the vote and became the largest party in the Reichstag. On January 30, 1933, von Hindenburg appointed Adolf Hitler Germany's chancellor. In the aftermath of the Reichstag fire, Hitler convinced von Hindenburg to pass the Reichstag Fire Decree, which severely curtailed the liberties and rights of German citizens. And then the Enabling Act of 1933 was passed by the Reichstag on March 23. This law gave the government the power to override individual rights prescribed by the Constitution, because of a so-called "state of emergency."

All this "came about within constitutional procedures and was enacted and implemented by and through democratically legitimized institutions." The judge did her best to stop me from reciting all that history in court, in order to prevent me from "relativizing the Holocaust" again, right there, in front of everyone, or to prevent the prosecutor from coming off as a jackass, but it was too late. Her questioning had opened the door.

A hilarious episode then ensued, in which the judge projected king-size enlargements of my tweets on a screen with an overhead projector, like the ones they used to use in elementary school, and then interrogated me at considerable length about whether the swastika in the offending artwork was "on the mask" or "behind the mask." For a moment, I considered requesting a recess in which to ask the artist, Anthony Freda, to prepare, sign, and telefax a notarized affidavit to the court explaining the details of his creative process and his state of mind at "the time of creation," but I remembered that it was only 6:00 a.m. in New York, which I thought might be a bit too early for Anthony.

Yes, the whole trial was as farcical as it sounds, but, the thing is, prosecutions like mine are never meant to make it into court in the first place. The game the German authorities were playing is somewhat like the plea-bargain game that the prosecutors play in the USA, which American readers will be familiar with from watching all those cop shows on television. The way this game works in Germany is, they charge you with a misdemeanor crime and hit you with a hefty fine, but one that is significantly less than what you will have to pay a lawyer to fight it in court. They are counting on you just paying the fine and avoiding a trial, where a judge can double or triple your fine or sentence you to prison. It doesn't matter if they have no actual legal arguments to support the charges. It's basically just a bullying tactic.

I have never responded well to bullies. I have an aversion to totalitarians, fascists, and other such authoritarian control freaks who get their rocks off intimidating, and dominating, and preying on the weak. My natural instinct, when threatened by bullies and other varieties of fascist creeps, is to get all up their faces and call their bluff.

Which doesn't always turn out so well. Cops, for example, will beat the living snot out of you if you get all up in their faces, as will most of your hardened criminal types. But it typically works with petty public officials and other such "respectable authorities," or at least those who are forced to maintain the appearance of adherence to the rule of law and fundamental democratic principles.

This is an important point, because it is the New Normal Reich's Achilles heel. I explained this in a previous essay, *Pathologized Totalitarianism 101*, back in November of 2021.

> New Normal totalitarianism—and any global-capitalist form of totalitarianism—cannot display itself as totalitarianism, or even authoritarianism. It cannot acknowledge its political nature.

In order to exist, it must not exist. Above all, it must erase its violence (the violence that all politics ultimately comes down to) and appear to us as an essentially beneficent response to a legitimate "global health crisis," and a "climate change crisis," and a "racism crisis," and whatever other "global crises" GloboCap thinks will terrorize the masses into mindless, order-following hysteria. . . . This pathologization of totalitarianism is the most significant difference between New Normal totalitarianism and 20th-century totalitarianism.

In other words, this new, emerging form of global-capitalist totalitarianism cannot afford to look like totalitarianism. It can't put on jackboots and black leather trench coats and start goose-stepping around with big fascist-looking banners and putting people up against walls and shooting them, at least not here in the heart of the empire.

The only way this new form of totalitarianism works is if people like my judge, and the countless thousands of New Normal Germans that have been out in the streets here displaying their unquestioning allegiance to the Reich, and demanding the banning of political opposition, and the segregation and persecution of "the Unvaccinated," or displaying solidarity with Ukrainian neo-Nazis, or supporting Israel's liquidation of Gaza, or whatever they've been instructed to unquestioningly support or display solidarity with tomorrow . . . the only way it works (i.e., this new totalitarianism) is if people, and not just German people, but Americans, and Brits, and Canadians, and Australians, and "Good New Normals" all throughout the West, are allowed to keep telling themselves and each other that they are "the good guys," the ones who are "defending democracy," as they march us down the road to totalitarianism.

Yes, I know, I'm repeating myself. I am going to keep repeating myself. Because the only way this doesn't all end in an extremely ugly and dystopian scenario is if we get through to those "Good New Normals." I'm not talking about trying to convince them of anything, or winning arguments about "the virus," or the "vaccines," or Israel, or Trump, or calling them names. I am talking about confronting them with what they are doing. I'm talking about short-circuiting their mental programming—even if just for a few fleeting seconds—by holding an accurate mirror up to them, and forcing them to look directly into it, and recognize what it is they've become.

That is what I did in criminal court last week. It's why the judge was forced to acquit me, and why she felt compelled to deliver that tirade and strap on her mask to make a big statement. She could have convicted me. She probably wanted to. In her mind, and in the minds of most New Normals, people like me are existential threats. However, to convict me, she would have had to watch herself make a mockery of the law and behave like a fascist . . . like a totalitarian functionary.

Call me a hopeless idealist if you want, but I have to believe that somewhere deep down inside even the most fanatical New Normals (or most of them anyway) is a decent human being, with principles, who does not want to be a fascist, or at least doesn't want to look like a fascist, and who can still be reached, if they can be forced into the position that judge was forced into last week. I have to believe that each brief short circuit, each momentary glimpse at themselves in the mirror, cumulatively, over the course of time, is eating away at their mental conditioning.

In any event, that's the theory I have been operating under for quite a while now. I guess I'll try it out again at my next show trial.

The Palestine Congress
April 14, 2024

Thank God for the German Hate Police! Or heil . . . or whatever the appropriate salutation is for these unsung heroes. They just saved us all from "hate" again!

Yes, that's right, once again, democracy-loving people here in New Normal Berlin and all across the New Normal empire were right on the brink of being exposed to "hate," and would have been exposed to "hate," had the Hate Police not sprung into action.

You probably have no idea what I'm talking about.

OK, what happened was, some pro-Palestinian activists organized a "Palestine Congress," and attempted to discuss the situation in Gaza, and call for solidarity with the Palestinians, and so on, right here in the middle of Berlin, the epicenter of European democracy, as if they thought they had a right to do that.

The German authorities were clearly intent on disabusing them of that notion.

Early Friday morning, hundreds of black-clad Hate Police descended on the congress location. Reinforcements were called in from throughout the country. Metal barricades were erected on the sidewalks. Hate Police stood guard at the entrance. The German media warned the public that a potential "hate-speech" attack was imminent. Berliners were advised to shelter in place, switch off their phones and any other audio-receptive communication devices, and wad up pieces of toilet paper and ram them deep into their ear canals to prevent any possible exposure to the "hate."

Sure enough, minutes into the congress, the anticipated "hate-speech" attack was launched! A Palestinian activist, Salman Abu Sitta, who had written an article that "expressed understanding of Hamas," and thus had already been placed on the official German "no-speak" list, started speaking to the congress on Zoom or whatever. Or . . . it isn't quite clear whether he actually started speaking. According to a Hate Police spokesperson, they raided the congress because "a speaker was projected who was subject to a ban on political activity," or because there was "a risk of a speaker being put on the screen who in the past made anti-Semitic and violence-glorifying remarks."[108]

Anyway, the Hate Police stormed the venue, pulled the plug, dispersed the crowd, and banned the rest of the "Palestine Congress," which was scheduled to continue on Saturday and Sunday. Then they arrested a Jewish guy who was wearing an embroidered Palestinian-flag-kippah, presumably out of an abundance of caution.

But the "hate-speech" attack wasn't over yet. It was one of those multi-pronged "hate-speech" attacks, or at least it involved one other prong. Earlier that morning, or perhaps while the Hate Police were still neutralizing the imminent threat at the venue, Dr. Ghassan Abu-Sittah, a prominent British surgeon who had volunteered in Gaza and was due to speak at the congress, was intercepted by the Berlin Airport Hate Police, refused entry into Germany, and forced to return to the UK. The Airport Hate Police informed the doctor that he was being denied entry in order to ensure "the safety of the people at the conference and public order," Abu-Sittah told the Associated Press.[109]

Kai Wegner, Berlin's mayor, presumably feeling a bit nostalgic for the fanatical days of 2020 to 2023, when one could persecute "the Unvaccinated" with total impunity, took to X to celebrate the Hate Police's thwarting of this "hate event."

---

108 Escritt, Thomas, "Police Shut Down Pro-Palestinian Gathering in Germany Over Hate Speech Fears," Reuters, April 12, 2024.
109 Jeffery, Jack and Geir Moulson, "Prominent surgeon says he was denied entry to Germany for a pro-Palestinian conference," Associated Press, April 12, 2024.

I would like to thank @polizeiberlin for their intervention at this hate event. We have made it clear which rules apply in Berlin. We have made it clear that hatred of Israel has no place in Berlin. Anyone who does not abide by these rules will suffer the consequences. —Kai Wegner, Twitter, April 12, 2024

The pro-Palestinian activist community also took to X and expressed their displeasure. Yanis "Vaccinate Humanity!" Varoufakis, who was one of the organizers and was scheduled to speak, was particularly incensed over the new German "fascism," which apparently he has just now noticed, despite the fact that it has been goose-stepping around in a medical-looking mask for the last four years.

Banned from speaking at the Palestine Congress (i.e., banned from physically entering Germany or even speaking to the Congress remotely), Yanis posted a militant video of himself courageously defying the German authorities on Instagram, despite the fact that, by posting the video, he "will be tried in Germany for breaking German law!" According to Yanis (who I don't recall speaking up about the new German "fascism" when the authorities were brutalizing the "Covid deniers" and on the verge of forcibly experimentally "vaccinating" every man, woman, and child in the country), his being banned from speaking to the people at the congress was "the death knell of democracy in the Federal Republic of Germany!"

Yanis was not alone in his outrage. An increasing number of mainstream German journalists, authors, artists, academics, and other members of the professional "progressive" classes are stunned that the new totalitarian society that they fanatically ushered into being during the so-called "Covid Pandemic" years (or just stood by in silence and watched as it happened) is now unleashing its fascistic force against them.

Which, OK, I get it. I mean, if I had just spent the last four years behaving like a Nazi, you know, persecuting "the Unvaccinated," demonizing everyone who refused to wear the insignia of my fascist ideology on their face, and parroting official propaganda like an enormous Goebbelsian keyboard instrument, or just stood by in silence while other people did that, I would probably want to act like that never happened, and pretend that

Germany was suddenly going "fascist" over the Israeli/Palestinian conflict, and just memory-hole the whole "Covid" thing.

I would probably be highly motivated to do that, if that were how I had behaved for the past four years, so that I didn't appear to be a fucking hypocrite who will start clicking heels and following orders the moment the authorities declare another fake "state of emergency" and jack up the Fear.

Sorry, I've been trying to be less vituperative, but this memory-holing bullshit makes me go ballistic. If there is one demographic that I do not need to hear sanctimonious exhortations to speak out against the global crackdown on dissent from, it is recently ex-Covidian-Cult leftists.

In any event, thank God for those Hate Police! If it weren't for them, well, just imagine the horror if the activists at that Palestine Congress had been allowed to express their opinions about Israel. They might have even said the word "genocide," or made reference to a "river" and a "sea." Who knows what that kind of hateful wrongspeak could lead to? Perhaps the end of Western democracy. Maybe even World War III.

Fighting Monsters

April 28, 2024

The following is a speech I gave in April 2024 at the opening of an art exhibition, "Make Art Not War," at the Musikbrauerei, organized by the Internationale Agentur für Freiheit in Berlin.

The name of this exhibition is "Make Art Not War." So I'm going to say a few things about art, and war. You're not going to like all of them. Or at least I hope not. If you did, I wouldn't be a very good artist, but I might be a pretty good propagandist.

I grew up in the 1960s and '70s. In the USA. The war was on television. In Vietnam. Cambodia. Cuba. The Middle East. Then in El Salvador. Nicaragua. Iran. Libya. Yugoslavia. Afghanistan. Iraq. The list goes on and on. I am almost sixty-three years old. All my life we've been at war. Not just Americans. All of us. People. Someone always at war with someone. And all my life there have been other people calling for peace. Protesting the war. Whatever war it was at the time.

If you read a little history, as I like to do sometimes, you will learn that someone has been at war with someone over something since the dawn of civilization. Certainly Western civilization. The history of Western art and literature begins with war. Genocidal war. The *Iliad* is a poem about a genocidal war. Rape. Mass murder. The slaughter of children. Most of Shakespeare's plays are about war, or are set during a war, or have something to do with someone killing someone over something.

Some of that history happened right here. There are bunkers below us where people sheltered during the bombing raids in the Second World

War. Legend has it the *Stasi* operated listening stations right here in these rooms. When I first arrived in Berlin, twenty years ago, I lived in a sublet on this street. This was my neighborhood, the *Bötzowviertel*. There were still bullet holes in the facades of buildings. People died here. Civilians. Children. Women were raped here. Families were dragged out of their homes and sent to the death camps here. This is Berlin. You know the history. I don't need to recite all the details.

What's my point? Well, my point is . . . that is war. Indiscriminate killing. Rape. Mass atrocities. That's what war is. That is what it has always been. And we've been doing it to each other since the dawn of civilization. It is not going to stop. We are not going to stop it. Art is certainly not going to stop it. We are, whether we like it or not, a violent species, human beings. It isn't all we are, but it is part of what we are. We are also lovers, teachers, healers, artists, and other beautiful things. But sometimes we are vicious killers. Monsters. Genocidal monsters.

A crazy old German philosopher once warned us, "Beware that, when fighting monsters, you yourself do not become a monster." He was joking, of course. There are no monsters. Or, rather, there are only monsters, on every side of every war. In a war, there are no good guys and bad guys. There is just our side and the other side. Our atrocities and their atrocities. And whoever wins gets to write the history.

That's it. The rest is propaganda. Their propaganda and our propaganda. Of course, our propaganda is not propaganda. Our propaganda is just the truth. Because we're not monsters. They are the monsters.

This is Day 202 of Israel's war on Hamas, or its liquidation of Gaza, depending on your perspective. I haven't said too much about it publicly. I said a few things about it when it began. That didn't go well. No one was listening. The propaganda from both sides was already deafening. I described the Hamas attack as mass murder. My pro-Palestinian readers didn't like that. I described Israel as a typical mass-murdering nation-state, no different than the United States of America, Germany, France, Spain, the Netherlands, the Soviet Union, the British empire, the Ottoman empire, the Holy Roman Empire, or any other mass-murdering nation-state or empire. My pro-Israeli readers didn't like that. Neither side wanted to hear about history. The history of asymmetric warfare, or terrorism, depending on your perspective. The history of nation-states and empires. They wanted to hear a story about monsters. About the monsters on the other side.

I told you you weren't going to like everything I said, right?

OK, let me say a few things about art now. If you didn't like what I said about war, maybe you'll like what I say about art. I can't speak for other artists, but I'll tell you why I think I became an artist, and what I have been trying to do as an artist.

I haven't been trying to stop any wars. Or to pacify the human species. I don't know how to do either of those things. And I am not a fan of propaganda. I confess, I have engaged in it from time to time, but mostly what I've been trying to do is deprogram minds, starting with my own.

We are all, by the time we realize we exist, the products of programming, ideological conditioning. I believe it is the job of artists to undo that, or at least to marginally interfere with it. That's what art, and artists, did for me. They introduced me to my mind. My programmed mind. They forced me to think, and to see, and listen. They taught me to question, to pay attention. They dared me to deprogram my mind, and provided me with the tools to do it. OK, sure, some mind-altering drugs also helped, but it was artists that introduced me to those drugs. Then they introduced me to the monster I've been fighting.

I have been fighting this monster, in my art, in my mind, and out in the world for as long I remember. You have to fight it everywhere at once. To fight it in your mind, you have to fight it out in the world. And to fight it out in the world, you have to fight it in your mind.

Let me tell you about the monster.

The monster is legion. It goes by many names. It wears many faces. They change over time. William S. Burroughs called it "the Control Machine." Some people call it the corporatocracy. I've been calling it global capitalism. The monster doesn't care what we call it. It doesn't care who we are, what our politics are, or which side of what war we think we are on. It doesn't care what we believe, which religion we profess. It couldn't care less how we "identify."

All it cares about is power. All it cares about is control.

It is everywhere, and nowhere. It has no country. No nationality. It doesn't exist. It is everything, and nothing. It is the non-existent empire occupying the entire planet. It has no external enemies because there is no outside, not anymore. So there is no real war. There are only insurrections, carried out by rebels, traitors, terrorists.

The monster, our non-existent empire, is the first global empire in human history. It is not a group of evil people. It is maintained by people, but they are all interchangeable. It has no headquarters. There is no emperor. There isn't any Bastille to storm. It is a logos. A system. An operating system.

It has no politics, no ideology. Its official ideology is "reality." Thus it has no political opposition. Who would argue against or oppose "reality"? Lunatics. Extremists. The terminally deranged. And thus there are no dissidents, no opposing political parties. There are only apostates, heretics, blasphemers, sowers of discord, "reality" deniers.

It manufactures "reality." Whatever "reality" it needs. The War on Terror. The War on Populism. The War on the Virus. The War on the Weather. The War on Hate. The War on Whatever. It doesn't matter. It is all the same war. The same "clear-and-hold" op. The same counterinsurgency. It has been for about thirty years.

If things seem crazy, if you're wondering what's happening, that is what's happening. That is all that is happening. That is all that has been happening since the end of the Cold War.

The empire is eliminating internal resistance, any and all forms of internal resistance. The monster is monsterizing everything and everyone. Transforming societies into markets. It doesn't have anything else to do. It is erasing values. It is dissolving borders. It is "sensitivity-editing" culture. Synchronizing everything and everyone in conformity to its only value . . . money. It is rendering everything a commodity.

It is the apotheosis of liberal democracy, the part where the monster does away with democracy, with the simulation of democracy, and proclaims itself "democracy." It is global-capitalist *Gleichschaltung*.

That's the monster I have been fighting.

Which makes me a terrorist. A conspiracy theorist. A Russian propagandist. A Covid denier. A right-wing extremist. An anti-vaxxer. An anti-Semite. A transphobic racist. An enemy of "democracy." A Hamas supporter. A Donald Trump supporter. An AfD supporter. Whatever the official enemy happens to be today.

It makes me a criminal. A thought criminal. An art criminal.

Which I literally am. The German authorities are prosecuting me for disseminating art. For tweeting art. Pictures. Words. They banned one of my books. So maybe I'm marginally interfering with their ideological conditioning, with their programming, with their New Normal *Gleichschaltung* op.

If so, good, because, if I can quote another German, "Art is not a mirror held up to reality, it is a hammer to shape reality with."

And I'll go a little further than Brecht. Every work of art we make shapes reality one way or another, whether we intend it to or not. It either feeds the monster or it fucks with the monster. The monster out there, and the monster in here, inside us, all of us . . . because it's all the same monster.

Thank you, all of you who are fucking with the monster.

That is all. Let's keep it up.

The Anti-Zionist Inquisition
May 9, 2024

Nobody expects the Anti-Zionist Inquisition!

Like their befuddled medieval Catholic progenitors in the classic Monty Python skit, they descend upon you without warning! Amongst their diverse weaponry are surprise, and fear, and ruthless efficiency, and fanatical devotion to the Church of Anti-Zionism!

Blasphemers, heretics, and other apostates of the Church of Anti-Zionism literally wee themselves at the thought of being publicly accused of non-anti-Zionism and subjected to their fearsome inquisitorial methods!

Yes, I'm speaking from personal experience, having recently survived a visit from the Anti-Zionist Inquisition on Twitter. What happened is, I noticed that the pro-Palestinian student protesters in the USA, or many of them, were wearing "Covid" masks at the protests. Suddenly, the newspapers of record and social media were flooded with photos of throngs of protesters in medical-looking masks, which I found disturbing.

So I tweeted about it.

I noted that protesters have been covering their faces with bandannas, balaclavas, and the like, to conceal their identities at protests for decades. I wondered why suddenly the only option to do that was a medical-looking "Covid" mask, the symbol of conformity to the New Normal Reich. Had Walmart run out of two-dollar bandannas?

I don't know what I was thinking at the time. I was probably possessed by a Zionist demon!

Anyway, the next thing I knew, the Anti-Zionist Inquisition was onto me. A semi-well-known anarchist writer who I had been friendly with for several years, and who is apparently a Cardinal in the Church of Anti-Zionism, sprang onto Twitter and demanded that I publicly "condemn the Zionist genocide," and answer to charges of potential Zionist sympathies, and otherwise recant my heresy and blasphemy.

I didn't do that for the Cardinal. I don't do that for anyone. I don't condemn things on command, not Hamas, not Zionism, not anything, for anyone. Nor do I perform any other kinds of tricks. If that's what you're into, get a fucking dog.

My unresponsive anti-authoritarian response did not sit well with this anarchist Cardinal, so he whipped out one of the Anti-Zionist Inquisition's most feared and most ruthlessly efficient weapons, the Online Character Assassination!

"Why is C. J. Hopkins now devoting all his efforts to attacking critics of the Israeli genocide?" he shrieked in a high-pitched Michael Palin register. Is C. J. Hopkins "controlled opposition"? Is he now, or has he ever been, a Zionist?

The Anti-Zionist faithful answered the call. I was instantly besieged by a swarm of fanatical morons demanding that I publicly deny that I'm a Zionist, and affirm that "Zionists" own the US government, and most other Western governments, and the banks, and the media, and . . . well, I think you're probably familiar with that narrative.

Wait . . . no, it's not what you're thinking. These people are not anti-Semites! They are anti-Zionists! They have absolutely nothing to do with the idiotic anti-Semitic garbage that, for example, white-supremacist groups like Aryan Brotherhood or Aryan Nations are into . . . you know, all that garbage about the "Zionist Occupation Government" and how "the Jews own everything," and "the Great Replacement," and all that.

I'm serious. I know some of these people personally. They are anti-Zionists, not anti-Semites. They just happen to be totally obsessed with the Jews, and Israel, and Zionism, to the point where anyone who refuses to conform to their simplistic worldview and political analysis is perceived as an enemy, or a "Zionist," or a "Zionist-entity sympathizer."

So, that was fun, my appearance before the Anti-Zionist Inquisition. Plus, it inspired me to conduct one of my online courses on basic smear-artist tactics, which I offer as a public service whenever the occasion arises.

It also moved me to tweet a few words of advice to my Anti-Zionist Inquisitors, which I will reproduce below for my readers who have the sense and the luxury not to be on Twitter.

It went a little something like this . . .

I hate to bum people out, but repeating the words "Zionism" and "genocide" over and over again is not a political strategy. If you want to stop slaughters like the one going on in Gaza someday, get a political strategy. Start with a political analysis. Use a map. A map of the Greater Middle East. Look at the countries on the map. Identify who is aligned with what.

For example, which of the Middle East countries on the map are playing ball with the global-capitalist empire? Which aren't? Which countries has the empire invaded, destabilized, and restructured since 1989? Why has it done that? Where are there still pockets of resistance?

Forget about ideology for a second. Every country has an ideology or a narrative to justify its actions. Try to look at the map through the eyes of the empire. Who is playing ball with you? Who is not? What needs to be done about that? What is your goal as an empire in this region?

Again, forget about ideology. Try to think strategically. Take Saudi Arabia. Saudi Arabia is an Islamic theocracy. And it's the largest US export market in the Middle East. The USA is its largest trading partner. Do you think the empire cares about its ideology?

Now take a look at Israel. What function does Israel perform for the global-capitalist empire? Do you think the empire cares about Israel's national ideology, i.e. Zionism, any more than it cares about Saudi Arabia's national ideology? If so, why do you think that?

Again, think strategy, not ideology. Does Israel maintain an arsenal of nuclear weapons because of Zionism? Why is the empire determined to ensure that Israel remains the only country with nuclear weapons in the Middle East? Does Israel receive billions in support from the empire because of Zionism? Did the empire invade, destabilize, and restructure Iraq because of its love of Zionism? Libya? Syria? Why is Iran such a problem for the empire?

Answer those questions and you may be on your way to developing something resembling a political analysis, which you can use to generate an actual political strategy. Then, someday, maybe, that political strategy might help you to stop slaughters like the one in Gaza.

Or, don't think about any of those questions, and simply keep shouting "ZIONIST GENOCIDE!" over and over and over again, and referring to Israel as "the Zionist entity." That's been working really well so far, hasn't it?

Oh, and, if anyone is still unclear about my political views and desperate to fix that . . . well, might I suggest that they actually read my books, or my online columns, or listen to what I've actually said in countless interviews.

Or, if it's too much work to do that, just ask some fanatical idiot on Twitter.

The Civil War Simulation
July 17, 2024

It has been slouching toward Bethlehem for the last eight years. The gyre has been widening, the falcon turning and turning, the center losing hold, and so on. Its hour has not quite come round yet, but something is rising out of Spiritus Mundi. No, not the beast from *The Second Coming*, but something perhaps just as rough and pitiless.

I've been calling it the "New Normal Reich." Others have been describing it with other names. No one can say exactly what it is, but at this point everyone feels it coming. Something resembling a new form of totalitarianism . . . or something resembling civil war.

One thing often leads to the other.

Every new totalitarian system is preceded by some sort of civil war. You can't just implement totalitarianism out of nowhere. In order to impose it on society, you need to tear society apart, pit the masses against each other, foment fanaticism, mass hysteria, and hatred. Above all you need to foment fear.

Once you have torn society apart and whipped the masses into a mindless paroxysm of fear and hatred and murderous rage, you can implement your new form of totalitarianism fairly easily, as people will be desperate for the restoration of "order."

One of the best ways to tear society apart and whip the masses into a mindless frenzy of fear and homicidal rage and hatred until they literally cannot think anymore and are reduced to a robotic state of cognition in which they shut down entirely or are transformed into shrieking fanatical zealots is to (a) terrorize them with fake existential threats, like the return of Hitler, or an apocalyptic virus, (b) demonize people who refuse to play along with the fake existential threats as yet another existential threat, and then (c) terrorize the masses all over again.

If you do that long enough, what will eventually happen is, the people you demonized as an existential threat because they wouldn't play along with the fake existential threats you were terrorizing the masses with will rise up against you and attempt to remove you from power.

At that point, you will be on the brink of civil war, which is exactly what you were trying to achieve. Because, once you're on the brink of civil war, you can justify the implementation of your new form of totalitarianism without too much trouble.

Basically, what you're looking to do, assuming you're the dominant power in this equation, is provoke whatever resistance to your dominance (or your rise to power) exists into forming something resembling a plausible oppositional (i.e., militant) force, which you need to suspend constitutional rights and the rule of law in order to contend with.

This civil war that you have instigated, or that you've brought a country or the world to the brink of in order to implement your new form of totalitarianism, is a simulacrum, but it is not fake. It is the actual civil war—or the actual imminent civil war—that conceals the fact that there is no civil war, because what is actually occurring is a "clear-and-hold" op.

What is actually happening is, a dominant power, a globally hegemonic dominant power in our case, is eliminating internal resistance throughout the territory it occupies, which in our case happens to be the whole planet. Any and all forms of internal resistance. The character of the resistance makes no difference ... Islamic fundamentalism, Christian fundamentalism, neo-nationalism, "populism," socialism, or whatever. Any form of resistance that interferes with the consolidation of its global hegemony and commodification of virtually everything.

In other words, the coming civil war (or the threat of civil war) is absolutely real, and is also a simulacrum concealing the fact that there is no coming civil war.

Yes, I know this is difficult to grasp. And I realize that people are all worked up at the moment, but bear with me if you possibly can. I am going to quote a French philosopher. Please don't freak out. I'll explain in a moment.

> The simulacrum is never that which conceals the truth—it is the truth which conceals that there is none. —Jean Baudrillard

Baudrillard is not saying that there is no truth. He is explaining how simulacra work, or one way that simulacra work. The fake thing (i.e., the simulacrum) exists to make the real thing seem "real." If you can copy something, then that thing must exist. The copied thing must be real, right?

Wrong. That's how this magic trick works.

How it works is, it generates a false dichotomy. It conjures an opposition into existence out of the ether. It summons up a simplistic binary equation (i.e., real/fake, true/false, left/right, us/them) and traps our minds within that equation. Either Disneyland is real or Los Angeles is real. Either you support Donald Trump or you support Joe Biden. Either the Palestinians or the State of Israel. MSNBC or X. And so on.

Or . . . OK, here's a simple analogy.

Imagine, if the authorities in charge of a prison instigated a war between two prison gangs, which were actually fighting for dominance in the prison. The gangs are real. The war is real. When it is over, one of the gangs will be dominant among the prison population. However, everyone will still be in prison, probably under a state of lockdown, which is what happens after a prison riot.

Does any of that sound familiar? I hope so.

Again, I realize emotions are high, what with the attempted assassination of Donald Trump,[110] and the ongoing liquidation of Gaza, and the

---

110 On July 13, 2024, a lone gunman with the obligatory three names attempted to assassinate Donald Trump at a campaign rally near Butler, Pennsylvania. Evan Vucci of the Associated Press snapped an instantly iconic photo of Trump defiantly pumping his fist with blood streaming down the side of his face as the Secret Service agents hustled him off the stage. The would-be assassin, Thomas Matthew Crooks, described by his neighbors as "a normal person," was shot to death by a Secret Service Counter-Sniper team. Speculation as to Crooks's motive continues.

ongoing left/right culture wars, and the rise of the Cult of Elon Musk, and the aftermath of the "Apocalyptic Plague of 2020–2022," and the "January 6 Insurrection," and so on . . . but maybe try, just for a few minutes, to step back from all the false dichotomies and all the thought-terminating clichés and the hatred and fear that we are being systematically inundated with, and reflect on where all this excitement is leading us, and how our passions are being instrumentalized, and by whom and for what purpose they are being instrumentalized.

If you think this all ends with America Made Great Again, or Palestine Free, or with Elon Musk marching into the White House with a bathroom sink, or some other revolution fantasy . . . well, it doesn't. It ends up where it ended up in January 2021, with soldiers in the streets of DC. It ends up with Gaza obliterated. It ends up with the prisoners back in their cells. It ends with "the restoration of order."

I do not know how to stop what is coming, what is slouching toward us to be born. I do not believe it can be stopped at this point. I will, however, be observing closely, and trying to make sense of events as they happen. I will probably be paying a fair amount of attention to whoever foments all that fear and hatred and murderous rage I mentioned above, and preys on people's emotions, and tries to trap people's minds within those false dichotomies, so that they wind up utterly unable to think and just shuffle around like robotic zealots cataloging who is "with us" and "against us."

I hope you won't find that too "negative" or "divisive."

And if you do, well, I wouldn't worry too much. My columns are getting less and less traction these days. I alienated the "10/7 Truthers" recently, so I'm in the doghouse with the "anti-Zionist" community, and I'm severely visibility-filtered on X, which, of course, is "the only real free-speech platform" (go ahead, enter that phrase into a search engine) and "a crucial historical force," and, of course, "the voice of the people," or "the new generation," and "all that stands between us and totalitarianism," or whatever cartoonish marketing gibberish Musk and his minions are whipping the new "resistance" up into a frenzy with at the moment.

But, seriously, those quotes are taken from tweets by Musk and other influential people, tweets which I will not reproduce here, so I don't get sued, or get my publisher sued, but which you can probably find online if you're curious.

The point is, we are watching a show. We're being molded into consumer demographics, mesmerized by marketing language devised by glorified PR flacks, and enlisted in a simulated civil war, a revolution that is being televised to prevent the revolution that will not be televised.

Sorry, I got all "divisive" and "negative" again. I think the kids call that "black-pilled" these days. Never mind all that stuff about simulacra, false dichotomies, and prison riots, and slouching beasts, and Spiritus Mundi. As they used to say, back in the day . . .

We now return to our regularly scheduled programming.

The People's Court of New Normal Germany

July 21, 2024

Just when I thought things could not possibly get more shockingly totalitarian here in New Normal Germany, where I'm being prosecuted, for the second time, for tweeting, the German authorities have gone and surprised me again.

No, they haven't established an actual Nazi-style People's Court of Berlin yet, and, of course, there is absolutely no similarity between the current German justice system, which is totally fair and democratic and a paragon of impartial justice and integrity and the rule of law, and the People's Court of Berlin during the Nazi era,[111] nor is there any similarity

---

111 \ "GERMANY: People's Court," *Time Magazine*, May 14, 1934. ("No sooner had the regimented millions of Berlin tramped home from Tempelhof Field to soak their tired feet than they had real news to read in their papers. Dissatisfied with the results of the famed Reichstag Fire trial in which all but one of the five defendants were acquitted, the Nazi government announced the establishment of a new 'People's Court' to take all cases of high treason from the penal division of the Supreme Court. Immediately after the Reichstag trial, Nazi papers snorted that Chief Justice Wilhelm Bünger and his associates were 'too legalistic, lacking the common touch.' To be sure that nothing like this should hamper the People's Court, it was announced that of its five members, only two had to be lawyers. The other three were to be chosen by the Chancellor from among those 'who have had special experience in fighting off attacks against the State.' The People's Court will have plenty of work. There is no appeal from its verdicts, and it must decree:

between Nazi Germany and New Normal Germany (i.e., modern-day Germany), and I would never, ever, imply that there was, as that would be intellectually lazy, and tasteless, and completely inaccurate, and illegal, and . . . well, let me fill you in on the latest.

The Berlin Superior (or Appellate) Court has set a date for my second thoughtcrime trial. As my regular readers may recall, my first thoughtcrime trial in Berlin District Court in January culminated with my acquittal. So the German authorities are putting me on trial again.

Yes, they can do that in Germany. But wait, that's not the best part.

The best part is, at my next thoughtcrime trial, this time in Berlin Superior Court, full-scale Anti-Terrorism Security protocols will be effect in the courtroom. Everyone will be subjected to TSA-style scanning, and will have to surrender all their personal possessions and hats and coats and head coverings to the Security Staff, and completely empty their pockets of all items. No computers, phones, smartwatches, or any other potential recording devices will be allowed in the courtroom. Pencils and sheets of paper will purportedly be provided to members of the press. Members of the press and public will be limited to thirty-five, and, after they have successfully passed their "screening," they will be cordoned off in the back of the gallery behind a wall of bulletproof glass and monitored by armed Security Staff.

For the benefit of any new readers unfamiliar with me, I'm not a terrorist. I'm an award-winning American playwright, novelist, and political satirist and commentator. I have lived here in Berlin for twenty years. The German authorities have been investigating and prosecuting

---

Death for all seeking to overthrow the Government, or the Constitution, by force or threats of force. Death for all who attempt forcibly to detach any part of the Reich territory or deliver it to any foreign power. Death for all who attempt to hinder the President, the Chancellor or any member of the Reich government from exercising his proper authority. Death for all who try to obtain a State Secret, publish it, sell or attempt to sell it to a foreign power. Death (or hard labor up to ten years) for all attempting to hamper the army or the police in doing their duty, or to influence them to this end through writings, pictures, radio messages or phonograph records. Hard Labor for all 'atrocity mongers' who publish in Germany or abroad 'false or grossly distorted statements' on conditions in the Reich.")

me since August 2022. My case has been covered in *The Atlantic*, *Racket News*, *Neue Zürcher Zeitung*, *Multipolar*, and other outlets, so I'm not going to reiterate every little detail again here. Basically, I am being prosecuted for "spreading pro-Nazi propaganda" because I criticized the Covid mask mandates and tweeted the cover artwork of one of my books.

Here's the cover artwork of that book. The other two images below are the recent covers of *Der Spiegel* and *Stern*, two well-known mainstream German magazines, which are not being prosecuted for "spreading pro-Nazi propaganda."

As anyone (even the German authorities) can see, the *Spiegel* cover artwork uses exactly the same concept as the cover artwork of my book. The only difference is, the *Spiegel* swastika is covered by the German flag, whereas the swastika on my book is behind a medical mask.

Both artworks are obviously intended as warnings of the rise of a new form of totalitarianism. *Der Spiegel* was warning about the *Alternativ für Deutschland* party (AfD), as was *Stern* with its swastika floating in a champagne glass. I was warning about what I dubbed "the New Normal Reich," the new nascent form of totalitarianism that emerged during 2020–2023, and which is still very much on the rise today, and which is thoroughly documented and analyzed in my book (which book was banned by Amazon in Germany at the same time the German authorities launched their criminal investigation of me and instructed Twitter to censor my tweets, which Twitter did, and which X continues to do).

The pretext the court is citing for ordering these Anti-Terrorism Security protocols at my trial is ridiculous, and infuriating. The court claims that the courtroom in which my trial is to take place is occasionally used for a certain "high-security" trial. Therefore, according to the Superior Court, my trial must also be subjected to Anti-Terrorism Security protocols. Seriously, the court sent my attorney a fax setting forth this "explanation," which is, of course, a load of horseshit. The Berlin Superior Court is a massive building containing many courtrooms, one or two of which are probably not subject to Anti-Terrorism Security protocols when "high-security" trials are not taking place within them.

No, the imposition of these Anti-Terrorism Security protocols is obviously a cynical ploy intended (a) to suppress coverage of the trial, (b) to discourage the public from attending, and (c) to intimidate and harass me and my legal counsel, and any members of the press and public who nevertheless attend the trial despite the "security procedures" they will be subjected to.

This cynical tactic, which is not an official press blackout, because journalists can still attend and attempt to scribble notes on their knees with the pencils and sheets of paper provided by the security staff, comes as no real surprise. As I mentioned above, my case and my first trial have generated a fair amount of attention from the international press, enough to put the court on notice that my prosecution was being watched. So it's no mystery why the German authorities would want to discourage any reporting on my "do-over" trial.

Also, the gallery was filled to capacity at my original trial in January, where I delivered a rather angry statement to the court, which was published and widely disseminated in Germany. So, again, it is no real mystery why the Superior Court would want to discourage the public from attending this new trial by threatening to subject them to these humiliating "security" protocols, and why it has limited the gallery size to only thirty-five seats.

I assume the German authorities—and by "authorities" I mean the Berlin prosecutor's office, the Berlin Superior Court (*Das Kammergericht*), and whatever other authorities are intent on punishing me, and making an example of me, for daring to criticize the government's edicts during 2020–2022, i.e., the suspension of constitutional rights, mask mandates, segregation, the banning of protests, et cetera—I assume these authorities are highly motivated to discourage the press from attending the proceedings of my second trial in Superior Court, because, from what I understand of the German legal system, they are going to "do" me (i.e., convict me) this time.

The way the German legal system works if they want to "do" you like they are going to "do" me is (1) you are tried and acquitted in the lower Criminal Court, (2) the state prosecutor appeals the verdict to the Superior Court, (3) the Superior Court overturns your acquittal, and (4) the prosecution goes back to the original Criminal Court, which stages a new trial, at which you will be found guilty, because once the Superior Court has overruled your acquittal, the Criminal Court will convict you based on the Superior Court's ruling. At which point you will appeal. And on and on and on it will go, until you are broke, or until you give up fighting because you are just so fucking exhausted.

I'm not making this up. This is how the People's Court of New Normal Germany (i.e., the post-Covid German justice system, which, again, bears no resemblance whatsoever to the People's Court of Berlin in Nazi Germany, or to the show courts in the Soviet Union during the Stalin era, or to any other totalitarian "justice" system) . . . this is how it works in New Normal Germany if you are a critic of the authorities and refuse to meekly accept whatever punishment they want to summarily dish out for whatever they deem to be your thoughtcrimes.

But, hey, at least they're not going to take me out, put me up against a wall, and shoot me, like they did with "political criminals" in Nazi Germany and the USSR, so I suppose I should be grateful.

I guess I'll have to work on that.

If you think my case is an aberration, it isn't. There are many, many other people, critics of the government's "Covid measures" during 2020–2023, who are being persecuted and made examples of. Most of these people do not have the financial resources to pay lawyers to fight these prosecutions, so they plead guilty to the charges and pay the fines, which are typically much less than what they would face in attorney's fees. Being somewhat of a public figure, I thought it was my responsibility not to do that. I'm extremely grateful to everyone who has donated to my legal defense fund, which is how I have been able to cover my legal expenses. There's enough left in that fund to cover my next trial in Superior Court, so I'm OK for now. I mention that because people are already asking how they can send me money.

What people can do, if they want to do something helpful, is make as much noise as possible about what is happening, not just in Germany, but all throughout the West. Because what is happening is . . . well, exactly what I tried to capture and analyze in my book.

The Powers That Be are going totalitarian on us. They are gradually, and not so gradually, phasing out the so-called "liberal" or "democratic" rights and principles that it was necessary to placate the Western masses with during the Cold War era, which it is no longer necessary to do beyond a certain superficial point.

I have published three books of essays documenting this transition to a new global-capitalist form of totalitarianism, so I won't go on and on about it here. But that is what all the censorship is about. That's what all the manufactured hysteria, fomented hatred, the fanaticism, the permanent state of "emergency" and "crisis," the "culture wars," the cults of personality, the bombardment of our minds with absolutely meaningless nonsense, the naked displays of force, the blatant instrumentalization of the legal system to punish political dissidents not just here in Germany, but all throughout the "democratic" West . . . that is what all of this is about.

I'll keep my readers posted on the details of my upcoming trial in Berlin Superior Court. My attorney is objecting to these "security protocols," of course. We'll see how that goes. In the meantime, instead of sending me money this time, maybe try to step back from all the mass hysteria and hatred that we are being inundated with and see the big picture. It isn't pretty.

Help spread the word about the new totalitarianism, about the phasing-out of our democratic rights. I don't care which "side" of whatever you are on—Trump, Biden, Palestine, Israel, the culture wars, the cancel campaigns, Covid, Elon Musk, Russia, whatever—and neither do The Powers

That Be. Take a step back and try to see the bigger picture . . . the forest, instead of just the trees.

And then make as much noise about it as you can.

We are heading somewhere very ugly, somewhere most of us can't imagine. Some of us will get there first, but all of us will be there, together, eventually. My story is just one example of what it will be like there, in that ugly place. It isn't really a story about Germany. It is a story about the end of the myth of democracy, and the rule of law, and all that good stuff. As Frank Zappa once so eloquently explained . . .

> The illusion of freedom will continue as long as it's profitable to continue the illusion. At the point where the illusion becomes too expensive to maintain, they will just take down the scenery, they will pull back the curtains, they will move the tables and chairs out of the way and you will see the brick wall at the back of the theater.

It's something to behold, that brick wall is, especially up close and personal. You'll see when you get here. I'll save you a seat.

Update: August 2, 2024

So, my second trial for alleged thoughtcrime-tweeting is going ahead as planned on August 15 in Berlin Superior Court (*Das Kammergericht*). Full-blown anti-terrorism security protocols will be in effect in the courtroom. That's right, the Berlin Superior Court denied my attorney's motion to rescind their Security Order, so the German authorities will be putting on an elaborate show of official force, which everyone is welcome to attend!

Or, actually, according to the Security Order, only thirty-five people are welcome to attend. That's one of the anti-terrorism security protocols. Also, if you do attend, you'll have to surrender all your personal possessions (i.e., notebooks, phones, wallets, pens, pencils, other writing instruments, wristwatches, hats, and other head coverings, et cetera) and any outerwear (i.e., jackets, scarves, et cetera) and totally empty your pockets of all items, presumably into a plastic bin like the ones they use at airport security, which the court's security personnel will carry away and store somewhere while you attend the trial, and which the Superior Court expressly denies any liability for (i.e., for your items). Once you have surrendered all your possessions, and have been body-scanned and metal-detected, and possibly physically patted down, you will be admitted into Room 145a, where you will have to sit in the rear five rows of the gallery, behind a bullet-proof security barrier, so that security staff can monitor you during the trial.

OK, I know what you're probably thinking, but the Superior Court's Security Order is not at all intended to prevent members of the press from attending and reporting on the proceedings. Members of the press are absolutely welcome! It's just that they will have to surrender their cameras and phones and pens and other writing instruments to the security staff before they enter the courtroom. But they are welcome to attend and report on the trial! The security personnel will even provide them with pencils—presumably those little child-sized pencils, which are harder to use as Jason-Bourne-style stabbing weapons—and sheets of paper that they can position on their knees and attempt to make notes on during the trial.

Same goes for all you members of the public. This Security Order is not in any way intended to discourage you from attending the proceedings, or intimidate or humiliate you by subjecting you to pointless "security protocols" and treating you like suspected terrorists. No, you are absolutely welcome to attend! You just might want to think about what you bring with you. Sharp objects are probably not a good idea. Likewise anything the court might construe to be a camera or an audio-recording device. The Security Order is clear about that. There is to be no photographic or audio record of the proceedings.

Oh, and definitely do not bring any state-of-the-art terrorist "wiretapping technology" with you. The court is particularly worried about that stuff. Hence the need to subject everyone to TSA-style body-scanning and pat-downs, and to confiscate their personal possessions, i.e., to ensure that no one smuggles in some sort of remotely activated wiretapping technology that will infect the judges' smartphones with some kind of untraceable surveillance software that will secretly record everything they say and transmit it to Tehran, or Moscow, or wherever.

You probably think I'm joking. I'm not. Here's how one of the Superior Court judges justified the Court's Security Order in his denial of our motion to have the Order rescinded:

> I cannot see the unreasonable restriction of the press and your defense that you are concerned about, nor any violation of the guarantee of a fair trial. I admit that the restrictions imposed by the Security Order are quite significant; however, they are by no means unreasonable. They are objectively required both by the overall tense security situation (e.g. publicly announced threats of attacks against judges of the Superior Court) and the increased special security requirements in at least one criminal trial conducted in the same courtroom. Since only the courtroom in question is assigned to the Criminal Division (and the other divisions) as a permanent courtroom, and a regular search of the courtroom following every session using suitable technology for recently introduced wiretapping technology represents an objectively unjustifiable burden, its introduction must be prevented from the outset if possible.

Yes, you read the judge's explanation right. Apparently, the court is worried that my readers, or maybe members of the German independent press, might be planning to launch an "attack" on the judges, presumably with their phones and writing instruments, or possibly their head coverings and outerwear, for example, their scarves, which I suppose, in the hands of trained terrorist assassins, could be used to strangle them. In any event, they clearly believe that an "overall tense security situation" exists, one which necessitates these anti-terrorism security protocols at the trial of a sixty-two-year-old playwright, author, and political satirist.

As I mentioned in part one of this column last week, I'm not a terrorist, or in any way terrorist adjacent. I'm an author and a political satirist. The German authorities are prosecuting me because I criticized them and their Covid mask mandates on Twitter.

My punishment for doing that has been, well, here I am, on trial, again, in the People's Court of New Normal Germany. The German authorities had my tweets censored by Twitter. They reported me to the Federal

Criminal Police Office, which is basically the German FBI. They reported me to the Federal Office for the Protection of the Constitution, Germany's domestic intelligence agency. My book is banned in Germany. They have damaged my income and reputation as an author. They have forced me to spend thousands of Euros in attorney's fees to defend myself against these trumped-up charges. And now they are going to subject me, and my attorney, and anyone who attends my trial, to this humiliating, ham-fisted, official show of force.

If you are American, or a Brit, or Australian, or whatever, and you're thinking this is just a crazy story about Germany or the EU, I am sorry, but it isn't. My case is just one of numerous examples of the criminalization of dissent that is being carried out all throughout the West. A lot of Americans and other people don't realize it, but freedom of speech is protected in the German Constitution.

My story is not about the differences between German and American freedom-of-speech protections. It is about the authorities prosecuting government critics like me on fabricated "hate crime" charges, banning our books, and censoring our political speech. Once a government starts doing that, the protections in its constitution no longer matter. You are no longer dealing with questions of law. You are dealing with the exercise of authoritarian power. That is what my story is about. Any Americans (and any other non-Germans) who have been paying attention to recent events will understand what I'm talking about.

As I've been saying, repeatedly, for the last four years or so, the global-capitalist power system (or the "corporatocracy," or "The Powers That Be," or whatever other name you need to call it) is going totalitarian on us. It dominates the entire planet, so it doesn't have anything else to do. It is conducting a global "clear-and-hold" op. It is neutralizing internal resistance, any and all forms of internal resistance. The criminalization of dissent is an essential part of that. I have been documenting this process in my columns and in my books, and specifically in *The Rise of the New Normal Reich*, which you can read, unless you live in Germany.

The point is, we are not in Kansas anymore. All that democracy and rule-of-law stuff is over. It is being gradually phased out. And sometimes not so gradually phased out.

I get that most people don't believe that. Most people won't until it's too late. That's how these transitions generally work. Most people can't see what is coming until it gets here. I can see it, but not because I'm a prophet. I'm just a loudmouth, and the loudmouths get crushed first.

Anyway, if you are in Berlin on August 15 and would like to observe the People's Court of New Normal Germany in action, or just get groped by a German law enforcement officer, the trial is scheduled to start at 10:30 a.m. Seating is on a first-come-first-served basis. So you may want to get there a little early, given all the scanning and screening and groping and the "overall tense security situation." The address is Elßholzstraße 30-33.

Update: August 14, 2024

And on and on and on it goes. Today, at the eleventh hour, the Berlin Superior Court postponed my trial—which had been scheduled to take place tomorrow—for reasons that remain unclear.

It would be wrong, and bad, for me to speculate about the Superior Court's reasons for this eleventh-hour postponement. Such unwarranted speculation on my part might even qualify as "misinformation," and call down the wrath of the German authorities, or the UK authorities, or, God help me, Thierry Breton Himself!

Nevertheless, here's what happened in the run-up to my now abruptly postponed trial.

On August 12, my attorney filed a motion alleging bias on the part of the Superior Court judge that issued the so-called Security Order that I reported on in part one and part two of this column. We filed this motion after our earlier motions to have the Order lifted were summarily denied.

And, this morning, a rather extensive article about my prosecution was published in the *Berliner Zeitung*, a mainstream German daily newspaper.[112] Despite the fact that this story has received a considerable amount of international press coverage, this is the first coverage it has received from the mainstream German press. Until today, they had been diligently ignoring the story, despite the fact that it has been

---

112 Hutter, Ralf, "Autor vor Gericht," *Berliner Zeitung*, August 14, 2024.

reported on in *The Atlantic*,[113] and the Foundation for Individual Rights and Expression just released a video feature and published a piece about it on their blog, and Sky News Australia[114] published a piece about it, and *Neue Zürcher Zeitung*[115] in Switzerland, also covered it, and Matt Taibbi in *Racket News*,[116] and Aya Velázquez,[117] a German independent journalist who, along with her colleagues Bastian Barucker and Stefan Homburg, has recently rocketed to fame for releasing the "Robert Koch-Institut Leak," which is currently shaking things up in Germany, and too many more independent media sources to mention.

But that *Berliner Zeitung* article (and all that other press) probably didn't have anything to do with the court's last-minute decision to postpone the trial. I mean, it's not like they are ashamed of what they're doing, i.e., criminally prosecuting an author for two tweets.

No, the impression I get is that the German authorities are extremely proud of what they're doing. After all, in the space of only one year, with the assistance of Amazon, Twitter, and now X, they have dragged me into criminal court, reported me to the German FBI and Germany's domestic intelligence agency, damaged my income and reputation as an author, forced me to spend over 10,000 Euros to defend myself against their trumped-up charges, had my book banned in Germany, censored my speech, and just generally made my life extremely stressful.

So it's unlikely that this one article, or this recent round of press, has shamed the court into postponing my trial at the eleventh hour. I'm sure

---

113 Kirchick, James, "What Happens Where Free Speech Is Unprotected," *The Atlantic*, January 3, 2024.
114 Mac Ghlionn, John, "Sound familiar Australia? Prosecution of novelist who dared to criticise Germany's authoritarian government sets a very dangerous precedent," Sky News Australia, August 4, 2024.
115 Neumann, Marc, "Der Autor C. J. Hopkins vergleicht die Corona-Politik mit jener der Nazis. Jetzt ist er von der deutschen Justiz wegen der Verbreitung von Nazi-Propaganda verurteilt worden," *Neue Zürcher Zeitung*, September 28, 2024.
116 Taibbi, Matt, "Madness: American Satirist C. J. Hopkins Sentenced in German Speech Case," *Racket News*, August 22, 2023.
117 Velázquez, Aya, "Acquittal for US author C. J. Hopkins," Substack, January 23, 2024.

the court does this all the time, you know, abruptly postpone a trial the day before it's scheduled for totally unspecified reasons. This is modern Germany, after all! It's New Normal Germany! Not old, bad Nazi Germany, where the courts were just an arm of the Nazi government! New Normal Germany is absolutely nothing like that! It's a totally democratic country where everyone is equal in the eyes of the law and "the Land of Poets and Thinkers" and "Unity and Justice and Freedom," and . . . whatever.

In any event, don't show up at the Kammergericht tomorrow. I mean, unless you're on trial yourself for something, or you just want to get groped by a German court officer.

I'll let you know when I receive a new trial date.

The New Normal Right
September 11, 2024

OK, this will be one of my non-satirical essays, or mostly non-satirical essays.

It will serve as a companion piece to *The New Normal Left*, another non-satirical essay that I published in April of 2023, which was basically just a reiteration of a speech I gave at a conference in London. It went over pretty well back then. I republished most of it in my latest Substack column, *A Brief History of Global Capitalism*. It didn't go over quite as well this time. Political perspectives appear to have shifted significantly over the course of the last year and a half. Or maybe it was just the word "capitalism" in the title, which, for some reason, annoyed a lot of people.

This essay will also annoy some people. However, that is not my intention, so if you're one of those readers who gets agitated if you see the word "capitalism" in anything other than an enthusiastically pro-capitalism context, you might want to give this essay a miss.

Also, if you're one of my regular readers, my apologies for the repetition of points that I have already made in earlier essays. Not everyone has read those essays, so I need to do that for the sake of clarity, which is what I hope to provide here, rather than just making people laugh.

The first thing I should probably clarify is what I mean by the term "New Normal." Naturally, people associate it with Covid. It doesn't have anything to do with Covid. Yes, the "New Normal" was ushered into being by the "state of emergency" that was imposed on the world from 2020 to 2023, but it didn't end in 2023, and it never had anything to do with a virus. You do not transform entire societies into pathologized-totalitarian police states and force people to submit to experimental "vaccinations" because of an airborne respiratory virus that poses no threat to the vast majority of humanity.

The "New Normal" was never about a virus. The term—which I did not make up; it was deployed by the authorities and the corporate and state media—means exactly what it sounds like it means. The "New Normal" is our new official "reality," just as "the War on Terror" was our official "reality" from September 2001 to 2016.

The "New Normal" is actually an evolution of "the War on Populism" that began in 2016, after Brexit and the rise of European populism, and Donald Trump in the USA. I've published whole books of essays on this subject, so I'm not going to reiterate all that here. Essentially, what happened in 2016 was, the global-capitalist system that we all live under switched "realities" like The Party switched official enemies in Orwell's *1984*. It happened over the course of a few weeks.

Most people have probably forgotten by now, but back in August 2016, we were still very much living in "the War on Terror." By October, "the War on Terror" was over, and "the War on Populism" was on. "The War on Populism" was our official "reality" from then until the Spring of 2020, when it morphed into the "New Normal" with the rollout of "the pandemic."

And now . . . well, here we are.

OK, let me try to clarify another point. When I say the "New Normal" is our official "reality," I mean "reality," not ideology. Ideologies are a dime a dozen. They exist in relation to other ideologies. "Reality" does not. There is only one "reality." If there is more than one "reality," they're just ideologies. "Reality" is singular. It is axiomatic. "Reality" isn't up for debate. If you debate "reality," you are a "crazy person." That's the whole point of having a "reality."

I realize this is a difficult concept. If you are having trouble with it, perhaps think of official "reality" as a supra-ideological ideology. I've often called it a "post-ideology." It's what an ideology becomes when there are no longer any other ideologies to put it in context (i.e., *as an ideology*). So it disappears *as ideology*, and becomes "reality," and becomes unassailable . . . or, in other words, "just the way it is."

Which, of course, is the ultimate goal of every totalitarian system, i.e., to overcode every element of society with its official "reality," eliminating any and all forms of dissent, which, at that point, no longer has to be suppressed, because it has become inconceivable, *literally* inconceivable, as in the mind can no longer formulate such thoughts (no more than fish could think critically about water, i.e., if fish could think like that).

The "New Normal" is our new official "reality." We are only in the early stages of it, but some of its features are unmistakably clear—the criminalization of dissent, corporate and state censorship, the devalorization of democratic rights and principles, the "pathologization" of political opposition, et cetera. I have described it as a new, nascent form of totalitarianism. A global-capitalist form of totalitarianism. I'm sorry if that agitates my "pro-capitalism" readers—as I mentioned, that is honestly not my intent—but global capitalism is the system that we all live within. We need to be able to call it what it is and try to understand how it is rapidly evolving.

It is evolving in an increasingly totalitarian fashion, which, given the circumstances, is not at all surprising. As I put it in one of my earlier essays:

> It's one big global-capitalist world now. It has been since the early 1990s. GloboCap has no external adversaries, so it has nothing to do but "clear and hold," i.e., wipe out pockets of internal resistance and implement ideological uniformity. Which is what it has been doing for the last thirty years, first, in the former Soviet bloc, then, in "The Global War on Terror," and finally, in our so-called "Western democracies," as we have just experienced up close and personal during the shock-and-awe phase of the rollout of the New Normal, and are continuing to experience, albeit less dramatically. In other words, GloboCap is going totalitarian. That is what the "New Normal" is.

If any of my staunchly pro-capitalism readers are still with me at this point, please, try to relax. I don't want to confiscate your private property, or raise the capital gains tax on billionaires, or any of that other "commie" stuff. I am neither "pro-capitalism" nor "anti-capitalism." I'm just trying to explain where we are.

Where we are is in the inceptive stages of the evolution of the first globally hegemonic power system in human history. Communism is dead. Nazism is dead. Every would-be ideological opponent to the hegemony of global capitalism is dead. There are only two major forces in play: (1) global capitalism, which is carrying out that above-mentioned global "clear-and-hold" op, and (2) the reactionary resistance to it.

The character of that reactionary resistance is decentralized and heterogeneous, as is the character of the global-capitalist system. Neither force is a monolithic entity. The basic differences are: (1) global capitalism, despite its heterogeneous elements and the perpetual intramural competition among them, comprises a single ideological system, whereas the reactionary resistance to it does not, and (2) the global-capitalism system is the occupying force, so it controls the territory—i.e., the entire planet—whereas the reactionary resistance is an insurgency, or, rather, a diverse array of insurgencies, many of which do not understand what they are actually "insurging" against.

Which brings us to the New Normal Right.

I have described the resistance to the hegemony of global capitalism as "reactionary." I do not mean that in a pejorative sense. Most of this reactionary resistance is an attempt to defend traditional values from the value-decoding machine of capitalism.

If I can quote from *The New Normal Left* again:

> Capitalism is a values-decoding machine. It decodes society of despotic values (i.e., religious values, racist values, socialist values, traditional values, any and all values that interfere with the unimpeded flows of capital. Capitalism does not distinguish). This is how capitalism (or democracy if you're squeamish) freed us from a despotic "reality" in which values emanated from the aristocracies, kings, priests, the Church, et cetera. Basically, it transferred the emanation and enforcement of values from despotic structures to the marketplace, where everything is essentially a commodity.

As the events of the last eight years have demonstrated, there are still a lot of people who have no interest in living in a global marketplace where there are no values, and anything means anything, and everything and everyone is essentially a commodity.

This is what the "culture war" in the West is all about. People are not quite ready to surrender their religious values, their cultural values, their national sovereignty, and other such concepts, and embrace a borderless, monomulticultural, supranationally governed, post-social society that is basically just an endless combination mega-mall and GloboCap theme park.

The thing is, the majority of the resistance in the West is staunchly "pro-capitalist," or at least staunchly "anti-communist," and thus is unable to face the fact that it is global capitalism and its values-decoding machine that it is actually resisting. Hence the desperate coining of alternative names to designate the adversary, "cultural Marxism," "communism," "wokeism," "crony capitalism" . . . the list goes on and on and on.

The same goes for the non-Western resistance. Most militant Islamic fundamentalists believe they are waging jihad against "the infidels," or "the Zionists," or against "the Great Satan, America." Populists in Eastern Europe believe they are resisting the USA, or NATO, which they are, but that's just intramural competition. What they are really up against is the values-decoding machine of global capitalism, which is desperate to get its hooks back into Russia, reprivatize the hell out of everything, and get those flows of global capital reflowing.

Anyway, that's the playing field, currently. You got GloboCap conducting its clear-and-hold op, neutralizing internal resistance to its global-capitalist *Gleichschaltung* campaign and implementing (post) ideological uniformity, and you got the internal, reactionary resistance to GloboCap.

So that works out pretty well for GloboCap. You can't carry out a clear-and-hold op if there's no reactionary resistance to "clear."

The catch is, most of the reactionary resistance is not quite scary and militant enough. I'm going to out on a limb here and say that most conservatives are not longstanding members of democracy-hating neo-Nazi militias. They're just regular folks who want to be left alone to live their lives as they please and raise their families according to their values, just like most liberals and, yes, even leftists, are not fanatical, mask-wearing, censorship-happy, shrieking, totalitarian freaks, but just regular people with good intentions.

But that doesn't work for GloboCap. Garden-variety, non-fanatical folks, regardless of their political persuasions, are as useless to the GloboCap clear-and-hold op as a one-legged monkey in an ass-kicking contest.

And so that's where the New Normal Right comes in.

If the New Normal Right did not already exist, GloboCap would be forced to invent it. It needs a convincing boogeyman—or, actually, a diverse collection of boogeymen—to serve as an excuse for its evolution into a pathologized-totalitarian system.

Fortunately for GloboCap, the New Normal Right does indeed exist and is becoming uglier and thus more useful by the day. Just like the New Normal Left are playing their part (i.e., as the New Normal's brownshirts), the New Normal Right are stepping into their role like seasoned Hollywood actors.

Their role in this drama is "the far-right extremists." The "bigots." The "anti-Semites." The "Holocaust deniers." The "neo-Nazis." The "neo-nationalist insurrectionists."

In other words, they are playing the part of "Hitler."

Naturally, GloboCap is playing "America" (i.e., the "good guys" who defeated Hitler), so it needs a "Hitler" to be at war with. It needs a "Hitler" to justify doing away with what is left of our democratic rights, transferring political power from nation-states to supranational global corporations and non-governmental governing organizations, censoring and visibility-filtering dissent, and otherwise continuing to metamorphose into its new totalitarian form. The terrorists are still playing "Hitler" abroad. It needs the New Normal Right to play "Hitler" at home.

Which the New Normal Right is increasingly doing. Emboldened in large part by Elon Musk and other prominent "influencers," they're letting it rip with the blatant bigotry, and anti-Semitism, and neo-nationalism, and strutting around like racist bull roosters. Holocaust denial is trending. Rumors of cat-eating Haitians are circulating. Elon, who has been consecrated "Free Speech Jesus," is "martyring" Himself in Brazil and the UK. His disciples are jet-setting around the planet, preaching the Gospel of Elon in their Free-Speech-X T-shirts and passing out pro-Bolsonaro stickers![118]

And now the Musk Cult is on its way to Washington to "Rescue the Republic" from tyranny![119]

Yes, the New Normal Right is salty! They are ready for action! The Rebellion is on! Unfortunately, they have no idea what it is that they are actually rebelling against. Intoxicated by a sense of impending victory over the "libtard commies" and their "woke mind virus," they are playing right into GloboCap's hands, or being led down to the Weser River, depending on how paranoid you want to get.

If I were the showrunner at GloboCap Pictures, I couldn't have scripted the set-up any better. All we need now is an inciting incident, you know, like terrorists attacking the World Trade Center, Russia invading Ukraine, Hamas attacking Israel, or neo-Nazis storming the Reichstag, or the Trumpians storming the US Capitol, or British racists running amok, or . . . well, I think you get the general idea. Something that will enable GlobCap to declare another "global state of emergency," re-suspend constitutional rights, unleash the goon squads and the New Normal Left again, and maybe even shut down the Internet to protect the public from malinformation, or extremism, or terrorism, or Hitler, or whatever!

Who knows? Maybe they'll even throw in another apocalyptic virus!

---

[118] On the advice of my attorney, and my publisher's attorney, I am not including a selfie photograph of a grinning Mike Shellenberger and a Free-Speech-X-T-shirt-wearing companion on the street in Brazil, brandishing a pro-Bolsonaro sticker, during the big PR "showdown" Musk had with Justice Alexandre de Moraes in August 2024 after Moraes ordered the banning of X in Brazil due to the company's non-compliance with Brazilian law. Two months later, Musk quietly complied with Moraes's demands, and access to X in Brazil was restored.

[119] Notheis, Asher, "Rescue the Republic event near Washington Monument aims to unite country," *Washington Examiner*, September 23, 2024. (Again, on the advice of legal counsel, I am not reproducing the promotional poster for this "Rescue the Republic" event, which depicted Musk and numerous other "Republic rescuers" crossing the Delaware in the style of Emanuel Leutze's famous 1851 oil painting, *Washington Crossing the Delaware*, but it's probably still up on the Internet somewhere.)

Political Justice

September 22, 2024

So, this came as a pleasant surprise.

A German judge, Dr. Clivia von Dewitz, published an opinion piece about my case and "political justice" in the *Berliner Zeitung,* a mainstream German daily newspaper. I've translated it below for any non-German readers who are not sick to death of reading about my case.

And, even if you're sick of hearing about my case, you should read her piece anyway, because (a) it will clear up any lingering misconceptions you may have about the law regarding the display of Nazi symbols in Germany—Dr. von Dewitz happens to be an expert on that law—and (b) she references the "RKI Leaks" (i.e., the Robert Koch-Institut Leaks), which are shaking things up here in Germany at the moment.

That's a whole story in itself, and I want to stay on track, but here's a translation of an excerpt from an article by two German lawyers[120] about what the RKI Leaks are exposing:

> To be clear: The first lockdown in the history of the Federal Republic of Germany was apparently based largely on political or ministerial influence on the RKI, which was sold to the public and the courts as an independent scientific risk assessment. . . . Since the

---

120 Lucenti, Sebastian and Franziska Meyer-Hesselbarth, "Corona und Recht: Die Pandemie der Unmenschlichkeit," *Cicero*, September 22, 2024.

RKI was bound by the instructions of and conformed its statements to the wishes of politicians, the minutes reveal that contradictions, ambiguities and inaccuracies in the official statements were systematically ignored, indeed had to be ignored. The publicly communicated protection of others through vaccination did not exist, nor did the extent of the risk to the general population from Corona infections postulated by the RKI. An objective look at the data published by the RKI in Germany in March 2020 showed no national medical threat.

So, yeah, the RKI Leaks are kind of a big story, and that story is the broader context of my story, which Dr. von Dewitz explains at some length in her article.

Oh, and if you're wondering about the phrase "political justice," it's mostly a German concept. I don't think the term is commonly used in English, or at least I couldn't find many references to it. It means exactly what it sounds like it means.

In a political justice system, the independence of the judiciary is overridden by the ruling authorities and thus fundamental democratic rights are violated. This independence [of the judiciary] is part of the separation of powers guaranteed to Germany by Article 20, Paragraph 2, of the Basic Law. Political justice is an abuse of executive power. The equality of political groups before the law is not taken into account, but rather, the justice system serves primarily to eliminate political opposition and thus expands the scope of the prevailing political system, rather than holding it in check. —Otto Kirchheimer: *Politische Justiz. Verwendung juristischer Verfahrensmöglichkeiten zu politischen Zwecken.* (1961 Political Justice) dt. Luchterhand, Neuwied 1965, S. 606.

Anyway, without further ado, here's the translation of Dr. Clivia von Dewitz's piece in the *Berliner Zeitung* [notes in brackets mine].

Judge on the CJ Hopkins Case: Using Nazi Comparisons Against Covid Policy—Is That Allowed?[121]

Our author wrote her doctorate on the Nazi-symbol ban and says: Hopkins's acquittal at his first trial was correct. Why is the Berlin public prosecutor appealing the verdict?

By Clivia von Dewitz, *Berliner Zeitung*, September 21, 2024.

The appeal hearing in the C. J. Hopkins case is scheduled to take place before the Berlin Appellate Court on September 30. The American-born man, married to a Jew, and living in Berlin for almost twenty years, is accused by the Berlin public prosecutor's office of violating the Nazi-symbol ban that has been in effect in Germany since 1968 with two posts on X [formerly Twitter]. The bone of contention is an image showing a white medical mask with a white swastika shining through in the middle of it. He published various accompanying texts, which will be relevant in the course of the trial. But more on that later.

Showing Nazi symbols still causes discomfort among a large portion of the population in Germany. Rightly so—these symbols represent an unjust regime of unimaginable proportions, which is responsible in particular for the Holocaust and the Second World War and thus for millions of deaths.

The [Nazi] Symbol Ban

Immediately after the Second World War, people understandably began to think about how to deal with Nazi symbols. The first criminal regulations that restricted National Socialist ideas and thus also Nazi insignia were the German military government's occupation laws for the American zone (such as Law No. 154). The law stipulated stiff penalties for the use of Nazi symbols on flags, banners and the like.

After 1949, only the Assembly Act of 1953 contained a ban on the use of National Socialist symbols. It was not until 1960 with the

---

121 Von Dewitz, Clivia, "Richterin zum Fall CJ Hopkins: Mit Nazi-Vergleichen gegen die Coronapolitik—ist das erlaubt?" *Berliner Zeitung*, September 21, 2024.

6th Criminal Law Amendment Act that the ban on displaying the symbols of former National Socialist organizations was introduced into the Criminal Code as Section 96a. In 1968, the insignia ban was introduced as Section 86a StGB as part of the party-ban provisions in the version that essentially still applies today, thus placing the standardization of the Nazi-symbol ban in the more general context of the party-ban law.

According to the ban on [Nazi] insignia (§ 86 Para. 1 No. 4, 86a Para. 1 No. 1 StGB), only those who distribute or publicly display Nazi symbols "which, based on their content, are intended to reflect the efforts of a former National Socialist organization" are liable to prosecution. This means that not every use of a Nazi symbol falls under the ban. On the contrary, the law confirms that only material, the content of which is directed against the free democratic basic order or the concept of understanding among nations, is considered [criminal] propaganda media (Section 86 Para. 3 StGB).

And, according to the criminal statute (Section 86 Para. 4 StGB), criminal liability is also excluded if the material serves the purposes of civic education, defense against unconstitutional efforts, art or science, research or teaching, or reporting on current events or history, or similar purposes (the so-called social adequacy clause).

It was in the 1970s that Nazi symbols were first used in a critical or ironic way. In these cases, jurisprudence failed to establish criminal liability, either at the level of the offense or by virtue of the application of the social adequacy clause. Because a critical and distanced use of Nazi symbols is not punishable, especially in view of Article 5 of the *Grundgesetz* [i.e., the German Constitution, literally "Basic Law"]. The fundamental right of freedom of expression and freedom of art enshrined therein is constitutive of a democracy.

The Verdict of the Tiergarten District Court: Acquittal

Given the above-described legal background, the Tiergarten District Court quite rightly acquitted C. J. Hopkins on January 23, 2024.

In its judgment, the court came to the conclusion that the defendant did not commit a criminal offense with his two posts, because, according to the verdict, in both of the posts cited by the Berlin public prosecutor's office, "when taking into account the text associated with the use of the mask, it can easily be seen that the connection to National Socialism is made in an emphatically negative sense." The posts are also unsuitable to promote a revival of National Socialist ideas or even former National Socialist organizations. Because people with neo-Nazi goals would never use the symbols of National Socialist organizations in an artwork that expresses their rejection. Therefore, any effect of the posts in a direction corresponding to the symbolic content of National Socialist insignia is ruled out from the outset. In short: The court found that an American citizen had used Nazi symbols without intending to glorify the Nazi regime in any way.

The question now arises as to how the Berlin public prosecutor's office is appealing this acquittal and summoning C. J. Hopkins to court again on September 30, 2024. According to the wording of the [Nazi] insignia ban, and the special importance, according to the Federal Constitutional Court, of freedom of expression and art for a democracy, there can be no other result than impunity for such posts.

In a ruling on April 11, 2024, in response to a constitutional complaint by Julian Reichelt, the Federal Constitutional Court noted the special importance of freedom of expression and made it clear that the state must also put up with harsh and polemical criticism. This must also apply when Nazi symbols are used to criticize state orders, regardless of whether the criticism is justified or not.

The Prosecution's Argument

The argument presented by the Berlin public prosecutor's office in the hearing before the Berlin district court—according to which distance from the Nazi era should not "only" become clear "when reading the text accompanying the image or when reflecting on it"—is not convincing. The criticism of the state expressed in the two posts through the use of the swastika clearly does not glorify the Nazi regime. On the contrary, the defendant is using Nazi symbolism to warn against a totalitarian style of government. This may seem extreme, but if you consider the government's actions during the Corona period, harsh criticism is at least understandable.

The minutes of the Robert Koch Institute (RKI) suggest that the government ordered significant parts of the measures restricting fundamental rights from 2020 to 2022 not on the basis of scientific findings, but out of political calculation, such that a new assessment of the government's actions from 2020 to 2022 is necessary.

This also and especially applies to the wearing of masks. For example, the RKI minutes of November 4, 2020, state: "FFP2 masks are very unlikely to be a protective measure. In addition, there is no reliable protection for laypeople without accompanying application!" And later, in the minutes of November 16, 2020, it states: "Can we still intervene? It is inconvenient and dangerous for masks to be used by laypeople. The German Society for Microbiology and Hygiene considers FFP2 masks, if they do not fit well, to be a less favorable means than MNS ('mouth and nose protection,' BZ editor's note), as they provide a false sense of security. (. . .) Influence is no longer possible, the deliberations are taking place now, RKI was not asked in advance." And in the very next sentence it states: "If a decision is made like this, the challenges should be pointed out, and disbursement by prescription should be recommended after prior consultation with the family doctor. The family doctor can check whether there is a cardiac or pulmonary risk and can provide instructions on its use."

Political Justice?

Given these statements by scientists in late 2020, how can the ongoing proceedings against doctors who issued mask-exemption certificates be justified? The suspicion of political justice or attitude-based criminal law arises.

The Osnabrück Administrative Court recently initiated a commendable new development in jurisprudence. The court introduced the RKI protocols in a trial regarding an employment ban as a result of the facility-related vaccination requirement. The RKI President was called as a witness. At the end of the hearing, the court found that there were considerable doubts about the scientific independence of the RKI, as it was operating according to the instructions of the Federal Ministry of Health. Because of massive doubts about the constitutionality of a paragraph in the then applicable Infection Protection Act, it has submitted the case to the Federal Constitutional Court for a decision (a so-called judge's submission). It remains to be seen whether the Federal Constitutional Court will take advantage of the opportunity and adapt its decisions to the actual state of scientific knowledge in the future.

Finally, it was recently highlighted by retired judge Manfred Kölsch that the damage to taxpayers caused by the ordering of 5.7 billion masks by May 5, 2024 (by the then Health Minister Jens Spahn), as well as by storage costs and by the likely economic consequences of the rulings by the Cologne Higher Regional Court on compensation for mask suppliers, is likely to total around ten billion Euros. The Federal Audit Office speaks of a "massive over-procurement" and further states that the masks were "of no use in combating the pandemic and therefore of no health policy value." At the same time, the RKI protocol of January 27, 2020, states: "It is not recommended to stockpile masks etc." Politicians ordered masks contrary to all economic reason and mandated the wearing of masks contrary to scientific findings and the professional assessment of the Robert Koch Institute. Regarding children, many experts even considered wearing masks to be harmful to their health right from the start.

In light of all this, the use of a swastika in conjunction with a mask as criticism of government orders may appear in a new light. If it is no longer possible to criticize government actions in an extreme way, what C. J. Hopkins was warning against with his posts has come true, namely the rise of new totalitarian government structures and thus the loss of democratic values. If *Der Spiegel* and *Stern*, which were not particularly critical of the government during or after the Covid period, and have not made a serious effort to educate, can use swastikas on their covers unchallenged, the same must apply to critics of the government.

Dr. Clivia von Dewitz is a German judge. Her doctorate thesis was on Nazi ideas and criminal law (§§ 86,86a and § 130 StGB).

Guilty

October 1, 2024

So, the Berlin Appellate Court overturned my acquittal today. I am now, officially, at least according to the New Normal German authorities, a "hate-speech" criminal. I'm officially a "hate-speech" criminal because I compared New Normal Germany to Nazi Germany, and I challenged the official Covid narrative, and I used the cover art of my book to do it.

The New Normal German authorities didn't like that, and were determined to punish me for doing that, and to make an example of me in order to discourage other people from doing that. It took them two tries, but they pulled it off. The judge in my original trial screwed up and acquitted me, but the Berlin state prosecutor's office didn't give up. They appealed the verdict, and this morning the Appellate Court overturned my acquittal and declared me guilty.

I'll report on all the ugly details of my day in court in a proper column sometime later this week, once I've sufficiently recovered from the hangover I am currently about to start working on.

In the meantime, here's the statement I read out in Berlin Appellate Court yesterday.

Statement to the Berlin Appellate Court, September 30, 2024

Ladies and Gentlemen, my name is C. J. Hopkins. I am an award-winning playwright, author, and political satirist. My work is read by hundreds of thousands of people all over the world. For over thirty years, I have written and spoken out against fascism, authoritarianism, totalitarianism, and so on. Anyone can do an Internet search, find my books, reviews of my plays, my essays, and learn who I am and what my political views are in five minutes.

And yet, I am accused by the German authorities of spreading pro-Nazi propaganda. I'm accused of doing this because I posted two tweets challenging the official Covid narrative and comparing the new, nascent form of totalitarianism it has brought into being—the so-called "New Normal"—to Nazi Germany.

Let me be clear. I did that. In August 2022, as Germany was debating whether to end its Covid mask mandates, I tweeted those two tweets. I challenged the official Covid narrative. I compared the New Normal to Nazi Germany. I did that with the cover art of one of my books. I did what anyone is allowed to do according to German law. I did what Karl Lauterbach has done. I did what German celebrities like Jessica Berlin have done. I did what major German newspapers and magazines have done.

A few months ago, *Stern* and *Der Spiegel* published covers of their magazines featuring swastikas. *Der Spiegel*'s cover featured exactly the same artistic concept as my book cover and my tweets. The only difference is, the swastika on *Der Spiegel*'s cover is behind a German flag, whereas the swastika on my book cover and in my tweets is behind a medical mask. That's it. That is the only difference.

Stern and *Der Spiegel* displayed swastikas on their covers in order to warn the public of the rise of a new form of totalitarianism, and that is precisely what I did. I compared the New Normal—i.e., the new nascent form of totalitarianism that came into being in 2020—to Nazi Germany. *Stern* and *Der Spiegel* compared the AfD to Nazi Germany. That is the only difference.

I'm not a fan of the AfD. I'm not a fan of *Stern* and *Der Spiegel*. That doesn't matter. *Stern* and *Der Spiegel* have the right to do what they did, and so do I. That right is guaranteed to us in the German Constitution. We all have the right, if we see a new form of totalitarianism taking shape, to oppose it, and to compare it to historical forms of totalitarianism, including Nazi Germany.

I don't follow German electoral politics very closely, so I don't know exactly what the AfD has done that prompted *Stern* and *Der Spiegel* to compare them to the Nazis. But I know exactly what the German authorities did during 2020 to 2023.

In 2020, the German authorities declared a national state of emergency, for which they provided no concrete evidence, and suspended constitutional rights. Nazi Germany also did that, in March 1933. From 2020 to 2022, the German authorities forced people to wear symbols of their conformity to the official ideology and perform humiliating public-loyalty rituals. The Nazis also did that. The current German authorities banned protests against their arbitrary decrees. With the help of the media, they bombarded the German masses with lies and propaganda designed to terrorize the public into unquestioning obedience. They segregated society according to who was and wasn't conforming to official ideology. They censored political dissent. They stripped people of their jobs because they refused to conform to official ideology and follow senseless orders. The German authorities fomented mass hatred of a "scapegoat" class of people. They demonized and persecuted critics of the government's decrees. They dispatched police to beat them and arrest them. They have instrumentalized the law to punish political dissidents. Nazi Germany also did all these things, as have most other totalitarian systems. I documented all this in my book. I spoke out against it. I published essays about it. I tweeted about it.

My punishment for that has been . . . well, here I am, on trial in criminal court for the second time. The German authorities had my tweets censored. They reported me to the Federal Criminal Police Office. They reported me to the Federal Office for the Protection of the Constitution, the German domestic intelligence agency. My book is banned in Germany. The German authorities investigated me. They prosecuted me. They put me on trial for tweeting. After I was acquitted, that wasn't enough, so they have put me on trial again. They defamed me. They have damaged my income and reputation as an author. They have forced me to spend thousands of Euros in legal fees to defend myself against these clearly ridiculous charges. And today, I, and my lawyer, and all the people in the gallery, have been subjected to this official show of force and treated like potential terrorists.

Why, rational people might ask, have I been subjected to this special treatment, while *Der Spiegel*, *Stern*, *Die Tageszeitung*, and many others who have also tweeted swastikas, have not?

This is not a mystery. Everyone knows the answer to this question.

You are not fooling anyone. Everyone understands exactly what this prosecution actually is. Every journalist that has covered my case, everyone in this courtroom, understands what this prosecution actually is. It has nothing to do with punishing people who disseminate pro-Nazi propaganda. It is about punishing political dissent, and intimidating critics into silence. I'm not here because I put a swastika on my book cover. I am here because I put it behind a "Covid" mask. I am here because I dared to criticize the German authorities. I am here because I refused to shut up and follow orders.

At my first trial, I appealed to the judge to stop this game and follow the law. She did that. She needed to publicly insult me, and then put on a "Covid" mask to display her allegiance to the "New Normal," but she acquitted me. She followed the law. And I thanked her. But I will not appeal to this court. I'm tired of this game. If this court wanted to follow the law, I wouldn't be here today. The court would have dismissed the prosecution's ridiculous arguments in its motion to overturn the verdict. You didn't do that. So I'm not going to appeal to this court for justice. Or expect justice.

Go ahead. Do whatever you feel you need to do to me. Fine me. Send me to prison. Bankrupt me. Whatever. I will not pretend that I am guilty of anything to make your punishment stop. I will not lie for you. I will not obey you because you threaten me, because you have the power to hurt me.

You have that power. I get it. Everyone gets it. The German authorities have the power to punish those who criticize them, who expose their hypocrisy, their lies. We all get the message. But that is not how things work in democratic societies. That is how things work in totalitarian systems.

I will not cooperate with that. I refuse to live that way.

As long as the German authorities continue to claim that Germany is a democratic country, which respects the rule of law and democratic principles, I will continue to behave like that is what it is. I will not be bullied. I will insist on my constitutional rights. I will continue to respect democratic principles and fight to preserve them. The German authorities can make a mockery of those rights and the rule of law and democratic principles if they want. I will not. Not for the Berlin prosecutor. Not for this court. Not for the German authorities. Not for anyone.

Totalitarianism, authoritarianism, tyranny, never win. Not in the long run. History teaches us that. And it is history that will judge us all in the end.

Fear and Loathing in New Normal Germany

October 5, 2024

The first rule of New Normal Germany is, you do not compare New Normal Germany to Nazi Germany. If you do that, New Normal Germany will punish you. It will sic the Federal Criminal Police on you. It will report you to its domestic intelligence agency. It will ban your books. It will censor your tweets. It will prosecute you on fabricated "hate-crime" charges.

I know this because that's what happened to me. I broke the first rule of New Normal Germany. I compared New Normal Germany to Nazi Germany. I did it with the cover artwork of my book.

Yes, there is a swastika on the cover of my book. A swastika covered by a medical mask. I tweeted that artwork in 2022. The German authorities prosecuted me for that, and have convicted me for that. So now I'm a "hate criminal," and an "anti-Semite," and a "trivializer of the Holocaust."

That's the second rule of New Normal Germany. You never, ever, display a swastika. Displaying a swastika is not *in Ordnung*. Displaying swastikas is totally *verboten*.

Unless you are the Health Minister of New Normal Germany and you are comparing your political opponents to the Nazis.[122] Or unless you are

---

[122] I'm referring to a tweet by Karl Lauterbach, the German Minister of Health, featuring two Nazi flags with big fat swastikas on them, in which tweet Lauterbach compares the *Alternativ für Deutschland* party to the Nazis. On the advice of my attorney, and my publisher's attorney, I have not reproduced

a popular German celebrity and you're comparing the Russians and their supporters to the Nazis.[123] Or unless you're a mainstream German magazine and you're comparing German populists to the Nazis . . .

. . . in which case, displaying a swastika is fine. And is not *verboten*. And definitely not a "hate crime."

And that's the third rule of New Normal Germany. If you agree with the government, obey their orders, and parrot their propaganda, you are not a "hate criminal." If you *are* the government, like an actual minister in

---

an image of the tweet here. Members of the current German government have a tendency to criminally prosecute or take other forms of vindictive legal action against their critics. I don't want to provide them with a pretext to go after this book.

123 This one was a tweet by Jessica Berlin, a German celebrity, who tweeted two side-by-side photos, (1) a bunch of little Nazi girls waving little Nazi flags with swastikas on them, and (2) people waving Russian flags at a demo in Frankfurt, with the message, "They're back," thus clearly comparing the Russia supporters to the Nazis. Again, on the advice of my attorney, and my publisher's attorney, I have not reproduced an image of Jessica Berlin's tweet, but I'm pretty sure it's still available on the Internet.

the government, like the Minister of Health, you're definitely not a "hate criminal." And, if you are part of the government's propaganda apparatus, needless to say, you are also not a "hate criminal."

However, if you criticize the government, or if you compare the government to Nazi Germany, and if you do that using your book-cover art featuring a swastika behind a Covid mask, then you're absolutely officially a "hate criminal," and an "anti-Semite," and a "trivializer of the Holocaust."

Here's how *Das Kammergericht*, Berlin's superior or appellate court, explained that in their press release,[124] after they convicted me of my "hate crime" [translation mine]:

> The swastika, one of the main symbols of the banned National Socialist Workers' Party (NSDAP), is used here exclusively to express criticism of the federal government's Corona policy; a clear departure from the ideals of National Socialism cannot be seen in the posts in question. The comparison of Corona measures, which are supposed to be embodied by the use of mouth-and-nose coverings, with the Nazi terror regime symbolized by the swastika represents a trivialization of National Socialism and the National Socialist genocide of millions of Jews, but not a criticism of it.

I remember when the presiding judge read that out in court. I remember it distinctly, because the judge to her right, a bespectacled woman with a military hairdo, was glaring at me with bone-chilling hatred. We got into a staring contest, which she eventually won, because I couldn't take it for very long. After a minute or so, I started having flashbacks of scenes from *The Pianist*, Roman Polanski's film, and of the eyes of medical-mask-wearing Germans when they saw the protest message I wrote on the mask I was forced to wear in grocery stores in order to buy food during the rollout of the "New Normal" in 2020–2022. That protest message read, "*Befehl ist Befehl*," which roughly translates as "orders are orders," and

---

124 "Kammergericht stuft Verwendung der Nutzung des Hakenkreuz-Symbols auf einer Corona-Schutzmaske als strafbar ein (PM 31/2024)," *Gerichte in Berlin* (Berlin.de), Pressemitteilung, September 30, 2024.

was the Nazis' infamous defense at Nuremberg (i.e., "I was just following orders"). If you have never been surrounded by mobs of medical-mask-wearing Germans all glaring at you with seething, utterly bone-chilling hatred . . . well, let me assure you, it is quite an experience. I experienced it, daily, for over two years.

I experienced it again in *Das Kammergericht*, where my acquittal in Berlin District Court in January was overturned at the insistence of the Berlin public prosecutor.

Yes, they can do that in New Normal Germany.

I'm going to spare you the procedural details, and legal arguments, and descriptions of the ham-fisted, anti-terror-style security protocols that *Das Kammergericht* ordered in effect for my trial. If you want to read about that, Aya Velázquez covered it in a recent extensive report,[125] and Dr. Clivia von Dewitz, a German judge and expert on the Nazi-symbol-ban laws, covered the legal questions in an article[126] before, and another article[127] after, the trial. I haven't translated the entire second article (as I did the first), but here's an excerpt:

> With this decision, the German judiciary is once again moving away from the principles of a liberal democracy, which thrives on the exchange of conflicting beliefs and opinions as well as criticism of government actions. If *Der Spiegel* and *Stern* are permitted to use swastikas on their magazine covers, the same freedom must apply to those who criticize the government. When, as here, the judiciary begins to apply double standards, and condemns obvious criticism of the government via the use of Nazi symbols, and conducts a trial under inappropriate "anti-terror conditions," one has to ask oneself

---

125 Velázquez, Aya, "Scandalous verdict: US author CJ Hopkins was found guilty," Substack, October 1, 2024.
126 Von Dewitz, Clivia, "Richterin zum Fall CJ Hopkins: Mit Nazi-Vergleichen gegen die Coronapolitik—ist das erlaubt?," *Berliner Zeitung*, September 21, 2024.
127 Von Dewitz, Clivia, "Autor CJ Hopkins verurteilt: 'Bedenkliche Tendenz der Gerichte, Regierungskritiker mundtot zu machen,'" *Berliner Zeitung*, October 1, 2024.

how far the judiciary in Germany has departed from fundamental democratic principles. In response to the court's ruling that such posts are not covered by freedom of expression or freedom of art, what, if not that, is freedom of expression or freedom of art? An American married to a Jew can hardly be accused of "trivializing National Socialism" or of "not expressing an explicit rejection of National Socialism."

Or you can read Eugyppius, another German, writing in English in *The Daily Sceptic*,[128] or an excellent piece in German by Milosz Matuschek,[129] which focuses on the legal arguments.

Or, if you'd prefer to hear from the enormous Goebbelsian keyboard instrument that is the majority of the mainstream German press, and you're able to read German, you can read all about how seditious and insane I am in *Der Tagesspiegel*, *Die Tageszeitung*, and the *Legal Tribune Online*, a legal journal. For some reason I can't possibly fathom, *Der Spiegel* were rather reserved in their coverage. I am sure it had nothing to do with the fact that they had printed that big fat swastika on their cover.

It was rather surprising that the mainstream German media turned up to cover the proceedings, as they had been studiously ignoring the story. Maybe the court's PR people contacted them ... or maybe they just smelled blood in the water.

In any event, the atmosphere in Room 145a of *Das Kammergericht* was dripping with sanctimonious, fascistic authority. It was clear from the outset that the three-judge panel was there to teach a "Covid denier" a lesson and remind the German public what happens when you break the rules of New Normal Germany. The judges had clearly already decided to overturn my acquittal, so the rest was just theater, which, apart from my attorney's lengthy arguments and my statement to the court, mostly consisted of the judges radiating imperious contempt and seething hostility down at us

---

128 Eugyppius, "On the Unjust and Ridiculous Conviction of C.J. Hopkins for Likening Covid Totalitarianism to Nazi Germany," *The Daily Sceptic*, October 1, 2024.

129 Matuschek, Milosz, "Causa Hopkins: Finden Sie die Straftat?," *Freischwebende Intelligenz*, October 4, 2024.

from the bench like an enormous three-headed Gila monster. The prosecutor mumbled two or three sentences in a monotone at the outset of the proceedings. She didn't bother to attempt to appear to present an actual legal argument, as that would have ruined the *fait-accompli mise-en-scène* effect they were obviously going for.

I have to give the court and the prosecution credit for their dramaturgy. The point of staging a public trial like this—which the prosecution demanded, which is unusual at the appellate level—wasn't to pretend to be carrying out justice. It was a show of force. A demonstration. A public humiliation ritual. And, all things considered, they staged it well.

It's embarrassing, but the truth is, they got to me. At some point during the bizarre proceedings, I started experiencing waves of disturbing flashbacks from 2020–2022, when hate-drunk New Normal Germans were chasing down maskless passengers on regional trains like the pod people in *Invasion of the Body Snatchers*, and goon squads (i.e., the German police) were savagely brutalizing anyone who protested against the "Corona measures," and government leaders, the state and corporate media, and the vast majority of the German masses were fanatically persecuting "the Unvaccinated" with a fervor not seen since the bad old days. So I was a little disoriented as I left the courthouse.

It has taken a few days, but I've mostly recovered. After consultations with my fearless attorney, I've decided to submit my case to the *Bundesverfassungsgericht*, i.e., Germany's supreme court, because, well, at this point, I kind of have to. If I don't, the precedent the New Normal German authorities are trying to establish will stand, and the right to freedom-of-expression in Germany will have become nothing but a sick fascist joke.

Yes, that right is guaranteed in the *Grundgesetz* (i.e., the German Constitution). It isn't quite the First Amendment, but it's good enough for Germany, and I'm not willing to let it be distorted and made a mockery of by a bunch of fascists, not without a fight.

The Revenge of Trumpenstein
November 8, 2024

So, it's déjà vu all over again.

That's right, he's back! Trumpenstein the Monster! Literal Russian-Agent Hitler! The Ayatollah of Orange Shinola! And this time he's not screwing around!

No, this time, he is really going to "drain the swamp"! He's going to rebuild that "big, beautiful wall"! Just you wait, you libtards, for the mass deportations! Yes, it's curtains for all those Mexican rapists, cat-barbecuing Haitians, and squirrel-murdering commies! There will be no more cross-dressing perverts perfidiously fluoridating our precious bodily fluids! No more egg-headed Cultural Marxists infecting our youth with their Woke mind virus!

This is the dawn of a Golden Age of Morning in America Made Great Again!

Seriously, this is not just a childish fantasy or a rebooted marketing campaign. Trump and Elon Musk, and their buddies on Wall Street, and in the Military-Industrial Complex, and Silicon Valley, are literally going to rescue America from Libtardism! They are going to kick some deep-state ass this time! It will be like the climax of one of those classic *Die Hard* movies that Bruce Willis used to do, in which the downtrodden working-class-hero cop beats the living snot out of the European bad guy, reestablishes the nuclear family, and then we all live happily ever after!

Of course, for liberals, it will be like one of those classic 1970s Hammer horror movie sequels with Peter Cushing and Christopher Lee . . . the

Return of the Revenge of the Curse of Trumpenstein! The Horror of the Curse of Trumpenstein! Trumpenstein Must Be Destroyed, Again!

The coming four years of recycled mass hysteria has already started. Jimmy "rest in peace wheezy" Kimmel is choking up on national late-night television.[130] Arnold "screw your freedom" Schwarzenegger has not been heard from and is probably in hiding. Some celebrity named Cardi B posted "I hate y'all bad" on the Instagram.[131] MSNBC's Joe Scarborough is blaming the Blacks and Hispanics for betraying Kamala.[132] Jason Stanley, the supercilious "fascism expert" who did that "Trump is Literally Hitler" video[133] for the *New York Times* in 2018, has proclaimed this "the End of US Democracy," again!

Militant liberals are digging out their solidarity safety pins and pink pussyhats and preparing to remount "The Resistance."[134] They will presumably all head out for California, which has been designated "Resistance HQ",[135] under the leadership of Subcommandante Gavin Newsom, who has vowed to "defend our Constitution" from Russian Hitler, or Literal Hitler, or the Return of the Revenge of Literal Hitler, or whatever new version of Hitler they come up with!

They're going to have wait a couple of months, though (i.e., the members of the anti-Trump "Resistance" are), because, technically, the Trumpians are still "The Resistance," and we can only have one "Resistance" at a time,

---

130 Taibbi, Matt, "In Election Aftermath, Hollywood Smashes Records for Lack of Self-Awareness—Jimmy Kimmel, one of the era's most infamous sources of misinformation, tearfully addresses a terrible night for 'journalism' and 'free speech,'" *Racket News*, November 7, 2024.

131 Stolworthy, Jacob, "Celebrities react as Donald Trump wins 2024 US election to become president," *The Independent*, November 8, 2024.

132 Keane, Isabel et al., "Liberal media outlets like CNN, MSNBC have meltdown over Trump win," *New York Post*, November 6, 2024.

133 Stanley, Jason, Adam Westbrook and Japhet Weeks, "If You're Not Scared About Fascism in the U.S., You Should Be," *New York Times*, October 15, 2018.

134 Reich, Robert, "A peaceful but determined resistance to Trump must start now," *The Guardian*, November 6, 2024.

135 Rector, Kevin and Angie Orellana Hernandez, "As with Trump's last term, California will lead the liberal resistance," *Los Angeles Times*, November 6, 2024.

or else "The Resistance" would end up resisting "The Resistance," which would make "The Resistance" the thing it is "resisting," which would make that thing (i.e., the thing it is "resisting") kind of like one of the official enemies in Orwell's *1984*, which the Party switches from time to time, which, of course, it is, but, well, ignore that for now. This is no time for critical thinking, or for any other type of actual thinking! No, it's time to Make America Great Again, or to Save the World from Hitler again, and respond to whatever other Pavlovian stimuli you happen to have been conditioned to respond to!

Which is why I'm going to wait a while before I publish anything serious on this topic. I do have a few thoughts about where we're headed, which I'm pretty sure no one is going to like. I'll publish them once things settle down a bit. For now, OK, the short version is, if you've been enjoying the Free-Speech-Twitter PSYOP, you're going to love the America-Made-Great-Again PSYOP!

If I'm right, it's going to be déjà vu all over again all over again! But whatever. Let's get back to the show!

A Tale of Two PSYOPS
November 15, 2024

Once upon a time, on a planet called Earth, there was born a global-capitalist empire. It was the first global empire in the history of empires. It dominated the entire planet.

No one knew what to call the empire, because there had never been anything like it in history. It had no external adversaries, so it had nothing left to do but "clear and hold," i.e., neutralize internal resistance and consolidate its domination of the planet.

So that is what it set about doing.

It did this first in the territories of its final ideological adversary, an empire called the Soviet Union, the ideology of which was known as "Communism."

This was known as the "Post-Cold-War Era."

It did this next in the Greater Middle East, where people were still trying to live their lives according to a religion known as "Islam."

This was known as the "Global War on Terror."

The Global War on Terror was originally intended to go on forever, and it would have, and it will, but it had to be temporarily suspended, and rebranded, because something unexpected happened.

One day, in the Summer of 2016 (theretofore officially "the Summer of Fear"[136]), the global-capitalist empire noticed that a new form of resistance

---

136 Connolly, Kate and Kim Willsher, "Summer of fear: the anxious mood in Germany and France," *The Guardian*, July 29, 2016.

to its domination of the entire planet had risen up, not in the former Soviet Union, or the Greater Middle East, but throughout the West, right in the very heart of the empire.

And so the War on Terror was suspended, and the War on Populism began.

The War on Populism raged for four years and culminated in the rollout of the New Normal, officially known as "the Covid pandemic."

For over two years, i.e., from March 2020 to approximately December 2022, the global-capitalist empire morphed into a new form of totalitarianism, a global-capitalist form of totalitarianism, which was not like any other previous form of totalitarianism.

This period was the shock-and-awe phase of the rollout of the New Normal Reich.

The transition to the New Normal Reich was broadcast throughout the global empire. The message was unmistakably clear. From now on, there would be a "New Normal." It would be like a permanent state of war, a permanent state of civil war. And so, from now on, everyone would need to pledge their allegiance to the New Normal Reich, and follow orders, or be labeled an "extremist," or a "science denier," or a "conspiracy theorist," or some other type of seditious deviant.

The vast majority of the citizens of the West understood the message, followed orders, and pledged allegiance to the New Normal Reich. But a sizable minority did not. The global-capitalist empire needed to neutralize this sizable minority.

The majority of this sizable minority was comprised of conservative, libertarian, and other basically right-leaning people. It contained a few old-school left-leaning people, but they were a minority within a minority, so they weren't really a factor when it came to neutralizing the larger uncooperative minority, which the empire promptly set about doing.

The Free-Speech Twitter PSYOP

In October 2022, Elon Musk, the multibillionaire military contractor, electric car salesman, and transhumanism enthusiast, and a coterie of serious global-capitalist entities and individuals[137] purchased the social media platform known as Twitter, Inc. for forty-four billion US dollars.

Musk walked into Twitter's San Francisco headquarters, grinning like a chimpanzee and carrying a bathroom sink, and the Free-Speech Twitter PSYOP began.

During the War on Populism and the shock-and-awe phase of the roll-out of the New Normal Reich, Twitter, Inc., and every other social-media platform and mass-media outlet in the Western world, had been functioning as the empire's Ministry of Truth, disseminating official New Normal propaganda, censoring dissent, and unpersoning anyone challenging the empire's official narratives. And thus, it provided the perfect stage for the PSYOP the empire was about to conduct.

Musk reinstated a number of prominent, primarily conservative Twitter accounts that had been deplatformed for "posting misinformation" about Hunter Biden's laptop and the "Covid vaccines," and for posting "incitement" and "glorification of violence," and bigotry and other such offensive content, among them, the account of Donald Trump, and tens of thousands of Trump supporters.

As Elon had promised, "the bird was freed"! Elon acolytes and grateful garden-variety Trumpians and other right-leaning persons poured onto Twitter to thank their savior for reversing the company's target demographic, thus saving America from "Cultural Marxism," and "Communism," and the "Woke Mind Virus."

The PSYOP continued with a textbook limited hangout known as the "Twitter Files." Musk let a few carefully selected journalists run a few searches at Twitter HQ, which exposed how the former staff of Twitter had been collaborating with elements of the Biden administration (i.e., not the global-capitalist empire) to censor and deplatform people, mostly those in the new "red" target demographic, and was part of some strictly USA-operated "Censorship Industrial Complex," which was absolutely not a global operation, and had nothing to do with any global-capitalist empire, or a "New Normal Reich," because all the censorship

---

137 Pringle, Eleanor, "Elon Musk was just forced to reveal who really owns X. Here's the list," *Fortune*, August 22, 2024.

and "shadowbanning," which was all in the past now that Elon was in charge, was the work of a cabal of deep-state libtard bureaucrats, who were a bunch of "Commies."

These revelations in the "Twitter Files" prompted Republicans in the US Congress to hold a series of subcommittee hearings into the possibly unconstitutional behavior of the Biden administration and its libtard proxies (i.e., not the global-capitalist empire), which had forced Twitter, Inc. and the other totally helpless Internet corporations to "shadowban" and censor Americans (i.e., not everyone else throughout the empire that these corporations were also censoring in a clearly globally coordinated fashion).

And then, right on cue, once the story had been framed within a USA-centric "red/blue" narrative, Musk shut the Twitter Files limited hangout down, i.e., before it could do any damage to the global-capitalist empire itself.

For the next two years, Elon and his cronies inundated their new target-demographic with "Free-Speech-Twitter" propaganda, sentimental Elon Muskhagiography, and a never-ending series of PR stunts. Twitter was officially rebranded as "X." Musk went to war with Brazil's Darth Vader, and Thierry Breton, and assorted other "Commies." Twitter users were besieged with memes of Elon dressed up as Captain Free-Speech America. Et cetera.

And so the Musk Cult was born.

Meanwhile, X is continuing to censor and otherwise "visibility-filter" content at the behest of governments throughout the empire, as well as in furtherance of its own objectives.

If you think that fact has had a negative impact on the Free-Speech Twitter PSYOP, on the contrary, the Musk Cult has only grown broader and stronger. Like any other cult, it is impervious to facts. All that matters is loyalty to the cult, and the leader of the cult, and the cult's official narrative. You can direct Musk cultists to the Twitter Safety pages where "visibility filtering" is explained, and cite countless examples of Musk's hypocrisy, and it will have absolutely no effect whatsoever. Like every other successful cult leader, Elon is beyond reproach, incapable of sin, a god made flesh.

But deifying Elon was not the primary objective of the Free-Speech Twitter PSYOP.

The primary objective of the Free-Speech Twitter PSYOP was to harness, corral, and establish control over the majority of the sizable minority of people who refused to follow orders and pledge allegiance to the New Normal Reich when it was rolled out during the "Covid pandemic." These people needed to be herded into a manipulable mass and redirected away from the global-capitalist empire and into a harmless cul-de-sac where they could scream and shout at the empire's designated scapegoats to their heart's content. The Musk Cult was just a means of herding and leading them into this cul-de-sac.

"Free-Speech Twitter" is this cul-de-sac, and is a microcosm of a larger cul-de-sac.

Which brings us to the second PSYOP.

The America Made Great Again PSYOP

One of the most effective ways to neutralize an opponent is to let them win. This is especially true when you're dealing with an opponent you can never entirely defeat.

What you do is, you lure your opponent into a battle you can afford to lose, because you need to actually lose the battle, and let your opponent actually win, i.e., not just trick them into thinking they have won, because . . . well, your opponent isn't stupid.

This battle that you lure your opponent into and let them win will be a battle over a territory within a territory, but which your opponent believes is "the territory." You can afford to lose control of this territory within a territory because you control the territory it exists within, and because your opponent doesn't know that.

The trick is getting your opponent to believe that, by winning this battle, they have won "the war," and that they now control "the territory," and have destroyed you, or have otherwise removed you from power, when, actually, all that your opponent has destroyed or removed from power is a corporeal decoy, a material incarnation of an invisible, immaterial adversary, an adversary they do not know exists, or which they refuse to acknowledge the existence of . . . assuming, of course, that is what you are.

At which point, you have neutralized your opponent.

For example, say you're a global empire, a supranational global-capitalist empire, and say your opponent is a populist insurgency, a potentially revolutionary mass, that you need to distract from contemplating your supranational, invisible, immaterial nature, and from the fact that the governments of nation-states are essentially administrative components of this invisible immaterial empire that you are, and thus it doesn't really matter to you which political party administers these nation-states or who the leaders of these parties are, because they can't really do much damage to you, because all they control are the material territories within the immaterial territory you control, which predetermines the context and the scope of their actions, and the parameters of their imaginations, and . . . OK, you probably see where this is going.

Or, I don't know, maybe you don't. So let me try to simplify it.

There is no "America" to make great again. "America" is a simulation. It is a map of a territory that does not exist. It is a dream within a dream in a film that no one can see because everyone is watching. It is a brand name for an imaginary product.

OK, that didn't make it any simpler, did it? Let me try this one more time.

We are living in a global-capitalist empire. One big global-capitalist empire. We have been for the last thirty-something years. All of us. Americans. Canadians. The British. The French. Australians. Germans. Russians. Israelis. Palestinians. Iranians. All of us.

The global-capitalist empire is not a cabal of powerful individuals. It is a system. And that system is evolving. Metamorphosing. Transmogrifying. Evolving into a new form of totalitarianism. A global-capitalist form of totalitarianism.

It is the system, and not its servants, that is driving . . . driving this systemic evolution. It makes no difference whether Elon Musk, or Donald Trump, or Macron, or Starmer, Netanyahu, Gates, Bezos, Soros, or any other political leader or powerful figure knows what they are doing. They serve the system, as the system requires, each according to their specific role and scope of action within the system.

Elon Musk did not "save free speech" or "rescue Twitter" from a "Woke Mind Virus." He purchased a corporation and rebranded its product for a new market demographic. In so doing, he corralled and neutralized most of the conservative populist resistance to the evolution of the global-capitalist system. Which is what the system needed to happen. It makes no difference whether Elon Musk understood his role. He played it perfectly. He is continuing to play it perfectly.

The Musk Cult is growing. Its apostles are preaching the Gospel of Elon throughout the empire, paving the road to The Privatization of Everything! Verily, it is the dawn of a golden age of "Freedom" ruled by global corporations and beneficent oligarchs!

However, before that golden age can begin, America must be made great again! And so the Free-Speech Twitter PSYOP has to be repeated on the macro-level. The same conservative populist resistance to the evolution of the global-capitalist system that Musk corralled and neutralized needs to be corralled and neutralized everywhere, not just in America, everywhere, all throughout the West and the rest of the empire.

Once it is corralled, and neutralized, and whipped up into a frenzy over "Wokeness," and "Cultural Marxism," and "Communism," it can be unleashed on the remnants of the dying age of nation-states, national sovereignty, constitutions, and so on, which will prompt the Global Powers That Be to take extreme measures to "defend democracy," which will prompt the Other Global Powers That Be to take more extreme measures to "Rescue the Republic," which will prompt the Global Powers That Be to take even more extreme extreme measures to "defend democracy from fascism" and . . . OK, this time, I do think you see where this is going.

Or, I don't know, maybe you don't. But I don't think I can make it any simpler. And I don't see any way to stop it or fix it. It isn't an error to be corrected. It is the organic evolution of a system . . . a supranational system evolving into a new totalitarian form.

So there you have it, a tale of two PSYOPS. I'm sorry that it isn't as comforting as a story about how Donald Trump and Elon Musk and their global-capitalist investors, and their respective subsidiaries, agents, and assigns, are going to "make America great again."

If it's any consolation, one thing is certain . . . whatever happens, it won't be boring.

The Year of the Zealot
December 17, 2024

It was the best of years, it was the worst of years, it was a year of brilliance, it was a year of buffoonery, it was a year of faith, it was a year of incredulity, it was a year of expectation, it was a year of tribulation, it was a year of uncertainty, and passionate intensity, and monomania, and paranoia, and fanatical fervor.

I'm designating it "the Year of the Zealot."

Now, before I review the cavalcade of bug-eyed zealotry that the year comprised, let me say a few words about zealotry. Because I get it. I understand the attraction. We live in chaotic and perplexing times. We are bombarded, on a moment-by-moment basis, by contradictory narratives, facts, fictions, baseless accusations, insinuations, official and unofficial propaganda, exaggerations, distortions, and bald-faced lies. Who has the time and energy to try to sift through the billion bits of bullshit blowing ceaselessly into our brains like random detritus swept up in some omnidirectional idiot wind? Is it any real wonder that so many people are retreating to the shelter of one or another ideological redoubt, some prefab bulwark, which can at least provide them with something resembling a coherent ontological structure, a lens through which to view and make some sense of our increasingly incomprehensible world?

No. I get it. I get the attraction. I do. But . . . well, this year is what that leads to.

For me, the zealotry began in Room 500 of the Berlin District Court, where I was on trial for the "crime" of tweeting the cover artwork of my bestselling book, *The Rise of the New Normal Reich: Consent Factory Essays,*

Vol. III (2020–2021). I have written about my thoughtcrime prosecution at considerable length, so I won't go on about it again here or reproduce the book cover art again. The short version is, the Covid zealots currently running the German government, and Germany's legal system, and most of its media, and comprising the vast majority of the German masses, do not appreciate being compared to the Nazis. I did that, so the authorities had my book banned, had my tweets censored, and prosecuted me for a "hate-crime."

In January, I was acquitted by a District Court judge, who, after delivering her verdict, explained to the press and observers in the gallery that my acquittal on the obviously trumped-up charge of "disseminating Nazi propaganda" proved that Germany is not the nascent totalitarian state that I had claimed that it was, and that, really, I am the totalitarian, and a babbling, Covid-denying idiot. Then she strapped on a Covid mask and stalked out of the courtroom. The prosecutor, who spent the proceedings behind a prophylactic "anti-Covid barrier" (like the Plexiglas panels they installed in stores to protect us from an airborne virus), and who appeared to be rather heavily medicated, was none too pleased with judge's verdict. So he crept back to his little prosecutorial office and started taking steps to have me tried again.

Yes, it was quite an absurd experience, my first thoughtcrime trial in Germany was. I'll tell you all about my second trial shortly, but, first, let's get to some of the other zealotry, of which there was no shortage this year.

Without doubt the primary source of zealotry in 2024 was the liquidation of Gaza, or Israel's self-defense of itself (or whatever people want to call it, depending on which side they fanatically support). It was like an International Zealot Convention. Zealots were everywhere, hooting and hollering, brandishing Israeli and Palestinian flags, accusing each other of genocide, attempted genocide, and other acts of heinousness. The Internet was awash with glossy color photographs of dead and mutilated bodies, blood-soaked kibbutzim, dismembered Gazans, inconsolable mothers clutching dead infants, terrified hostages being dragged out of their homes, sheet-covered corpses in hospital parking lots, grinning IDF soldiers posing in Palestinian women's underwear, Palestinian militants parading the corpses of their victims around in pickup trucks, and so on, all of which was of course the fault of "the other side," who are inhuman monsters who need to be wiped off the face of the planet.

Here in Germany, pro-Palestinian activists staged demonstrations and other events, or attempted to, until they were descended on by the Anti-Anti-Zionist Thought Police, who were determined to protect the German public from "hate speech" (including, but not limited to, specific "hate words," like "river" and "sea"). Immigrant neighborhoods were flooded with riot cops. Terrorist-adjacent kebab shops were raided. Goon squads went around stomping on people's votive candles at outdoor vigils. The whole fascist "state-of-emergency" show that we were treated to during "the Covid pandemic" was back on, but the official scapegoats had been changed.

Anti-Zionist Covid zealots, who had applauded the rollout of the new totalitarianism during 2020–2022 (or stood by in silence and watched as it happened) suddenly found themselves face-to-face with the New Normal Reich they had ushered into existence. Artists were disinvited from exhibitions! Filmmakers were demonized by the media! Masha Gessen's literary award ceremony was rescheduled! Yanis Varoufakis, banned from speaking at a "Palestine Congress" in Berlin, took to social media to alert us to the fact that "fascism is alive and well in Germany!"

Meanwhile, in the USA, mobs of medical-mask-wearing Anti-Zionists were occupying Academia, which, personally, I found unsettling, having been relentlessly harassed by fanatical mask-wearing Covidian Cultists for the preceding four years. I was foolish enough to tweet about it, which prompted a visit by the Anti-Zionist Inquisition!

"Are you now, or have you ever been, a Zionist?" the inquisitors demanded to know. "Do you renounce the Zionist Entity and all its works?" And so on. This went on for days. Swarms of ardent anti-Zionist zealots besieged my Twitter feed, accusing me of heresy, until, finally, I was declared "apostate" and excommunicated from the Church of Anti-Zionism.

For the record, I am neither a Zionist nor an anti-Zionist, nor a member of any other ideological faction or movement. I don't believe Israel is any more or less legitimate than any other nation-state. I am no more or less horrified by its behavior than I am by the behavior of any other nation-state, for example, the United States of America, which, unlike Israel, I am a citizen of, and which has slaughtered millions of people throughout its history. I'm not a big fan of nation-states, generally. I'm not obsessed with the Jews, or any other religious groups. My sympathies lie with the Palestinian people, and the Israeli people, and the American people, and the German people, and the French and British and Iranian and Syrian and Russian and Ukrainian and Italian and Chinese and the Greek and Irish and Australian and Canadian people, and all the other people that are being fucked over by their own or other nation-states, or by the supranational global-capitalist empire that has been destabilizing, restructuring, and privatizing the planet for going on the last thirty-five years.

But that kind of namby-pamby, old-school-lefty, both-sides bullshit doesn't cut it with monomaniacal zealots like the Anti-Zionist Inquisition, or the 10/7 Truthers, who claim, among other things, that, actually, it was the IDF that mass-murdered everyone on October 7, while the mostly peaceful Hamas guys were conducting interviews with prospective Israeli hostages and handing out garbanzo-bean Slurpees to the kids.

Seriously, people propagated this fantasy . . . OK, not the part about the garbanzo bean Slurpees, the part about Israel "Hanniballing" everyone. As if Israel didn't provide its critics with an overabundance of actual atrocities to report.

But this is what comes of fanaticism and zealotry. It makes no difference whether it's Israeli propagandists lying about "forty beheaded babies"[138] or anti-Zionist propagandists lying about Hamas. The point is not to deceive anyone. It's just to whip your side up into a frenzy of hatred of the other side, and reinforce unquestioning allegiance to your side, because you're the "good guys," and the other side is "evil," or "eviler," or "they started it," or whatever.

Oh, and, speaking of unquestioning allegiance, the other primary source of shameless zealotry in 2024 was the Musk Cult. I have to tip my hat

---

138 Tenbarge, Kat and Melissa Chan, "Unverified reports of '40 babies beheaded' in Israel-Hamas war inflame social media," NBC News, October 12, 2023.

to Musk, and to the formerly secret consortium of global-capitalist behemoths that took over Twitter. They saw an opportunity, and they seized it.

There we were, a multiplicitous mass of opposition to the New Normal Reich, righties, lefties, inbetweenies, people of every color and creed, united in defense of our democratic rights, pushing back against a weird new form of totalitarianism, and . . . well, that couldn't be allowed to continue.

It was obvious what had to be done. As Vladimir Lenin famously noted, "The best way to control the opposition is to lead it ourselves."

It took two years, but that multiplicitous mass of opposition has been torn asunder. It has been branded, commodified, purified, and controlled. It has been taxidermied. Its organs have been harvested. Its lifeblood has been hypodermically extracted, distilled into an innocuous elixir, and sold back to its desanguinated self. It has been zombied. Its soul has been scooped out. It has been replaced with a simulacrum of itself.

All that remains of it now is the Musk Cult.

Notwithstanding the fact that it is massive, and global, the Musk Cult works like any other cult. Cultists' brains are relentlessly barraged with infantile AI-generated Elon memes. Elon as Ceasar. Elon as Jesus. Elon as Captain Free-Speech America. Elon as the right hand of Trump. Elon as the Martian Führer. They are inundated with Elon's thought-terminating clichés and mind-numbing platitudes throughout the day. "X is the only source of truth." "The hammer of justice is coming." And so on. Dare to post anything critical of Elon and you will be set upon by Musk-Cult zealots, or visibility-filtered into the void. Milieu control, demand for purity, loaded language, dispensing of existence, and all the other classic hallmarks of cults and operant conditioning are in effect.

God forbid you challenge the Cult's official narrative. You will be branded a "libtard," or a "cultural Marxist," or a "communist," or a "leftist," which are the Musk Cult's versions of a "suppressive person" in the Church of Scientology.[139] No, this is no time for division or doubt or

---

139 Challenge Elon and you'll be "unverified" and censored, because . . . well, as one senior cult member explained recently, "While, of course, censorship is bad, we have to avoid disruption."

negativity or critical thinking! Our heroes are literally rescuing the republic! Musk and Trump and their millionaire buddies, and the stockholders of that formerly secret consortium of supranational global-capitalist entities, and Saudis, and assorted other oligarchs—i.e., that consortium I mentioned above—and Musk's military-industrial complex associates, and the "defense" corporations they are stockholders of, and their subsidiaries, agents, and assigns, and the CEOs, CFOs, COOs, and presidents of those companies, and their attorneys, and the consultants and think-tank guys and gals they all have lunch with occasionally—not to do any actual business, of course, just to keep in touch with old friends and colleagues—and the Wall Street honchos, and the CEOs of the six corporations that own the US media, and the big five publishers that decide what you can read, and diaphoretic transhumanist billionaire tech geeks, oh, and let's not forget the pharmaceutical industry with their miraculous mRNA vaccines, and all the other "freedom fighters" who care so much about our democratic rights, and each and every one of us, personally, that they are going to go mano a mano with the Woke Cabal and the Cultural Marxists, vanquish the Axis of Libtardism, and Make America Great Again!

Jesus, I got myself all worked up there. I was almost about to buy a subscription to X and start pumping out Elon memes on Grok, or start searching for "ghost gun" parts on eBay, or obsessing about whatever we've been prompted to be obsessing about by the time you read this—squirrels, drones, cat-eating Haitians, whatever Musk and his disciples decide to anesthetize their followers' minds with today.

But, seriously, all this zealotry is exhausting. Or maybe I'm just getting old. I confess, I'm feeling slightly worn out, and disillusioned, and kind of blue these days. Maybe it was my second thoughtcrime trial, at which the Berlin Superior Court overturned my acquittal, so that now I've been forced to submit my case (which, remember, is about two tweets) to Germany's supreme court, the *Bundesverfassungsgericht*. Or maybe it is just being forced to watch as GloboCap's New Normal Reich rolls on, and that curtain at the back of Frank Zappa's theater gets pulled closed over that brick wall again, and we retake our assigned seats, and the show continues . . .

If you will allow me to bastardize one of my favorite bits from *Fear and Loathing in Las Vegas*—for a moment, in early 2022, it felt like we had all the momentum again, like we were riding the crest of another high and beautiful wave, as Hunter Thompson put it. Now, almost three years later, you can scroll back through your Twitter timeline, and with the right kind of eyes you might just see the high-water mark—that place where the wave finally broke and rolled back.

But, whatever, as the doctor said, "Buy the ticket, take the ride."

OK, that's it for 2024. Merry Fanatical Christmas and a Happy Zealous New Year!

Acknowledgments

Heartfelt thanks to Julie Blumenthal, Matt Taibbi, Friedemann Däblitz, Tony Lyons, Hector Carosso, Robert F. Kennedy Jr., Jay Bhattacharya, Gavin de Becker, Catherine Austin Fitts, Anthony Freda, Toby Young, Jeffrey Tucker, Drew Pinsky, MD, Nico Perrino, James Kirchick, Ralf Hutter, Clivia von Dewitz, Aya Velázquez, Bastian Barucker, Trish Wood, Eva Sudholt, John Mac Ghlionn, Sascha Freudenheim, Integrity Media Group, Peter LaTona, Dr. Jan Harrell, Mathias Bröckers, Dirk Pohlmann, Max Blumenthal, Mike Freedman, Milosz Matuschek, Aaron Reese, Kit Knightly, Catte Black, Jerzy Ziolkowski, Marc Neumann, Michael Ballweg, Andrew Doyle, Stefan Millius, Clifton Duncan, Angie Tibbs, Tyler Durden, Nick Hudson, Heike Brunner, Abir Ballan, Piers Robinson, Fabio Vighi, Emily Garcia, Henrik Hjulgaard, Sören Kristoffersen, Max Stadler, Jessica Hamed, Eugyppius, Erik Rusch, Margaret Anna Alice, James Howard Kunstler, Chris Martenson, Elza van Hamelen, Meghan Murphy, Marcus Aurin, Bernd Volkert, Christine Black, John Leake, Hugo Fernandez, David Josef Volodzko, Boris Reitschuster, Jens Fischer Rodrian, Alexa Rodrian, Jill Sandjaja, Anselm Lenz, Patrick Henningsen, Ahmad Malik, Robert Cibis, Ciarán O'Regan, James Freeman, Viviane Fischer, Wolfgang Wodarg, Chris Klotz, Chris Best, Hamish McKenzie, and everyone at Substack HQ, Manova, Apolut, Radio München, Free21, and all the other independent outlets that have translated and republished my essays, and special thanks to all the generous readers who have contributed to my "legal defense fund" and have otherwise supported my work.